THE CODE FOR

GLOBAL
ETHICS

RECENT BOOKS BY
Rodrigue Tremblay, PhD

Le Code pour une éthique globale, vers une civilisation humaniste
   (in French)

*The New American Empire: Causes and Consequences
   for the United States and for the World*
   (in English, French, and Turkish)

Why Bush Wants War: Religion, Oil and Politics in World Conflicts
   (*Pourquoi Bush veut la guerre*, in French)

The Way It Is: The Shock between Politics, Economics and Morality
   (*L'Heure Juste*, in French)

Modern Macroeconomics, Facts and Theories
   (in French)

Africa and Monetary Integration
   (in French and in English)

Introduction to Economics
   (in French)

THE CODE FOR

GLOBAL ETHICS

TEN HUMANIST PRINCIPLES

RODRIGUE TREMBLAY

PREFACE BY
PAUL KURTZ

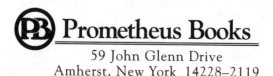

Prometheus Books

59 John Glenn Drive
Amherst, New York 14228–2119

Adapted from the French edition, Rodrigue Tremblay, *Le Code pour une éthique globale, vers une civilisation humaniste*, Éditions Liber, Montreal, Quebec, Canada, 2009. ISBN: 978-2-89578-173-8. First English Edition.

Published 2010 by Prometheus Books

Inquiries should be addressed to
Prometheus Books
59 John Glenn Drive
Amherst, New York 14228–2119
VOICE: 716–691–0133
FAX: 716–691–0137
WWW.PROMETHEUSBOOKS.COM

14 13 12 11 10   5 4 3 2 1

Library of Congress Cataloging-in-Publication Data

Tremblay, Rodrigue, 1939–
    [Le Code pour une Éthique globale, French]
    The code for global ethics : the ten humanist principles / Rodrigue Tremblay. —1st English ed.
        p. cm.
    Includes bibliographical references (p.   ) and index.
    ISBN 978–1–61614–172–1 (cloth : alk. paper)
    1. Humanistic ethics. 2. Social ethics. I. Title.

BJ1360.T74 2010
171'.2—dc22

                                                            2009050900

Printed in the United States of America on acid-free paper

This book is dedicated to

GIORDANO BRUNO
(1548–1600)

and to all those who have died
at the hands of religious zealots.

THE TEN PRINCIPLES FOR A GLOBAL HUMANISM

T he ten personal and social rules of rational humanism for a more harmonious and just world.

1. DIGNITY: Proclaim the natural dignity and inherent worth of all human beings.
2. RESPECT: Respect the life and property of others.
3. TOLERANCE: Be tolerant of others' beliefs and lifestyles.
4. SHARING: Share with those who are less fortunate and assist those who are in need of help.
5. NO DOMINATION: Do not dominate through lies or otherwise.
6. NO SUPERSTITION: Rely on reason, logic, and science to understand the Universe and to solve life's problems.
7. CONSERVATION: Conserve and improve the Earth's natural environment.
8. NO WAR: Resolve differences and conflicts without resorting to war or violence.
9. DEMOCRACY: Rely on political and economic democracy to organize human affairs.
10. EDUCATION: Develop one's intelligence and talents through education and effort.

CONTENTS

ACKNOWLEDGMENTS

I would like to express my deepest gratitude and admiration to the successive generations of thinkers and philosophers who have paved the way to establish the intellectual foundations for improving the human condition. I would like also to thank the Quebec Humanist Society which, by bestowing upon me the Condorcet prize for political philosophy, has given me the opportunity to outline the ten basic humanist moral commandments, which serve as the chapter headings of this book.

I cannot be grateful enough to Dr. Paul Kurtz, a great humanist who has devoted his entire life to teaching and promoting the principles of global humanism. I thank him sincerely for devoting the time and energy to write the inspired preface of this book. Dr. Kurtz has summarized beautifully the wisdom the three humanist manifestos have given the world. I sincerely hope that this book is a modest complement to the tremendous accomplishments of Dr. Kurtz's career.

Two outstanding individuals were gracious enough to read the entire manuscript of the book before its publication. They are Michel Lahaie, MA, and Dr. Gaston Gravel. They provided critical suggestions on some relevant topics covered in the book. I am happy to acknowledge their valuable contributions.

My thanks go also to Mr. Giovanni Calabrese, editor of the French version of this book *Le Code pour une éthique globale*, (Éditions Liber), for his diligent work and valuable advice.

Steven L. Mitchell of Prometheus Books has provided invaluable assistance in preparing *The Code for Global Ethics* for publication. I am very grateful for his suggestions and helpful encouragement. I wish also to express my sincerest thanks to Jade Zora Ballard, assistant editor, for seeing the manuscript through to publication.

Finally, even though she knows without my saying it (but it's nice to see it in black and white), my warmest thanks go to Carole, my wife and indefatigable first reader, copy editor, and sounding board for numerous discussions and ideas developed in this book.

PREFACE

TOWARD A NEW
PLANETARY HUMANISM

Humankind is confronted by two possible scenarios: the first is humanistic. It adopts an optimistic and courageous forward-looking stance regarding the Human Prospect, placing confidence in the ability of human beings to solve their problems. Humanists emphasize reason, science, and technology as vital to improving the human condition. They recognize that many societies are embroiled in political and economic wars and conflicts, and that ignorance and mistrust often dominate flash points, such as in Africa and the Middle East today. Meanwhile, environmental problems present awesome challenges as economic growth gallops ahead: global warming, melting glaciers, disappearing rainforests, desertification, and the population explosion evoke dire prognostications of Armageddon. Yet humanists believe that we can and must solve these problems. If we are to do so, however, it is essential that we advance education for all children on the planet, extend genuine democracy and human rights everywhere, and strive to overcome the ancient religious, ethnic, nationalistic, racial, and ideological divisions of the past.

Humanists have welcomed the disappearance of the colonial empires of Europe, and the rapid emergence of Asia—Japan, South Korea, China, and India—though they recognize that economic and political conflicts for natural resources (oil, gas, water, and mineral resources) will most likely intensify. Humanists are critical of the uni-lateral hegemony of the American Empire, and they maintain that *a new humanistic global ethics needs to be developed* if the future is to be bountiful. Rodrigue Tremblay eloquently defends this form of rational humanism. We need to work together, he recommends, if we are to contribute to the continued amelioration of human life on the planet. He prescribes ten basic principles embodied in a code of global ethics to guide us.

Pitted against this affirmative humanistic outlook is a second pessimistic scenario rooted in dogmatic religions of the past. Espe-cially troubling is the resurgence of intolerant fundamentalist reli-gions that block human progress and have little confidence in the capacity of human beings to solve their problems or to contribute to a better life. These reactionary religions wish to return to the ancient "sacred books" of bygone ages. Their texts were spawned in premodern rural and nomadic cultures that were rooted in fear and superstition and burdened by economies of scarcity. They were contrived in a prescientific age before the industrial, democratic, and information revolutions of the modern age, or the emergence of the Enlightenment in the eighteenth century. It is clear that the world needs to assert a *New Enlightenment* in the twenty-first century that expands reason and science, education and democracy. But this will not happen easily until we recognize our mutual interdepen-dence and make the case for a new global ethics. Especially neces-sary in this great task is a new commitment to Planetary Humanism and the need to accept the "natural dignity and inherent worth of all human beings" as a first premise. This universal principle is based on reason but inspired by empathy. If the humanist scenario is to suc-ceed, we need to embark upon a vigorous campaign devoted to the well-being of humanity as a whole.[1]

Historically, many authors—secular and religious—have praised the "brotherhood of men," no doubt an anachronistic term today. Nevertheless, stoicism in the Hellenic world recognized the importance of a universal moral principle, as did Christianity and other patriarchal religions. Too often, however, the latter are tied to creeds anchored in faith—Christianity, Judaism, or Islam—which implicitly presupposed the concept of "the chosen people." Regrettably, this was limited to only those who were committed to *their* religious faith; they alone would receive the keys to the gates of heaven, the divine rapture, or salvation. All others would be condemned to hell. How discriminatory and destructive this apocalyptic vision has been, for theologians have consigned to perdition those who did not accept the divine commandments, allegedly revealed to this or that prophet or sect. Too many wars have been waged in the name of divine sanctions—it is time that humankind declares its independence of them all.

Dr. Tremblay points out in this book that we need to abandon selective moralities concocted in the infancy of the species. We need to move to a higher plane in which all members of the human family are treated equally as persons, "ends in themselves,"—as Immanuel Kant postulated in his second categorical imperative. The salient point that is evident today is the urgent need to bring a *universal* ethical code to fruition.

A compelling reason why this is the time to develop a new global ethics is that scientific studies have for the first time empirically demonstrated that *Homo sapiens* has common roots. Beginning in Africa, humans migrated some sixty thousand years ago to Europe, Asia, Australia, and across the Bering Straits to North and South America. Genetic studies of our common DNA indicate that we are truly members of the same *Homo sapiens*. We share a global songline based on genetic markers that indelibly point to our unitary origin. Thus our species is not divided along fixed racial lines; constant migrations tie us indelibly together. Humans traversed the continents by foot, caravan, camel, donkey, and chariot, and in modern times by ship, airplane, and spacecraft. Invading armies on land and armadas on the high seas, as well as peaceful trade, commerce, immigration and emigration enabled humans to continuously intermingle and intermarry.

Today North and South America, Europe, Asia, Australia, and Africa are open to peaceful transactions, and now, we live in an interdependent world. We breathe the same air, share the same atmosphere, and we need uncontaminated drinking water, food and shelter to survive. Although there are geographical differences, we share the same generic history as a species. Accordingly, each of us, no matter where we live, has a stake in the preservation of our planetary abode. Vividly dramatized by space travel, for the first time we can view our blue-green planet from afar and realize that the historical-political-socio-economic boundaries that divided humankind for millennia are fictitious. Geologists have demonstrated that the continents are shifting, however slowly, that our Earth is undergoing constant processes of change, and that all species need to adapt if they are to survive. The intricate fossils preserved in the Burgess Shale of Canada for 500 million years show that millions of species are extinct. Will the human species survive? Only if we take the bold steps necessary to achieve progress.

We have developed the scientific method that powerfully enables us to make wise choices. Unfortunately, there exists a great disparity between the continued discoveries of the sciences on the one hand, and the cultural lag of inherited moral doctrines rooted in theistic religions on the other. Will we overcome this dualism between science and morality that persists? Only if we develop what this insightful book recommends, a new rational humanistic ethics. Scientific technology makes this feasible today because of the invention and proliferation of new communications media. There are no longer isolated pockets of humans living in remote regions of the world; radio, television, the iPod, and especially the Internet bind us instantaneously together. Whether Canadian or American, Latin American or African, Chinese or Russian, French or Indian, we can come to know and appreciate each other today as never before.

"No deity can save us, we must save ourselves," states *Humanist Manifesto II*.[2] We need a realistic appraisal of the human condition and a resolute determination to take responsibility for our own destinies— as far as we can—in our own hands. This is the Prometheus model, the myth of the Titan who challenged the gods and bequeathed fire and the arts and sciences so that primitive humans might leave the caves in which they huddled and enter the world with the courage to change it. Today we have the power to do so. We need as never before to recognize the necessity of developing shared values and working cooperatively to bring about a better world. But if we are to do so, we need a new code of global ethics. This book issues a powerful clarion call to do just that.

Dr. Paul Kurtz
Founder of the Center for Inquiry,
Founder of the Council for Secular Humanism,
Amherst, New York

INTRODUCTION

THE ETHICAL INFRASTRUCTURE OF EVERY SOCIETY

We are discussing no small matter, but how we ought to live.
—Socrates (ca. 469/470 BCE–399 BCE)
in Plato's *Republic*

A man's ethical behavior should be based effectually on sympathy, education, and social ties and needs; no religious basis is necessary.
—Albert Einstein (1879–1955)

Why is humanism not the preeminent belief of humankind?
—Joyce Carol Oates,
American Humanist of the Year, 2007

The world faces a crisis of civilization, which is in reality a moral crisis. The modern moral worldview that has evolved since the eighteenth-century Age of Enlightenment seems to be weathering. There is a recrudescence of the old moral formulas that encourage conflicts and wars. Humanity is in need of a new moral revival, free of sectarian references, in order to pursue its long march for survival in a climate of progress and liberty.

The Code for Global Ethics proposes an imperative and more explicitly universal code of rights and obligations for all individuals, whether they be ordinary citizens or leaders of countries, of corporations, or religious organizations. It outlines the principles of *rational humanism* to be applied within the global context of a shrinking and politically and economically interdependent world. Such a universal and global code of conduct is then compared to alternative moral codes—codes usually based on sectarian religious systems—with a demonstration of why such narrow or ethnically centered moral systems have failed humanity in the past. In our view, humanism is about idealism, compassion, and mutual tolerance, in a true spirit of humanity.[1] It is a truly universal vision of humankind.

Since our worldview affects how we interact with others, any moral code must be judged as to how its adherents treat other people and whether or not it improves people's lives. If the adherents treat others badly and their moral values reduce others' quality of life, it is a bad moral code; if the adherents treat others with dignity and respect and their actions improve the lives of the greatest number, it is a good code of ethics. This is the ultimate pragmatic test of reality and results.

It would seem that there is not necessarily an irreconcilable antagonism between humanism as a universal philosophy and religion as a personal human experience.[2] It is only when religion becomes an aggressive political movement that crushes human liberty and dignity that it becomes hostile to the humanist worldview. In other words, it is only when religion turns against humanity that there is a conflict between humanism and religion. The centuries-long Inquisition in Europe, which was responsible for the deaths of thousands of individuals guilty only of following their conscience and personal beliefs, is a good example of the kind of conflict that can arise between humanism and organized religion.

In the past, the principles espoused by organized religions were often intended to apply to a particular ethnic group, to members of a particular nationality, or to coreligionists and insiders of a religious denomination. In almost all cases, these moral principles were not meant to be universal, applicable to all humans without distinction of race, sex, language, birth, property, culture, or nationality—especially when it was a matter of politico-religious morality. It seems that, historically, religious or political leaders use religious laws and precepts to increase the social and political cohesion and unity of their own group or community, and its eventual survival, while at the same time emphasizing their differences with, and often their hostility toward, other groups and other communities. As South African archbishop emeritus Desmond Tutu put it, "Religion is like a knife. If you use it to slice bread, it's good. If you use it to slice off your neighbor's arm, it's bad." Unfortunately, throughout history, the knife of religion has been used just as often to cut other people's throats as to cut bread.

One can easily arrive at such a conclusion after reading the books that support the monotheist religions of Judaism (the Torah), Christianity (the Bible), and Islam (the Qur'an or Koran). History is replete with calls to kill in the name of some god. In these three professed revealed books, one discovers, for example, that while it is written, "do not kill," what is really meant is do not kill the insiders or allies. But anything goes regarding the outsiders—the members of opposing religions or coalitions, the foreigners, the strangers, the infidels, the nonbelievers, the miscreants, the pagans, the enemies.

Human ethics is indeed complex, essentially because morality and cooperation tend to come much more naturally within groups than between groups. The challenge of civilization and of humanist ethics in particular is to extend in-group morality to a harder to achieve between-group morality, in a truly global context.

After that of being turned against the "others," the second flaw found in faith-based moral codes is the erroneous idea that human beings are not only at the top of all living species, but that they happen to be the center and the masters of a Universe especially created for them by mysterious divinities. This egocentric and anthropomorphic vision of things has unfortunately separated humans from the rest of the physical world and from other living species. By separating man from nature, indeed, the theory of "man-center-of-the-Universe" has caused us to lose respect for all other forms of life, and has prevented us from perceiving our true place in the Cosmos. We must not only have respect for our fellow humans, but we must also have respect for all forms of life and for the environment.

A third major flaw of religious morality is the subtle distinction that it often introduces between individual or private morality, and public or state morality. There is one morality for ordinary people in their daily lives and another morality for leaders and government agents acting in their official capacity. This moral dichotomy may explain more than anything else why humanity is still saddled with murderous wars.[3]

Why such à la carte morality? My answer is that the medieval religious concepts of morality are fundamentally inadequate for modern humanity living in an integrated and multicultural world and on an ever-shrinking planet, a planet that requires global solutions to global problems. Such concepts belong to another age, when each human group had a circumscribed geographical horizon and when the moral rules for survival were crueler and more primitive. Over the coming centuries, moral rules must adapt in order to maximize the chances of humanity's survival in the new environment of global economic, political, and cultural cooperation, and in the face of the new challenges of global climate change. Suffice it to say that from a humanist point of view, the state has no special moral status in relation to its actions, as compared to any other human action.

A fourth defect of religion-based morality comes from the fact that it relies on the fiction of an eternal hell not only to terrorize the faithful, but also to intimidate and demonize nonbelievers who refuse to submit to the dicta of the religious authorities. This is quite a sadistic, immoral, and unjust threat, because it condemns without appeal two-thirds of humankind to exclusion and possibly to persecutions, religious wars, and genocide. This is a very serious defect of religion-based morality, since this ideology of hell and the hatred it may have encouraged against others may have caused, directly or indirectly, countless conflicts and millions of deaths.

A fifth weakness of religion-based morality arises from its philosophical stance regarding a hypothetical separation between the human mind and the human body. Much of the negative religious morality concerning the human body comes from this erroneous distinction that has no scientific basis.

Faced with such an entrenched but flawed morality and considering the huge challenges that humanity must overcome, it would seem that we need a new moral code of conduct, one that transcends traditional religion-based morality and that adopts a posture of global awareness and sensitivity to human problems. The rational humanist principles of morality can provide such guidance. Some may argue that universal humanist principles of morality are self-evident and intuitive and need not be presented in an orderly fashion. I disagree. I believe that such principles are superior to any other system of moral values, especially those based on the old concepts of ethical duality and in-group morality inspired by religion. I believe these principles should not only be proclaimed, they should also be compared to other flawed moral codes that have come down to us from an often dark past. They derive from the conviction that in these times, when greed and egoism are elevated to the level of public policy and private morality, it is urgently necessary to look for a better moral code.

The question of human morality has been with us ever since humans began living in groups and in more or less organized societies, where survival depended upon mutual assistance. In this sense, morality is perhaps the oldest philosophical question. But what is *morality*? What is *ethics*? What is *empathy*?

Morality is the set of written and unwritten rules to enable humans—and other species—to get along in groups or in communities. *Religion* is only one source of morality, since obviously morality exists without religion. In fact, *humanism* is probably a more natural source of morality when this takes the form of spontaneous altruism, compassion, self-sacrifice, cooperation and mutual aid within the group, basic sentiments of justice, respect for territorial rights, sexual rights, and so on. We can even say that some form of morality exists in animals.[4] All species must necessarily have followed some elementary moral code and developed a moral instinct in order to have survived the long evolutionary process.

Human morality is an attribute of human conduct; it establishes why some actions are deemed to be wrong and others are considered right. It is the ability to do good because it is the right thing to do, beyond and above simple social convention. Morality can be general or specific. A general or basic moral code exists intuitively in a person's mind and is independent of any deity or supernatural world.[5] For example, people know naturally that to kill another human being is wrong and that to steal from others is also wrong.[6] This comes from millennia of evolution and step-by-step progress in human nature. People have also a natural and intuitive feeling that their behavior and their interactions with others must be honest, fair, and just, above and beyond any legalistic or religious subtleties. In this general sense, basic human morality relates ideally to how people do what is right in their private activities and in dealing with their fellow human beings.

Ethics deals with questions of moral judgment and of moral behavior, with putting into practice a given set of mutually shared values and rules. The word ethics derives from the classical Greek *ethicos*, which means character. Depending on the degree of complexity of human societies, there can be more specific, more comprehensive, and more complete codes of ethics that specify in detail what it means to be moral and to behave morally. As human societies become more developed, they also become more vulnerable and naturally require more elaborate moral systems.

Empathy toward others is the capacity to feel for others by imagining ourselves in their place.[7] Indeed, to have empathy for others and see things from their perspective is the foundation of a humanist civilization. Morality and empathy are buried deep in our genes, but so are other, antisocial traits such as savagery and cruelty. Humans have to learn how to develop their moral judgment and their more positive tendencies, and, at the same time, learn how to repress their darker impulses and refrain from immoral behavior. That is why we can say that human morality is both an intuitive phenomenon and a learned attribute of human behavior.[8]

The fundamental purpose and meaning of life is to be happy, to live fully and morally. Indeed, for each human being, the central purpose of life is to aim for the highest level of happiness, self-esteem, character development, personal fulfillment, and human accomplishment that one's natural endowments and potential make possible. It is natural, therefore, that for many individuals, such fulfillment will be found in their work, trade, craft, profession, or in the demanding art of raising a family. Provided that such devotion does not become an absolute or an obsession, to the exclusion of all other activities and responsibilities, striving for success and accomplishment is a most moral and worthy goal. However, the journey is more important than the destination. Thus, doing one's best along the way is more important than success itself.

The happiest among us are often those individuals who accept to devote their time, talents, and energies to building something greater than themselves and who strive to make the world a better place for everyone. In fact, the more moral and the more altruistic a person is, the more he or she will be open to find true happiness. In that sense, doing good is its own reward. There are many roads to happiness and self-esteem, but to do good and to be moral is the surest way. And what is more, our actions cumulatively shape our relationship with the world. Indeed, if one strives to do good, one will also become a better person.[9]

It is my contention that old moral codes, religious or philosophical, are ill adapted to the complex and multicultural world in which we live presently. In the new global age, I think that a universal humanist code of ethics is better adapted to the present human condition than any other approach to human morality.[10]

For the purpose of this book, I define *humanism* as a philosophical worldview about humanity and human existence that affirms the inherent dignity and inherent worth of all human beings, without reference to superstition and the supernatural. Applied humanism, in essence, translates into fraternity toward all human beings. Similarly, *rational humanism* is a philosophy that relies upon logic and science to understand the Universe and to solve life's problems, and aims at motivating everyone to live a moral and fulfilled life.[11]

To be moral in a specifically humanistic way is much more than the obligation to obey the law or to practice decent human sexuality. Humanist moral standards are truly universal and apply to all human beings living on this planet and to all human activities, whether carried out individually or collectively.[12] The fundamental humanistic laws of conscience and humanity apply in all circumstances and to all individuals, whatever their role and wherever their location. There is no "adaptable morality" for a person acting in one capacity and another one when fulfilling another function. By extension, there is not a domestic morality that is different from an international morality. This is the basic message of the humanist code for global ethics.[13]

In many quarters it is taken for granted that harsh religious systems of heavenly rewards and religiously inspired guilt and punishments are required for people to behave morally. One might think that such rules are necessary to overcome humans' alleged natural tendencies toward wickedness and depravity. If this were true, we would observe that religion-driven societies behave more morally than secular societies. This is patently not the case, since very often it has been the most pious and religious societies that have acted in the least moral way. This is an indication that the source of human morality need not be found in religions, but in a more rational moral philosophy based on human reason and the need for moral humanist rules for survival.

Indeed, it is not true that if religion-based ethics is replaced by rational, humanism-based ethics the result is necessarily an egocentric approach to morality. Contrary to what many philosophers have thought in the past, I do not think it is a practical necessity to believe in a deity for people to act morally, nor that the mass of people must be scared into being moral.[14] Some modern philosophers, such as Jean-Paul Sartre,[15] go from one extreme to the other. They argue that when man rejects the fiction of a transcendental God, each individual becomes *de facto* a god, perfectly free and responsible for all humanity. They cite approvingly Dostoievsky as a starting point, "If God didn't exist, everything would be possible," to argue for a moral anarchy where each person, alone, must invent his or her own values, since there are no inherently true natural values. These are dangerous exaggerations. Humans are free, but within moral limits. And natural, universal, humanistic, and inherent values exist within all rational human beings. These values are not exterior, but constituent parts of the natural condition.[16]

Today, with the increase in education and literacy, and therefore intellectual independence, it is easier for people to understand the need and the rewards for being moral. Even though moral perfection doesn't exist and will never be totally possible, most people understand that it is in humans' best interest to be moral. It is the surest way to foster individual and collective survival and to attain happiness for all.

Secular and humanist-oriented societies are certainly as moral as religion-centered societies. For example, on the whole, secular Sweden is certainly as moral, if not more so, as fanatically religious Iran. Historically, who would pretend that the more secular Switzerland was less moral than the more religious Nazi Germany?[17] Principles of living need not be of a religious origin for the average individual to behave morally. As a matter of fact, human morality predated the advent of organized religions. It is not derived from them, and it will outlive their eventual replacement.[18]

Humanity would not have survived if it had not devised moral codes. This was the case in the past, and it will still be the case in the future. What is at stake here is not which moral code was best suited for the past, but which moral code is better suited for the future and for humanity's survival.

That is why I will develop in this book the proposition that basic humanist living principles are superior to any religion-based principles in guiding individuals in their daily moral decisions. There truly exists such a reality as a humanistic code of global ethics and a set of civic moral rules without religion.[19] It is not necessary to be religious to be moral. On the contrary, to be fanatically religious is to be immoral.

The fact that humans have survived in such great numbers—more than six billion individuals and counting—is no guarantee that they will survive as a species in the future. It is in this sense that humankind may be in need of a new morality that meets the new requirements for survival and progress.

The world has changed profoundly since the events of Hiroshima and Nagasaki in the fateful summer of 1945. We now know that humans have the terrible power and the moral capability to destroy themselves with nuclear weapons, with no credible morality standing in their way. To kill and destroy with nuclear weapons not only requires technology;[20] it also requires a moral vacuum all too frighteningly present in today's shortsighted elites who are obsessed with power, self-indulgence, instant gratification, and crass materialism.[21]

This book is a modest contribution to the never-ending task of building a better world for humankind. It codifies some moral principles better suited for a globalized and shrinking world. In this modern code of conduct, one can find some well-known and tested classical rules of behavior, going back in time to ancient philosophers, while others will appear cast in a new light, reflecting new realities.

ONE

DIGNITY AND EQUALITY

FIRST HUMANIST PRINCIPLE:
PROCLAIM THE NATURAL DIGNITY AND
INHERENT EQUALITY OF ALL HUMAN BEINGS.

Equal and exact justice to all men, of whatever state or persuasion, religious or political; peace, commerce, and honest friendship with all nations—...freedom of religion; freedom of the press; freedom of person under the protection of the habeas corpus; and trial by juries impartially selected—these principles form the bright constellation which has gone before us and guided our steps through an age of revolution and reformation.
        —Thomas Jefferson (1743–1826), third US president

However little it may often appear to be true, the social world is governed in the long run by certain moral principles on which the people at large believe. The only moral principle which has ever made the growth of an advanced civilization possible was the principle of individual freedom, which means that the individual is guided in his decisions by rules of just conduct and not by specific commands.
        —Friedrich A. Hayek (1899–1992)

I think that on balance the moral influence of religion has been awful. With or without religion, good people can behave well and bad people can do evil; but for good people to do evil—that takes religion.
        —Steven Weinberg, Nobel laureate, physics

33

T he first humanist rule deals with basic human dignity. It is the most important; all the other rules are derived from this first one. Respect for human dignity is the fundamental principle that should govern relations between individuals and among nations. Every human being, irrespective of culture, nationality, birth, property, race, sex, or creed, has a natural right to personal dignity, including the right to be free of ill treatment, brutality, and cruelty. As French statesman Lazare Carnot (1753–1823) once advanced, we should strive to "elevate to human dignity all members of humankind."

In practice, this means we should treat every human being with dignity, as we as individuals would like to be treated with dignity by others. This also means that we should never treat human beings as tools, objects, or instruments, but always as autonomous entities endowed with inalienable and inherent rights.[1] This need to treat all human beings with dignity is analogous to the famous "golden rule" of universal morality. According to the fundamental reciprocity principle, each one of us should attempt to treat others as we would have others treat us. The corollary is also true: we should not treat others as we would not like to be treated by them.[2]

HUMANIST MORALITY

Morality is about what is and is not acceptable in social and individual behavior. One's morality is heavily influenced by one's perception of future uncertainty and the desire to remove as much of this uncertainty as possible. Morality is a social necessity. In a world of anarchy and moral decay, no individual's life, family, and property are secure. Social disintegration and economic regression follow. In these circumstances, what is socially wrong is what hurts the common good. What is socially right is what enhances the common good. For practical, ethical decision making, what is individually wrong is what diminishes the common good, and what is individually right is what enhances the common good. Because we are social animals, human morality is about how we treat others. Pretending to be moral while treating others badly is sheer hypocrisy.

Most religions have a core moral code that teaches kindness toward other human beings, along with the promise of eternal life. The problem comes from the fact that religions rarely extend this goodness to people who oppose their faith-based certainties. Moreover, they usually have two or three sets of contradictory moral principles to choose from, depending upon their immediate interests and circumstances.[3]

How can we aspire to a nonsuperstitious and nonmystical guide to moral living? The answer lies in a global, rational, and modern humanism that emphasizes the intrinsic value of human life and establishes human morality outside of a religious framework. Such a morality rejects the supernatural, mystical, and transcendental claims made by traditional religions in favor of rational and scientific explanations of the laws of the Universe and of the meaning of life. Humanist morality establishes a set of ethical rules of conduct that are designed to promote the greatest individual good and the greatest social good for the advancement and progress of humanity as a whole, with no reference at all to supernatural entities.

How to give purpose to one's life, how to treat others, and how to live in a civilized society are questions that assume a moral content, which implies that a few essential principles of what is right and what is wrong are needed to guide personal and social behavior.

There are of course some universal principles that belong to common sense. For example, it is wrong to kill other persons or to steal from them. But what does equality between people mean in practice? What is the meaning of solidarity among humans? What does it mean to have personal freedom? Can public morality—that is the morality of persons in power—be different from ordinary morality? Does the moral code change for a person who attains social or political power?

THE HUMANIST PRINCIPLE OF EQUALITY
BETWEEN MEN AND WOMEN

In many cultures, women do not have the same individual, social, and economic rights as men. Only in democracies where secular humanist morality is followed do we find real equality of rights between men and women. In certain churches and in theocracies, in general, women are treated as inferior. Why?

To begin with, one has to remember that all religions are human inventions. As such, they are institutions that reflect the traditions and superstitions found in their cultures. It isn't surprising that their rules tend to treat men better than women. Since moral principles tend to reflect the power structure of the society, if only men have access to power, the prevailing morality will assign a higher status to men than to women.

Historically, the idea that women are inferior to men may have originated in the premium placed on physical strength, which was required for hunting and waging war. Men, being more immediately essential for the group's survival, held a privileged position.

But there is also an ideological reason, analogous to defamation, prevalent in many cultures, which placed the blame for humanity's problems on the shoulders of women. Even before monotheist religions invented the concept of original sin as the source of all humanity's trials, the Greeks imagined the myth of Pandora's box to denigrate women. The gods created Pandora in order to punish men for having stolen fire from them (with the help of Prometheus). Pandora's curiosity led her to open the box containing all the diseases, sorrows, vices, and crimes that could befall humanity. According to the myth, it was because of Pandora, the first woman, that evil entered the world.

Various religions have adopted similar myths, for example the legend of original sin, which explains why so many religions, even in this day and age, show contempt for women and are obsessed with sex. The most vivid example is the order that followers can read in the Bible about burning women accused of witchcraft, a practice taken seriously during the sixteenth and seventeenth centuries in Protestant countries.[4]

Religions have often considered women less "pure" than men. For many years, the Roman Catholic Church denied mothers entry to a church for a month after a birth if the child was a boy, but for two months if the baby was a girl. The men running the church considered human birth, the most natural of all events, to be something impure and shameful. Some even went so far as to declare the birth of a female child to be a form of birth defect, the model being a male child.

The same detachment from women, the same fear of women, lay behind the requirement of celibacy for the entire clergy of the Roman Catholic Church. For many years, it was thought that only an unwedded way of life could lead to sanctity. The early Church had married priests (and even some bishops), as does the Orthodox Church of today. When the Second Lateran Council, during the European Middle Ages, definitively proclaimed the Church's clerical celibacy requirement, it was in fact a break from centuries of Christian tradition.[5] Practical considerations led the Catholic hierarchy to change the clergy's civil status. It was in part a reaction to Catharism—a new heretical religion growing fast in the Southwest of France—which prided itself on having unmarried priests. It was also a way to avoid the break-up of the Church's huge properties, especially land, through multiple inheritances among the priests' children.[6] Of course, in another case of discrimination against women, the Roman Catholic Church has never accepted that they be ordained and join its clergy.

The long tradition of misogyny is still alive in the Roman Catholic Church. It comes down from the teaching of Paul of Tarsus, who wrote letters in the first century confirming the traditional subordinated role reserved for women. In ancient civilizations, it was common practice to consider that women were owned, bought and sold as pieces of property, by fathers and husbands alike. Therefore, the apostle Paul invented nothing new when he wrote in the first century, "Let a woman learn in silence with all submissiveness. I permit no woman to teach or to have authority over men; she is to keep silent" (1 Timothy 2:11–12). It was a basic tenet of both Hebrew and Roman law that women had no civic rights. Fathers or husbands had, *de jure*, the power of life or death over them.[7]

No other organized religion, however, treats women, in practice, with less respect and consideration than Islam. Indeed, this religion often imposes on girls and women a series of detailed constraints which at times obliges them to hide their face in public, sometimes forbids them from practicing sports and, in the end, frequently forces them to relinquish any hope of living a normal life in society because they are prevented from exercising a profession. In the most fanatical Islamic countries, the official religion mandates to women a status that is tantamount to slavery. For instance, in Afghanistan, when the country was under Taliban control, girls were formally forbidden to go to school. And to underline the total and symbolic submission of women to men, Islamist religious extremists force women to bury themselves under a *tchadri*, sometimes called a *burqa* or *jalbab*, an opaque veil that covers them from head to foot, with only a small opening at the level of the eyes.

Certain Muslim countries have retained the old, barbaric tradition of stoning to death girls and women accused of sexual transgressions, or who have simply shown themselves in public without wearing the approved costume. It is thus true, even in these modern times, that certain men use religion to control and maintain women in a discriminatory system of perpetual submission and dependence. The violence perpetrated against women and sanctioned by certain organized religions remains a great human scandal in the twenty-first century.

Historically, the attitude of organized religions toward women has closely paralleled their position regarding slavery. In both instances, slaves and women were admonished to submit to their masters. It was only after the advent of the Renaissance, and especially after the Enlightenment, when the secular principles of basic human equality and of democracy became widely accepted, at least in the West, that women were granted equal civic rights and that owners were forced to free their slaves.

RELIGIONS AND SLAVERY

The revealed books of religions, whether in the Bible, the Torah (the word *Torah* means "law"), or the Qur'an (Koran), have all condoned slavery. The Bible permitted owners to beat their slaves severely, even to the point of killing them. However, as long as the slave lingered longer than twenty-four hours before dying of the abuse, the owner was not regarded as having committed a crime, because, after all, the slave was his property. One of the biblical passages that was the favorite of theologians who wished to justify slavery on biblical grounds was Genesis 9:25–27. It purports that it is alright to make generations of slaves: "Cursed be Canaan! The lowest of slaves will he be to his brothers... Blessed be the Lord, the God of Shem! May Canaan be the slave of Shem. May God extend the territory of Japheth; may Japheth live in the tents of Shem and may Canaan be his slave."[8] The Jewish Torah is even more explicit: "You may, however, take as your booty the women, the children, the livestock, and everything in the town—all its spoils—and enjoy the use of the spoil of your enemy which the Lord your God gives you." (20:14–15)

In the New Testament, there is no outright condemnation of slavery. Jesus himself is not reported to have said anything negative about the practice prevalent in his times nor to have hinted that masters should free their slaves. His principal proselytizer, Paul of Tarsus, never wrote an Epistle saying that slavery was profoundly immoral. This moral ambivalence may have contributed to the American Civil War (1861–65). Indeed, the president of the Confederate States of America, Jefferson Davis, had this to say about the legitimacy of his fight: "[Slavery] was established by decree of Almighty God... it is sanctioned in the Bible, in both Testaments, from Genesis to Revelation... it has existed in all ages, has been found among the people of the highest civilization, and in nations of the highest proficiency in the arts."[9]

For its part, the Roman Catholic Church accommodated itself to the institution of slavery for a very long time. While it is true that the church spoke out against slavery at various times throughout history, it reserved its condemnation for new colonies and regarding certain peoples. It was only in 1839 that Pope Gregory XVI finally condemned the slave trade as a social evil, but he did not push for the emancipation of those slaves already held in bondage. As late as 1866, the Vatican still considered that "slavery itself, considered as such in

its essential nature, is not at all contrary to the natural and divine law."
It was only in 1888, and again in 1890, that Pope Leo XIII came out
unambiguously against slavery, declaring the enslavement of native
peoples and blacks to be an evil practice. Nearly a century later, in
1962–65, the Second Vatican Council definitively closed the books on
the question, declaring slavery a grave offense against human dignity.
This was, however, nearly twenty centuries after the founding of the
Christian religion.[10]

Such is also the case with Islam. Islam has retained the principle
of slavery and sanctioned the practice in the Qur'an. Even the
prophet Muhammad took slaves. He owned many slaves, both males
and females, after he moved from Mecca to Medina. Islam retains
slavery for two reasons: because slavery is part of *jihad* and it is
believed that infidel prisoners of war may be enslaved after a war; and
because the sexual propagation of slaves naturally generates more
slaves for their owner, who can then sell them. It is an historical fact
that one of the reasons Muslims invaded black Africa was the search
for slaves. Many Qur'anic verses condone and attest to Islam's
approval of slavery. For instance, it is only in 1962 that some Islamic
countries such as Saudi Arabia and Yemen finally abolished slavery.

The first humanist moral rule precludes and rejects any idea of
having human beings considered as objects that can be owned, abused, or
exploited. Slavery and slavery-like systems are anathema to humanism.[11]

A SOURCE OF CONFLICTS: IMAGINARY GODS WHO TAKE SIDES

The principle of equal rights among all human beings is far from
being universally accepted. And, in many cases, the main obstacle is
religion. Indeed, some peoples have not only invented gods, but they
have gone one step further in inventing theories according to which
they have been chosen by such imaginary deities and thus deserve a
special status among human groups. Such pretensions have consequences. Those who believe in them naturally come to develop a
sense of superiority toward everyone else. On no account should the
lucky chosen few mix with lesser people for fear of being contami-

nated and corrupted by them. Discrimination, segregation, and loathing of the inferior people ensue. The seeds of permanent conflicts and wars are sown.

People identify with the gods they have invented, gods who are the image of themselves and who can help them pursue their own selfish interests. Those who indulge in such myths delude themselves, since they are but means to justify their often very obvious interests.[12] The destructive ideology that some people are especially chosen by abstract deities and are elevated to a special level of importance and authority is particularly pervasive among certain Judaists and certain evangelical Christians. For instance, the belief in innate Jewish superiority has a long tradition in some Jewish religious and political thinking, central to which was the Judaic notion of the Jews as Yahweh's chosen people. Moshe Ben Maimon (1135–1204) was the main proponent of such a theory.[13] But partisans of Islam find in their own holy book, the Qur'an, passages that incite them to scorn the Jews. For example, the Jewish people are charged with "falsehood" (Surah 3:71), with distortion (Surah 4:46), and of being "corrupters of Scripture" (Surah 2:75). The Qur'an goes even further and admonishes Muslims not to make friends with people of other faiths: "Do not take the Jews and the Christians for friends; they are friends of each other; and whoever amongst you takes them for a friend, then surely he is one of them; surely Allah does not guide the unjust people." (5:51)

Because this hegemonic ideology implies a particular sense of superiority, it has been a curse that Jews have had to carry for centuries. Even nowadays, in Israel and elsewhere, the popularly accepted theory of Zionism is based, to a large extent, on the self-serving myth of the chosen people. Such notions of innate superiority are, of course, in direct negation of the humanist principle of the equality of all human beings and should be rejected a barbarous relic of ancient times when ethnocentrism, imperialism, and racism prevailed. Indeed, there is no better recipe for conflicts and wars among humans than such backward-looking illusions. For this reason, it is deplorable that some still find solace in such self-serving myths.

In the United States there exists a similar dangerous sentiment of religion-based superiority, found especially in religious Puritanism: Americans are seen to be an "almost chosen" people, their country a "city upon a hill" supposedly guided by a providential hand. Such a concept of American exceptionalism, mixed with the concept of Puritan millennialism, was incorporated historically into the myth of Manifest Destiny. This convenient and self-deluding ideology was used during the nineteenth century to dispossess the American Indians of their lands and to launch imperialistic wars abroad, as in the Philippines at the turn of the nineteenth and twentieth centuries.[14]

Adopting Puritan millennialism—a theory of Anglo-Saxon or Teutonic racial superiority—some religious Americans persuaded themselves that the United States was a sort of new Israel. It was a convenient theory that justified the slaughter of American Indians for the sake of a higher Christian civilization. According to this racial theory of history, popular not only in late nineteenth-century America but also in early twentieth-century Germany, according to historian John Burgess, the Teutonic nations were destined "to carry the political civilization of the modern world into those parts of the world inhabited by unpolitical and barbaric races." This divine theory of Manifest Destiny was spawned by Christian America's conviction that the Christian god wished the white peoples of Europe and America to dominate the world.

In 1886, a period fertile with delusional authors, Josiah Strong published a book titled *Our Country*, in which he advanced the idea that English-speaking peoples have the mission to evangelize the world. A few years later, Brooks Adams published a similar ethnocentric theory of history in a book titled *The Law of Civilization and Decay*, whose main thesis was that nations oscillate historically between barbarism and civilization. In a surprisingly frank development, the author then went on to extol barbarism, arguing that barbarism was necessary to develop empires and subjugate colonies. Adams then envisaged the emergence of an Anglo-Saxon alliance between the US and Great Britain that would dominate the world.

The reader will have recognized the old self-serving colonialist idea that dark-skinned people in foreign lands are unable to govern themselves and need external military intervention to do so. It is incredible that such ideas are still being relied upon to support new forms of zealous nationalism at the beginning the twenty-first century. For example, they serve to justify American-led wars of aggression in the Middle East, viewed by some as crusades against evil, but which are more realistically being waged to protect the state of Israel and to secure access to energy resources.[15]

Such eccentric and archaic ideas are not inconsequential, for sooner or later opportunistic politicians think of using them as stepping-stones to power. For instance, in 1889, an imperialist American politician, Theodore Roosevelt, in a book titled *The Winning of the West*, wrote that the 1864 slaying of several hundred Cheyenne women and children was "on the whole as righteous and beneficial a deed as ever took place on the frontier." For this politician, drunk with millennium ideas, the extermination or genocide of the Americans Indians served to advance civilization! When he became president in 1901, after the assassination of William McKinley, Theodore Roosevelt applied his racial theories of civilization in the Philippines where, for fourteen years, the United States fought a nationalist insurgency. Perhaps not surprisingly, the American Protestant missionary press was most supportive of the brutal Philippines war, a war that resulted in the killing of hundreds of thousands of Catholic Filipinos. Of course, in the realm of genocide, the German Chancellor Adolf Hitler outdid all the other millennium imperialists.

At the beginning of the twenty-first century, a similar wind of folly blows in certain American quarters. The powerful Jewish-inspired neoconservative movement, for example, is driven by the same sense of moral superiority and by an apology of world imperialism for the good cause. The cause this time—which conceals more down-to-earth interests—is the spread of democratic universalism, especially in the oil-rich Middle East.[16] Irving Kristol, one of the original neocons, advances that America needs a twenty-first century version of Manifest Destiny. For Kristol and his cohort, just as it was Manifest Destiny for the United States to reach the Pacific Ocean in the nineteenth century, so it is today America's Manifest Destiny to seed democracy around the world. The shaky assumption underlying such thinking is that a democratic state can be imposed from above by an imperialist and militarist power. For the neocon missionaries, force must be used to convert the world to democracy. This is the new religion: freedom from the barrel of a gun.

This is of course a fundamental contradiction in terms, for in a democracy, power originates from the people, not from armed foreign invaders, and the law, not force, regulates the interactions between individuals and between nations. In fact, imperialism is the antithesis of democracy. Nevertheless, with such open-ended patronizing and condescending hubris, American neoconservatives can justify any imperialistic war. Indeed, the neocon theological version of Manifest Destiny is also a theology of war. As such, these old theories in new clothes represent a grave danger to world peace and human dignity because they run counter to the principle of equal rights among all human beings.

Two

RESPECT LIFE AND PROPERTY

SECOND HUMANIST PRINCIPLE:
RESPECT LIFE AND PROPERTY OF OTHERS.

The care of human life and happiness, and not their destruction, is the first and only object of good government.
—Thomas Jefferson, third US president

And reason . . . teaches all mankind who will but consult it, that being all equal and independent, no one ought to harm another in his life, health, liberty, or possessions.
—John Locke (1632–1704)

The ultimate end of all revolutionary social change is to establish the sanctity of human life, the dignity of man, the right of every human being to liberty and well-being.
—Emma Goldman (1869–1940), Lithuanian-born American anarchist

The second humanist rule is really two rules in one. Since life is the most important property that a human being can possess, respect for human life, and respect for all forms of life for that matter, along with respect for property, translate into not killing each other and not stealing from each other. This second rule is also a prerequisite for rule 7, which commands us not to waste the Earth's resources, and rule 9, which mandates democracy and free markets as the best institutions for guaranteeing human dignity, freedom, and liberty.

45

THE MOST IMPORTANT PROPERTY IS LIFE

The natural right to property, beginning with the ownership of one's own life, is the foundation of human liberty. People have an unalienable right to life. No human being, in whatever capacity, has the right to take away someone else's life. Not to kill is a basic humanistic value.

Also, there cannot be individual freedom without people having the liberty to own what is needed for their survival and development, while being responsible for what they own. To own something is to be responsible for it, to be free to have control over it, and to be able to dispose of it and to enter into voluntary contracts with others. Ownership is therefore the foundation of voluntary economic exchange, of commerce, and of free functioning markets. When despotic governments or other authorities deprive people of their natural right to property, they deprive them of their natural right to be free. That is why the rule about not stealing is also a humanistic value. The institution of property has taken many forms in the past, some good and some less desirable.

The respect for life encompasses the means to sustain life, to raise a family, to be independent, and to have privacy. Every individual owns him or her self. In the past, however, certain societies developed the terrible idea that persons could be the property of others. This was the monstrous institution of slavery, as mentioned previously.

The right to life would be somewhat theoretical if the fight against human diseases and illnesses was not a social responsibility and if access to health services were reserved to the rich. Before wasting money on unproductive investments, such as armaments or grandiose monuments, governments should make it a priority to complement individual efforts to improve health conditions in their country. This also means, internationally, that richer countries have a moral obligation to assist poorer countries in improving health conditions and health standards. As we shall see in chapter 10, this also applies to education standards.

The natural right to property also means that killing a fellow human being—in effect, robbing him of his life—is the supreme act of stealing and the most reprehensible act of all. This also means that collective killing and genocide are the most abominable acts that can be committed. Religions usually forbid the killing of individuals but often will make exceptions for people who are evil and allow governments or authorities to kill and murder. Indeed, when people are demonized and portrayed as nameless, cold-hearted, immoral, worthless and bad, then theocratic rules could authorize killing them. Killing in such circumstances is done to get rid of evil. It is with such nonhumanistic sophisms that religious wars were born. Indeed, in religious wars, each side inevitably invokes its own sacred text and tries to take over the other side, not through persuasion, but by force of arms. With such an attitude, religious people might feel justified in bombing and machine-gunning other human beings, and still keep a good conscience.

To a certain extent all wars are religious in nature, since the enemy is first demonized before being killed. That is why we can say that wars and military murders are the last refuge of the religious scoundrel. Humanistic thinking makes no distinction between killing another human being in a private gesture in daily life, or in response to a military command. Except in the case of genuine self-defense, both constitute crimes against humanity.

RATIONALISM, COOPERATION AND PROPERTY

All this is in line with the thinking of the great liberal economist, Ludwig von Mises, who mapped out the foundation of liberty in his book *Liberalism*, which initially appeared in 1927. Mises said that the foundation of liberty is private property, including the private ownership of the means of production. If property were protected from the discretionary power of governments or other authorities, all else in politics would follow. First, the state could not be coercive and imperialistic because it couldn't raise the funds necessary to finance military adventures in foreign lands.

Second, the more the state and its rulers are given control over private property, the more they will be tempted to impose their authority via arms and war. Indeed, governments generally do not hold referendums on the opportunity or not to wage war. This is still the most undemocratic decision made by governments. As Tolstoy wrote, "In all history there is no war which was not hatched by the governments, the governments alone, independent of the interests of the people, to whom war is always pernicious even when successful."

Economist Mises is to be commended for his defense of rationalism and voluntary cooperation as the essential foundation of the liberal political order. In Mises' view, peace, liberty, and free enterprise are cut from the same cloth. They are the result of a society with a decentralized political system that respects the privacy, property, associations, and wishes of the population.

Such a liberal society trades with foreign countries rather than waging war on them. It proclaims the right of peoples to self-determination and the right of secession and emphasizes that no government can rule over a people without consent. It respects the free movement of persons. It does not intervene in the private religious affairs of people but rather endorses a complete separation of church and state and adopts a rule of tolerance. Therefore, the natural right of property is the foundation of liberty and peace, while statism, theocracy, and militarism are synonymous with slavery and war.

PUBLIC AND PRIVATE PROPERTY

One of the great achievements of human civilization was the advent of production specialization according to comparative advantages, leading to the commercial exchange of goods and services. This generated a huge increase in human productivity and living standards. A doctor could specialize in treating the sick, while buying his milk from the dairyman. The baker could concentrate on making bread, without wasting his time and resources on making shoes, better left to the shoemaker, and so on. Between regions and nations, warm regions could produce fruits and exchange them for minerals extracted from mines in colder regions rich in iron and other minerals.

In other words, the advent of private markets and of relative prices for goods and services according to supply and demand changed forever the fate of humanity. It allowed for population growth on a scale that self-sufficiency would never have made possible. But to produce and to be productive, humans had to save and invest in techniques and means of production. They had to invent and innovate. And to be motivated enough to sacrifice and to make the necessary efforts, they had to be able to expect a certain probability of rewards for their undertakings. And it is here that the institution of private property plays a role.

Indeed, the farmer who owns his land is more motivated to get up early to do his chores than if he is only the renter of the property. Ownership is responsibility. To own means to preserve, to maintain, and to improve. Every owner has an inherent interest in seeing his or her property improve in value and in utility.

This may be the greatest distinction between collective property and private property: what belongs to everybody belongs in practice to nobody, and the responsibility for upkeep and improvement is diffuse. Only a strong central authority, a government endowed with collective property rights, can assure that collective capital goods do not degenerate and lose their value to society. And whoever speaks of collective ownership also implies a great concentration of economic and political powers, with all the risks to personal freedom that such a political concentration entails.

There are social goods, goods that are consumed simultaneously by all—such as the justice system to preserve law and order, roads to move people and goods from one place to another, public parks for the continuous enjoyment of all, and so on—that are more economical when centrally owned and administered. Economists have a general rule to decide when public ownership is superior to private ownership: when the total social benefit of public ownership is higher than total social cost, as compared to private ownership, then the former is to be chosen over the latter. In practice, for most goods, the total net social benefit derived from private property surpasses by far the total net social benefit that can be derived from collective ownership. Essentially, this is due to the difficulty of managing public enterprises in an efficient manner, as compared to the tighter management observed under private ownership. A grand scale demonstration of this principle was carried out during the twentieth century when the economies of state-owned and centrally planned communist countries in Eastern Europe and elsewhere collapsed, as compared to the market-driven and decentralized economies of Western Europe, America, and Asia, which adjusted and prospered over time.[1]

PROPERTY, ECONOMIC EFFICIENCY, LIBERTY AND SOCIAL JUSTICE

A discussion of the institution of property raises several questions. What is the nature of ownership, and should there be limits to the rights that attend it? Should property always be held privately and never in common, or should some combination of these two types of ownership prevail in certain circumstances? To what extent does the legitimacy of a system of private property depend on considerations of economic efficiency or distributive justice?

The US Constitution, for instance, protects "life, liberty, and property," in its Fifth Amendment: "No person shall ... be deprived of life, liberty, or property, without due process of law; nor shall private property be taken for public use, without just compensation."

In the Sixth Amendment, the US Constitution also protects the right of habeas corpus for all people: "In all criminal prosecutions, the accused shall enjoy the right to a speedy and public trial, by an impartial jury of the state and district wherein the crime shall have been committed, which district shall have been previously ascertained by law, and to be informed of the nature and cause of the accusation; to be confronted with the witnesses against him; to have compulsory process for obtaining witnesses in his favor, and to have the assistance of counsel for his defense."

Criminal justice based on the British Magna Carta of 1215 denies government the power to imprison people without trial. Indeed, Anglo-Saxon Common Law since the Magna Carta proclaims that the government, as represented by a king, a prime minister, or a president, cannot imprison an individual without due process. This is the cornerstone of individual liberty in a democratic society.

Respect for individual private property as a principle of freedom and liberty is undoubtedly more prevalent in the Western world than elsewhere. In the old English tradition, the principle holds that "a man's house is his castle." It follows that being a renter doesn't have the same advantages as being a property owner, perhaps even involving an infringement on a person's freedom of action. Indeed, when farms, lands, and houses are owned and controlled by a few, the risk becomes high that corruption, despotism, and tyranny will ensue.

For many centuries, individual private property rights have been the foundation of economic cooperation, of private commercial markets, and of ways to economize scarce resources. This tradition is deeply rooted in British common law. The main exception to this principle is when the government, acting in an overriding case of public interest or public good, resorts to its right of eminent domain. It can then forcefully, albeit with just compensation, take over a private property for a public project, such as building a highway or a railway, or other social projects.

Therefore, private property rights are not absolutes in themselves. They only are acceptable if they foster the common good and are not incompatible with social justice. Basically, public property is required in order to establish the common economic infrastructures for all inhabitants living in a given territory (courts, police, national defense, public education, etc.) and to protect the public interest. Private property is also necessary in order to have an efficient economy based on specialization and voluntary exchange. In a well-functioning economy, people own their own labor and talent for innovation and can apply them, with capital, knowledge, and effort, to produce goods and services useful to society. The mechanism of freely fluctuating prices provides the signals for economic agents to produce more of what is more valuable and less of what is less valuable. Users and consumers are the final arbiters of what is valuable and what is less valuable, through their purchasing decisions.

In this perspective, we may ask what should be the line of demarcation between public and private property? Also, how can society obtain both economic efficiency and social justice (usually defined as the avoidance of large and excessive inequalities in wealth and income)? The answers to these two questions usually depend on whether free markets can function efficiently and therefore enhance the common good. However, this is not always the case, and public intervention may thus be required to correct any imbalance.

We then face what economists call market failures. There are many instances when market failures result in reductions rather than increases of the common good. A legitimate government, representing the democratically expressed will of the people, must then step in and protect the public interest. This action can span from simple government regulation to the complete nationalization of an industry.

Economists have long identified five main types or causes of market failure, when private markets do not bring about economic efficiency and must be regulated to avoid socially undesirable consequences.

The first instance is the existence of public or collective goods and the means of financing their production. It is in the nature of public goods to be accessible to all once they exist—clean air to breathe, for example—but users have a built-in incentive to refrain from paying for a public good that is freely accessible once in existence. In a purely private market, therefore, insufficient financing would result in the public good being provided in insufficient quantities.

Other instances of such public goods, besides a clean environment, are national defense, city-street lighting, lighthouse protection for ships, police services, the public roads system, public airwaves for radio and television, public libraries, the provision of general inoculations against diseases, and the system of public parks and beaches. In such cases, the government is justified in either regulating the private production of such public goods, financing their production through general taxation, or, as a last resort, providing them directly for collective consumption, at marginal, cost-covering prices.

The second instance is the existence of monopoly or cartel power in the hands of private interests. Monopolies and cartels can exert significant influence over prices or production, depriving society of goods or services produced at the most efficient level.

As a rule, price is higher and output is lower under monopoly conditions than in a competitive market. Relying on public regulation of monopoly or cartel behavior may be justified, through antitrust policies, for example. Alternatively, adequate taxation of monopoly profits may be required or policies may be designed to introduce more competition into existing markets though deregulation. In the case of recently privatized utilities, public interest may require some temporary price controls.

The third instance occurs when a production or consumption activity results in externalities or neighborhood or spill-over effects, that is, when market prices do not reflect the impact of an economic activity on third parties. Such economic externalities can be either negative or positive. An example of a negative externality would be a firm that emits pollutants during production and doesn't incorporate the damage to the environment in its costs of production or in the price consumers pay for its product.

The fourth instance of market failure occurs when market participants have incomplete or asymmetrical information. For example, government may have to regulate the introduction of new medications because consumers may be negatively and irreparably affected, due to a lack of information about this category of products.

A fifth market failure is more social and political than purely economic. It may arise when there is an excessive inequality in the distribution of wealth and income. Excessive wealth and income inequality is dangerous for social peace, for the survival of democracy, for the preservation of individual freedom, and for the continuance of economic dynamism. Indeed, private markets are inherently more valuable to those with the most wealth and income, and least to those without much purchasing power. In a dynamic sense, if the operations of private markets lead to ever-increasing inequality of wealth ownership and income over time, this may be seen as a social and political market failure. The government may consider such a gross inequality in the distribution of wealth and income to be against the public interest and use the taxation system to rectify the situation.[2]

Economic market failures do not necessarily imply that government should always attempt to solve them on its own because the costs of government failures might be higher than those of the market failures it attempts to fix. This may be the result of the failure of the

democratic process itself. Indeed, when special-interest groups succeed in taking control of the government apparatus for their own private benefits, government may cease functioning for the common
good. In such instances, government intervention may make matters
worse. A government reform should precede its involvement in regulating private markets.

OWNERSHIP RIGHTS AND THE HUMAN GENOME

The discovery of the structure of DNA (deoxyribonucleic acid) in
1953 was one of the greatest leaps of all time in biological science.
The discovery uncovered the molecular structure of the double-helix
DNA molecule in each of the 46 chromosomes in human cells. The
technique of DNA sequencing in living organisms, and especially the
sequencing of the human genome and the identification of individual
genes, is of great importance. For the first time, it opens up the possibility of knowing, in advance, the genetic strengths and weaknesses of
every single individual. Indeed, in a not-too-distant future, it will be
possible for every human being to have his or her genetic background
decoded, revealing, for instance, any susceptibility to particular diseases. On the positive side, this has the potential to completely trans-
form the preventive, diagnostic, and therapeutic medicine of the
future. However, this new knowledge, and especially the use we make
of it, raises many social and moral concerns.[3] Obviously, as with any
new knowledge, it can be used productively or destructively. The
most recent example is nuclear technology, which can serve either to
produce energy or to build atomic bombs to kill people.

Genetic knowledge has the same double-edged potential. It can
lead to new cures for previously intractable human diseases, such as
the debilitating Huntingdon's or Alzheimer's diseases, or it can give
more tools to governments and organizations to thwart personal privacy and freedom, leading to genetic discrimination of all sorts. For
example, might insurance companies use genetic knowledge to deny
certain individuals health or life insurance? Might employers deny
employment to an individual known to have "bad" genes? Will private

companies acquire a monopoly position on certain genetic material and reap enormous profits? And, if so, for how long?

Attempts at patenting DNA sequences and privatizing their ownership are particularly troubling. In some countries, notably in the US, there has been a rush to apply ordinary intellectual property laws to the field of genomics. Researchers and corporations who artificially isolate individual human genes have tried to use these laws to obtain monopoly patents on certain genes. However, the property of a patent on a human gene is not at all comparable to ownership of an invention or a new product. In the latter field, competition can give rise to similar inventions and similar products, and the consumer is somewhat protected from exploitation over time.

In the field of genomics, however, a life patent on a human gene creates a potentially dangerous monopoly situation because these genes cannot be duplicated. The granting of such monopoly patents could be seen as antisocial. Without strict regulations, it could lead to human exploitation through the charging of exorbitant licensing fees, royalties and rents. It's one thing to grant a patent on a technique or an identification method but quite another to grant a patent on the gene itself. No one owns human life, and private industrial researchers do not invent the genes they try to patent and profit from. This is a case where public property should prevail, and research licenses should be freely granted to biologists and other users. Antiquated patent laws should be modified accordingly to protect the public and sustain the common good.[4]

THE ENVIRONMENT AND PROPERTY RIGHTS

To own a property is to have a direct interest in having the value of that property maintained and increased. Property automatically begets responsibility. As a famous economist once put it, "In the history of the world, no one has ever washed a rented car."[5] An owner has an inherent incentive to exploit resources responsibly: owners are rewarded when they conserve and when they invest time and money for the upkeep of their properties. Individual property rights usually promote socially sustainable behavior. It doesn't pay to kill the goose that lays the golden egg. Indeed, an owner has the necessary incentive to manage an asset for the long term and not only for the short term. A farmer-owner, for example, will pay careful attention not to overuse the land in one year to the detriment of future years' production; he will enrich it and till it to make it more productive. A homesteader-owner will maintain and repair his house to preserve its value and good appearance.

The right of ownership also entails the right of not having one's property harmed or destroyed by external interventions. The principle that one may not harm a neighbor's property allows courts to rule on matters of pollution and contamination of the environment. The right to have a clean environment has been incorporated into nuisance laws, which prevent one's property from being encroached upon by others. Sometimes, the most efficient situation is to guarantee constitutional protection for individual private property, subject to an overriding clause of public interest. In general, however, it can be said that a person's property rights end at the neighbor's border and that one has no right to use one's property in a way that injures the property of others.

There are many examples that can illustrate this principle. For instance, individuals owning land adjacent to a body of water have a right to an uninterrupted and unpolluted flow of water beside or through their properties. Therefore, if someone upstream pollutes a river, downstream landowners have the right to petition a court of law either to receive appropriate compensations or to have sanctions imposed on the polluters, including cease and desist orders that may result in a relocation or the discontinuance of the polluting activities. This has the effect of raising the cost of polluting with the result that there is less pollution.

THE RIGHT TO DIE WITH DIGNITY

In 2001 Holland became the first country to legalize the right to die with dignity, reaffirming the humanist principle that such a right belongs to the individual, not to politicians or priests. Belgium followed in 2002. In both of these humanist countries, the law protects a doctor who performs euthanasia from criminal charges within certain narrow parameters. The patient, who must be an adult, must be suffering constant and unsupportable physical or psychic pain, as the result of an incurable condition. He must be conscious, and his request to die must be well thought out and persistent. No outside pressure is tolerated, and the patient must be assured that palliative care will be provided for as long as necessary.

Life on this planet is in a constant state of change and renewal. Even if humans are more intelligent than other animals, the laws of birth and death nevertheless bind them. After all, if life is a repeated victory over matter, death itself is an abhorrent reality. It is nothing less than an unavoidable surrender to the overwhelming forces of nature. Therefore, should not human intelligence permit us to organize the circumstances of our death in order to turn its inevitability into a more humane and tolerable experience?

Regarding euthanasia, there is a chasm between public opinion and the views of the religious, legal, and political elites. In Europe as well as in the United States and Canada, those in power do not hesitate to place their judgments and values above those of the person who is the most concerned in such a vital decision: the patient. Even when the proper safeguards are being followed, doctors and other caregivers who are close to a patient can be imprisoned for assisting people who suffer from painful and incurable illness to die.

In the most publicized example, in 1999, Dr. Jack Kevorkian was condemned in the United States to ten to twenty-five years in prison for helping a person with Lou Gehrig's disease to die. Dr. Kevorkian was paroled in June 2007.

In 2001 former American Attorney General John Ashcroft even tried to use the Drug Enforcement Administration agency to render it illegal for doctors to help terminally ill people end their own lives. The clear intention was to prevent Oregon—the only state that allows doctor-assisted suicide for terminally ill patients—from implementing its Death with Dignity law, a measure that was adopted by ballot initiative in 1994, then again by a large majority in 1997. Fortunately, on January 17, 2006, in an important victory for physicians, pharmacists, and patients everywhere, the US Supreme Court sided with the people and ruled that politicians, clergymen, and bureaucrats may not define the scope of legitimate medical practice, even in cases where terminally ill patients personally request aggressive treatment to suppress intolerable pain or to arrange for a gentle, and inevitable, death.[6]

Even today, politicians, clergymen, and judges paternalistically refuse to lose control over the people up to the very end, denying them the right to decide when to cease treatment and seek a dignified death. It is perhaps a vestige of the religious past that such apparatchiks seem to think they hold a divine power to decide for others on questions of life and death. This is but another example of the pernicious influence of organized religion on our daily lives.

THE ISSUE OF ABORTION

There are few countries where abortion is uncontroversial. The right of a woman to control her own body and reproductive life presents a moral dilemma. In the Bible, there is very little concern for a woman's right to possess her own body. For example, the crime of rape is treated as an offense against the property of the father or husband, rather than as a attack on the dignity of the victim. As for abortion, the Bible remains mute.

Nevertheless, abortion involves morality, legality, and constitutionality, and it is debated worldwide. Indeed, the incidence of abortion around the world has been estimated to be about 26 induced abortions per 100 known pregnancies.[7] It is a complex issue because it opposes two perceived human rights; a woman's right to her own physical and mental health and the natural right of a future human being, the fetus, to be born. In the past, when reliable and safe contraceptive means were rare and costly, therapeutic medical abortion replaced makeshift or self-induced abortion procedures to terminate unwanted pregnancies. This was justly considered a great improvement in medical care.

Nowadays, however, with the widespread availability of many forms of contraception and birth control, including even retroactive means, the need for therapeutic abortions should be significantly reduced. It remains that abortion should no longer be used as a birth control device. For their part, governments have a responsibility to diminish the need for and the incidence of abortion, not through severe legal prohibition, which can be futile and dangerous, but through sex education and by making modern contraception methods easily available.[8]

From a humanist point of view, it can be said that while women have ownership of and control over their own body and can make individual choices accordingly, they also have an overall responsibility to show respect for human life. However, nobody—and certainly not the government or religious authorities—should dictate to women how they should manage their own body.

HUMANISM AND TEN CONTEMPORARY MORAL DILEMMAS

Here are ten contemporary moral dilemmas for which the second humanistic rule can provide guidance and answers.[9]

Birth control and family size. Birth control devices have existed from time immemorial. However, it was only during the twentieth century, with the advent of hormonal oral contraceptives, that safe and reliable birth control methods became available. For the first time, women could decide when to become pregnant without being subjected to chance and randomness. Women also gained the freedom to distinguish between their sexual life and the decision to bear a child.

For overpopulated countries mired in poverty and misery, a better control over the rate of population increase, coupled with better education, may be the principal avenue to escape their predicaments. The empowerment of women in every society must be considered a great step forward in human civilization.

This is subject to the important caveat that proper sex education is necessary to teach young persons that sexual promiscuity is incompatible with sound emotional development, that it may be detrimental to their health, that it is inimical to their self-esteem, and, therefore, that it should be avoided. Such a warning is consistent with humanist rule 1.

Therapeutic abortion. The right of a woman to own her own body supersedes the right of an unborn fetus. However, abortion should not be a substitute for responsible birth control, but should only be resorted to when a woman's physical or mental heath is seriously at stake. Modern contraceptive methods should be made easily available to all women who wish to use them. This is consistent with humanist rule 2.

Euthanasia. Death is a living experience from which none can escape. On the one hand, it is never permissible to kill another human being. On the other hand, each individual owns his or her body and can elect to put an end to existence through circumscribed assisted suicide methods. To render such an extreme decision truly a choice of last—and exceptional—resort, proper assistance and care should be provided to individuals who encounter otherwise solvable physical, psychiatric, emotional, or other types of personal problems and difficulties. This is consistent with the first two humanist rules.

Animal rights. Humans should have respect for all forms of life and avoid cruelty to animals. However, animals are not rational, moral agents and do not have the same rights to life as humans. Nevertheless, humans have an obligation not to treat animals brutally. As for the future, although animals are still presently a source of food and protein for most humans and, as such, the practice is a natural phenomenon, it should be expected that the necessity for using animals for food will become less and less so for economic, health, and moral reasons.

Economically, the production of butchery animals requires a lot of land and thus will likely become less feasible in the future. Nutritionally, meat consumption is not a true necessity and is less healthy for the human body than alternative sources of food. Morally, the act of killing animals for human consumption is a legacy of times when humans were dependent on animal protein for their survival. As this necessity gradually disappears, the philosophical rationale for eating animals will also disappear. This is consistent with humanist rule 2.

War. Wars of aggression and war killings are to be prohibited and are contrary to humanist morality, the only case for war being a circumscribed situation of legitimate defense (see chapter 8). This is consistent with humanist rule 8.

State-imposed capital punishment. The execution of another human being for the motive of revenge or retribution is contrary to humanist morality and is a legacy of more barbaric times. Only in situations of imminent self-defense can someone take the life of a fellow human being. This is consistent with humanist rules 1 and 2.

Genetic diseases and genetic research. Genetic diseases are caused by gene defects in an individual. Examples where genetic inheritance is a cause (or plays a role) can be found in diseases such as Huntington's, cystic fibrosis, Lou Gehrig's, Parkinson's, Alzheimer's, and certain types of cancer. Genetic testing has made it possible to seek out preventive healthcare for some one thousand diseases. Under proper professional supervision and with prudence and caution, DNA technology and other technological means, including synthetic biology, genetic therapy, genetic surgery, and the creation of new forms of life, should be encouraged and supported, from a humanistic point of view, as means to fight and eradicate many debilitating diseases. Human diseases in general have nothing to do with the supernatural world, and have certainly nothing to do with the notion of an original sin as the source of human disease and suffering. Old and antiquated religious codes should not stand in the way of scientific research and scientific progress.

Nevertheless, there are certain practices of procreation that can result in negative spillover effects for society as a whole, and which, therefore, require public supervision or, in some cases, prohibition. For example, social fads or cultural biases leading to the uncontrolled prenatal selection of the sex of children before birth have the potential to negatively impact the sex balance in a given population. Such an activity, therefore, needs to be properly regulated to avoid irreparable damage to society. Preimplantation genetic diagnosis (PGD), when done for nonmedical reasons, such as for sex selection, cannot be considered ethical. Parents need to be reminded that they do not own their children but are only their natural custodians until they reach adulthood.

Similarly, the biological cloning of individuals would violate the basic principle of human dignity and should not be practiced. It is not because a procedure is technically feasible that it becomes morally permissible. A cloned person, as an artificially engineered biological copy of somebody else, would be robbed of his individuality. This would be a negation of his fundamental right to be an autonomous and distinct human being. This is consistent with humanist rules 1 and 2.

Family units, marriage, divorce, and so on. There are many reasons why two persons might want to live together on a permanent basis. A first motivation may be to solidify a mutual long-term commitment of love, exclusive affection, and caring. A second reason, often related to the first, but not exclusively, is for the purpose of having children and raising a family. Third, two people may want to commit themselves to one another in order to create a permanent environment of intellectual, emotional, and moral support. A fourth reason may be more social and economic, in the sense that a family, as a social and economic unit, offers its members the promise of mutual assistance and of enhanced financial security.

Although circumstances do change and errors are sometimes made, and therefore adjustments are necessary, the ideal situation for raising children and forming a family is for two individuals to enter into a stable life-long commitment. However, this is not always possible when situations of incompatibility, unfaithfulness, or neglect arise.

Whatever the motivation for entering into a contract of marriage, or for dissolving it, such decisions belong to the individuals involved and not to third parties or government agencies. It is true that the state has the responsibility to assist families with children to make sure that the children are properly fed, clothed, and educated because they are future citizens. However, it has no business in dictating how two free and consenting adults wish to live their lives together. Marriages of any kind are private contracts between individuals, and no government interference is warranted. The state should limit its involvement to the creation of the proper legal framework within which such intimate decisions are made and carried out. This is consistent with humanist rules 1, 2 and 3.

Honesty and objects found fortuitously. An example of a minor moral dilemma is that of objects found by chance. Suppose one finds a pencil on a crowded street, and there is no easy way to find out to whom it belongs. What should be done? Suppose again that someone finds a wallet containing $100 with the name and phone number of the rightful owner in it. What to do? An easy moral rule can be applied here: when the rightful owner can be identified, or when there exists a Lost and Found facility, a found object should always be returned to its rightful owner or to the Lost and Found. This is always the case when the marginal value of a found object is higher than the marginal cost in time and money required to find its rightful owner. In situations where the owner is impossible to find and when there is no Lost and Found available, and if the marginal value of the found object is lower than the marginal cost in time and money required to find its owner, the found object can be kept. This is consistent with humanist rule 2.

The use of judgment in reference to moral principles. To decide according to rigid principles without reference to one's better judgment may have unintended negative consequences. As Kant once said, "Among men there are but few who behave according to principles—which is extremely good, as it can so easily happen that one errs in these principles, and then the resulting disadvantage extends all the further, the more universal the principle and the more resolute the person who has set it before himself." There are circumstances, indeed, in which no rigid or absolute principle should be followed, but rather decisions must be made for the best result.

Consider the case of a doctor's vow of confidentiality. If he diagnoses a deadly contagious disease, it is his duty to disregard his promise and inform the relevant authorities in order to protect the public welfare. The same applies to a lawyer who learns that one of his clients is about to commit a murder. In many moral decisions, personal judgment has to be exercised in balancing the advisability of an action according to general moral principles and the seriousness of consequences that would follow. Moral principles are never substitutes for one's judgment and personal responsibility.

THREE

TOLERANCE
The Empathy Principle

THIRD HUMANIST PRINCIPLE:
PRACTICE TOLERANCE AND OPEN-MINDEDNESS
TOWARD THE CHOICES AND LIFESTYLES OF OTHERS.

Laws alone cannot secure freedom of expression; in order
that every man present his views without penalty there must
be spirit of tolerance in the entire population.
—Albert Einstein (1879–1955)

Tolerance implies a respect for another person, not because
he is wrong or even because he is right, but because he is
human.
—John Cogley (Commonwealth, April 24, 1959)

Begin every day by telling yourself: Today I shall be meeting
with interference, ingratitude, insolence, disloyalty, ill will,
and selfishness—all of them due to the offender's ignorance
of what is good and evil.
—Marcus Aurelius (121–180 CE),
Roman emperor from 161 to 180 CE

How people choose to live their life is their own personal decision, provided they do not hurt others. However, to be truly
moral, people must be tolerant of each other. The first manifestation
of tolerance is showing respect, empathy, and compassion for other
people who happen to have different feelings, different philosophies,
different interests, or different views of the world. To be tolerant, a
person must develop a capacity to feel what others feel and be able to

share other people's sentiments, concerns, joys, and sorrows. Therefore, the *empathy principle* in human relations means that people put themselves in the place of others and see things from their point of view.[1] Indeed, according to the empathy principle, one must aim at treating others as if one were in their place. The empathy principle can thus be framed this way: "Do to others what you would wish to be done to you, if you were in their place." That is why we say that empathy is the foundation of humanist morality. It is the awareness that most humans develop that other people can suffer and flourish as they do and that they should treat others accordingly.[2]

THE EMPATHY PRINCIPLE

The empathy principle is derived directly from the first rule of humanist morality and the reciprocity principle. However, it goes further than to simply say that everyone should treat others the way they would like to be treated by them and should refrain from treating others in a way they would not like to be treated. While the reciprocity principle is self-centered in nature, the empathy principle comes less naturally and may have to be acquired and learned through reasoning and teaching. Both are necessary to arrive at the *Super Golden Rule* of humanist morality, which is the sum of the two principles. Therefore, the Super Golden Rule of humanist morality is as follows: "Not only do to others as you would have them do to you, but also do to others what you would wish to be done to you, if you were in their place." In practice, this humanist moral principle requires that we judge whether an act is moral or not *as if* we did not know in advance if it would apply to us or to others. Thus, racism is wrong because you would not want people to treat you badly if you were of another race; sexism is wrong because you would not want to be treated disrespectfully if you were of another sex; torture is wrong because you would not want to be tortured, and so on.

The Super Golden Rule of humanist morality does encompass moral reciprocity, but it goes much further toward genuine altruism, compassion, and human empathy. It truly defines our moral obligations to others in positive terms about what should be done. As human beings living on the same planet, we have a humanist moral duty to be responsive to the needs of others.

When one applies the empathy principle, indeed, one recognizes that one's own rights and needs are also everyone else's rights and needs.[3] The empathy principle is the foundation for the rule of tolerance in our complex and pluralistic world. As such, the fundamental right of freedom of conscience means that people have a right to their own thoughts, their own beliefs, their own philosophy, and their own religion. The only requirement is that they do not impose these beliefs on others and do not use these beliefs to foster violence and intolerance toward others. Fanaticism, extremism, and proselytism are the opposite of tolerance, trust, and open-minded attitudes in human relations.

TOLERANCE IN OPEN AND DEMOCRATIC SOCIETIES

Tolerance, generosity, and understanding toward others, including religious tolerance, are the civilized ways to avoid conflicts in the world. Even though it is natural for people to look after themselves and their families, toward whom they have a primary duty and to whom they owe affection, they should never let their own immediate ambitions and interests blind them to other people's legitimate interests. The natural tendency to selfish behavior should be counterbalanced by a high degree of disinterestedness and understanding in our dealings with other human beings.

What should be our attitude, however, when facing ideologues, extremists, and fanatics who would use violence or other unconstitutional means to abolish freedom of thought, conscience, and speech, thereby posing a threat to everyone's freedom? Then it becomes a moral duty to resist their open calls for dictatorship, theocratic government, and totalitarianism, and to foil their attempts to enslave the people. Indeed, the humanistic rule of tolerance toward individuals does not mean that democratic and open societies should embrace a suicidal tolerance of totalitarian ideologies or legalize intolerant movements that openly threaten to abolish freedom and democracy because when individual freedom is abolished, it is very difficult and costly to reestablish it.

One of the greatest threats to freedom and democracy nowadays comes from the fallacious ideology of multiculturalism and its underlying false tenet that all cultures are equal. According to this ideology, the different ethnic groups that arrive in a given society through immigration must be encouraged to preserve their cultural identity, even in cases when such cultural values are diametrically opposed to freedom and democracy. Another related but abusive idea consists in defining cultural values and religious beliefs as being immutable and beyond the realm of reason and critical analysis. This can go as far as to consider such values and beliefs as being uncontestable propositions or characteristics as immutable and unalterable as race, sex, ethnicity, or skin color. In the long run, the adoption of such flawed ideologies in a democratic society could sound the death knell for freedom and democracy and the prosperity that ensues.[4]

Individuals with set, entrenched religious and political opinions, and motivated by transcendent ideas about the afterlife, eventual salvation, and even martyrdom, can sometimes become fanatical in these views and intolerant toward other human beings who hold different beliefs. As Indian-born author Salman Rushdie observed, "When religion gets into the driving seat, all hell breaks loose."[5] Such people consider their cause so important and supreme that anything that stands in their way in promoting it can be dispensed with, including, if need be, freedom and democracy. An example of such thinking is this quote from a religious Islamic author who admonishes fellow Islamists in these terms: "The unbelievers, idolaters, and others like them must be hated and despised. We must stay away from them and create barriers between them and us. The Qur'an forbade taking Jews and Christians as friends, and that applies to every Jew and Christian, with no consideration as to whether they are at war with Islam or not."[6]

Such religious hatred and frenzy are in opposition to the fundamental right of free thought and free speech in a democratic and open society. They contradict the famous quote on humanist tolerance and freedom of speech attributed to Voltaire, "I disapprove of what you say but I will defend to the death your right to say it." They are basically inimical to the good functioning of a modern, pluralist society.

The religious frame of mind may explain why religions, spiritual or political, have so often been the cause of oppression, massacres, persecutions, and wars throughout the history of humankind. It is because religions, especially the proselytizing and politicized ones, are based on the premise that each religion has total absolute truth, and other creeds are necessarily in error. Therefore, they are intrinsically incompatible with one another. They encourage the frame of mind of us-against-them: either you belong to them, or you are against them. Therein lies the fundamental basis for conflicts and wars, which originates from a religion-based world vision. This may be an important reason why religious ethics, even if it has had some influence in preventing violence between individuals within the same group, has failed so miserably in preventing collective violence.

It is indisputable that wars dehumanize people and, as such, are the principal enemy of humankind. In this narrow sense, organized religions, by encouraging exclusive behavior and conflicts between people, have also been the curse of humanity. This is because all religions have within them exclusionist tendencies that make them impenetrable to other views and other beliefs—and often closed even to the small compromises of daily life. This characteristic breeds exclusion and hatred. Throw in the self-interests of self-appointed leaders who use religion as a ladder for their own social, economic, or political climbing, and it is easy to understand why some positive emotions such as forgiveness and altruism can be transformed into meanness and cruelty toward the dangerous others who are considered less pure or less worthy.

TOLERANCE AND THE RULE OF LAW

In a society of rights where the rule of law prevails, peaceful competition of ideas can be a source of enrichment. However, there is a fundamental opposition between a free and open society and the imposition of an absolutist and totalitarian religious morality and belief system.

That is why freedom of religion and freedom from religion (the right not to practice any religion) should be inscribed in all modern constitutions. Indeed, there cannot be true religious liberty if the liberty not to be religious is absent. All democratic constitutions should clearly specify that the government of all the people should never support or encourage any particular religion and should never become the proselytizing tool of any religion. There should be a very strict separation between the state and religion.[7] Indeed, the state is completely incompetent to give rulings upon the validity of any religion. It is only within the framework of guaranteed individual freedom for all that tolerance can become a *modus vivandi*, preserved for all, even in the presence of religious or ideological extremism. It is also the best way to avoid social conformity and repression, which lead to intellectual and economic stagnation.

FOUR

SHARING

FOURTH HUMANIST PRINCIPLE:
SHARE WITH THOSE WHO ARE LESS FORTUNATE
AND HELP THOSE WHO ARE IN NEED.

Principle of Social Justice: Social and economic inequalities are only acceptable if such inequalities benefit the least-advantaged members of society, and if there exists a "fair equality of opportunity" in society to acquire skills and to be rewarded according to merit.
—John Rawls (1921–2002), *A Theory of Justice*

Justice is as strictly due between neighbor nations as between neighbor citizens. A highwayman is as much a robber when he plunders in a gang as when single; and a nation that makes an unjust war is only a great gang.
—Benjamin Franklin (1706–1790)

The test of our progress is not whether we add more to the abundance of those who have much, it is whether we provide enough for those who have too little.
—Franklin D. Roosevelt (1882–1945),
Thirty-second US president

E ven though nature itself is neutral, blind, cold, indifferent, and amoral, caring and altruism are natural human attributes. This does not mean that humans are disinterested and are never selfish; but they can act out of love, kindness, fairness, consolation, compassion, solidarity, or sympathy for other human beings. Some are more

71

inclined to make sacrifices and to care for others, but all can feel good when helping others. As the popular dictum says, "giving is its own reward," essentially because when we help others, we help ourselves in many ways.

No man is an island, and no nation is an island either. Humans increasingly form an enlarged family. This engenders the necessity to care for each other, to be kind and generous, and to share with each other. It is a humanistic obligation to help the less fortunate, especially children, the poor, the sick, the aged, the suffering, the displaced, the refugees, the isolated, and the lonely.

Because they needed to live in groups to survive in an inhospitable environment, early humans had to develop a capacity for sharing and mutual assistance in order to overcome the harsh forces of nature. Humans would not have survived without such a culture of sharing, at least within their immediate group, be it a family, a clan, or a tribe. Initially, all that was required was sharing the means of subsistence within a small group of related people. Over time, the concept and practice of sharing evolved to embrace larger communities, especially as conflicts for survival between groups became more frequent and deadlier.

The same moral requirement for sharing to survive exists today, except that our living group now encompasses all humankind. Sharing among humans is a requirement for the survival of all on planet Earth; it cannot be uniquely and principally an in-group and xenophobic practice, but must translate into a universal endeavor. Not only do we have a basic moral obligation to help friends in need, but this obligation extends to any person who suffers and requires assistance.

This raises the question of how to achieve a situation of maximum social justice without reducing the self-interest-centered incentives required for an economy to function efficiently. How can we be just, fair, and efficient without at the same time making everybody poorer? In this we subscribe to John Rawls' *maximin* principle of social justice, which says that economic incentives should be established in such a way as to benefit not only the producers themselves, but also the least-advantaged members of society.[1] This means that public support for individuals should not be such that it gives rise to a problem of *moral hazard*, where people come to depend on society and on government handouts, knowing that even if they act irresponsibly and behave as parasites, the government will always bail them out.[2] In any society, there is a moral requirement to be productive, just as there is a moral requirement to be fair and generous.

Fundamentally, a well-organized society should have as much equality of opportunity and the most equitable distribution of goods among its members compatible with the working of an efficient economy. Such is the objective of a just social and economic order, which provides an equal chance for everybody to reach full potential as a human being. This means that all children should receive the education and professional training that their talents and motivation warrant, irrespective of the wealth or income of their parents. A fair and equitable society should make sure that wealth and social status are not obstacles to implementing the principle of equal opportunity for all. This also means that no one should fall victim to starvation, homelessness, or lack of healthcare.

WHY PRIVATE CHARITY IS NOT ENOUGH

It is a well-established assumption in welfare economics that private charity and corporate philanthropy are not sufficient to correct the wide income disparities between the rich and the poor arising from the natural functioning of markets. First, there is the "freeloader" problem, which translates into people avoiding being generous when the burden of charity giving can be shifted to somebody else. Second, charity without an intermediary is rare. For example, excluding church dues (which are not really in the same category as redistributive charity) direct giving to the poor accounts for only 10 percent of all charitable donations registered in the United States.[3] Moreover, many private charities are tax deductible or are managed by tax-exempt institutions or foundations, with the end result that a certain proportion of them are indirectly publicly financed. Third, most individual charity donations tend to be localized and cannot be relied upon alone to alleviate poverty, with the end result that rich communities tend to receive more funds than poor communities. The rich tend to donate to "rich" charities; the poor tend to donate to "poor" charities.

Thus, private charity alone cannot correct these distortions. A collective effort must complement private efforts to fight poverty and deprivation, and to develop a true culture of solidarity and mutual support. And the democratic means to correct income and wealth inequalities is the democratic state. Since the rich often profit disproportionately from the work of the poor, it is only natural for the state to tax the rich to give to the poor. Such are the requirements of social justice. That is why we say that cooperation and risk sharing in a true social and economic partnership are to be encouraged in any society— because they generate social integration and economic security. The state, of course, is an important institution for achieving that goal. But other institutions, such as cooperatives, can also help alleviate poverty and empower individuals.

IN PURSUIT OF THE GREATEST SOCIAL GOOD

The purpose of government is to make decisions and formulate policies in a democratic environment for the greatest common good, or general welfare. That is the profound meaning of the principle of the "government of the people, by the people, and for the people." Government does not exist to serve the special interests of kings, aristocracy, or bourgeoisie, but for the greatest common good of all. Special-interest politics is the antithesis of true democracy.

Economists have a decision-making rule that governments can apply to maximize total welfare: total social benefits derived from a project must be greater than total social costs. For that, expenditures must be allocated so that for all government programs, the marginal social benefit should equal or surpass the marginal social cost. Social benefits and social costs include both private benefits and costs, and any external benefits or costs reaped or supported by the community as a whole. If the marginal social benefits derived from a given program are superior to its marginal social costs, it could be expanded; if it is the contrary, it should be scaled down or abolished.

THE RISE OF WESTERN CIVILIZATION

In 1648, after 150 years of religious warfare, Europe officially emerged from the medieval and feudal world into what has since been called "Western civilization." It was the Treaty of Westphalia that triggered this fundamental change. For the first time, the functions of a government in a modern nation-state were outlined. First, the government existed not to promote the interests of one class or one group over the others but rather to seek the general welfare of all the people. This is the practical application of the principle that, in a civilized society, each person is responsible for the welfare of all others. "Do unto others as you would wish others do unto you" became an applied principle rather than a pious wish. Government became the instrument for implementing mutual responsibility for promoting the general welfare of all citizens.

The Treaty of Westphalia in its entirety contained many principles designed to promote peace between nations. Its guiding principle for peace was the *principle of benevolence*, meaning that a country's policies should always take into consideration "the benefit of the other." The treaty established two other innovative principles: the principle of the sovereignty of independent nation-states and the principle of equality among nations. This recognized, for the first time, that all sovereign nation-states had equal legal standing, and their independence was to be guaranteed by a mutually acceptable system of international law, based on internationally binding treaties and on mutually beneficial commercial trade and economic development. This was designed to forbid the intervention of one state in the internal affairs of another sovereign state solely for its own benefits. Before the Peace of Westphalia, autocratic states had relied on brute force and the right of the strongest to regulate interactions between states. The advent of the independent nation-state also meant that people had the right of political self-determination. Political and social democracy could finally emerge as a political system.[4]

INTERNATIONAL SOLIDARITY AND SHARING

In the context of economic globalization and international capitalism, it can be expected that the winners in the outcomes of markets would be called upon to compensate the losers. Nations-states do contribute to international income and wealth redistribution, but this is done on a much smaller scale than is necessary to substantially alleviate human misery and underdevelopment. In my opinion, super rich individuals—those who profit the most from the social functioning of markets and who reap the largest sums from the economy—should contribute a small portion of their enormous wealth to international solidarity and international sharing.

In 2007 *Forbes* magazine estimated that there were some 946 billionaires in the world, for a total private fortune in excess of $10 trillion. Even though such wealth holders do pay taxes in their home country and some are personally very generous, many use tax heavens and various schemes to escape social contribution altogether, both local and international. There exist also numerous individual tax-free foundations in many countries that serve to concentrate wealth on an ever-growing scale and that shield such private wealth from a just taxation.[5] In the name of social justice and international human solidarity, measures should be taken in the future to eliminate such huge concentrations of wealth.

Yale University economist James Tobin has proposed the levy of a special tax on international currency transactions of between 0.1 percent and 0.25 percent. Such a tax would not only collect funds, it would reduce short-term speculation on currencies. This international tax could provide the United Nations with a large source of reliable funding, independent from the annual donations from participating states. While not disapproving of such an international currency tax, its implementation poses special difficulties, and it could be mired with obvious problems of avoidance. Large financial centers would oppose such a special tax, making it impracticable for other countries to implement it. And even if applied, such a tax could turn out to be regressive if it were to be applied only to currency holders unable to avoid it.

An alternative would be to establish a United Nations International Solidarity Organization (UNISON) that every country wishing to be a member of the United Nations would be obliged to join and support through statutory annual transfers. UNISON would then be empowered to finance education, health, and basic development infrastructures in the poorest countries of the world, and its operating budget would be approved by the United Nations General Assembly, restructured into a true international parliament.

It would be logical that the richest individuals and the largest tax-free foundations participate in supporting such an effort of international solidarity and sharing. For example, a minuscule annual tax of 0.1 percent on individual fortunes and on tax-free foundations in excess of $1 billion could serve to establish a special UN fund to permanently support UNISON. Its functioning budget of international redistribution could also partly come from a minuscule consumption tax of one tenth of 1 percent levied in all participating countries.[6] Even on such a small scale, this international initiative would represent a giant step toward international solidarity and international social justice.

In effect, UNISON would act as a permanent Marshall Plan for the poorest countries. If the Marshall Plan could be implemented after World War II for European countries, its equivalent could certainly be implemented in the future for the poorest countries. What it takes is political will and leadership, and a genuine desire to share in solidarity with the rest of the world, in a worldwide effort of mutual aid and assistance.

FIVE

NO DOMINATION, NO EXPLOITATION

FIFTH HUMANIST PRINCIPLE:
USE NEITHER LIES, NOR TEMPORAL DOCTRINE,
NOR SPIRITUAL POWER TO DOMINATE AND EXPLOIT OTHERS.
PROCLAIM THE PRINCIPLE OF EQUALITY
OF OPPORTUNITY FOR ALL.

> So long as the people do not care to exercise their freedom, those who wish to tyrannize will do so; for tyrants are active and ardent and will devote themselves in the name of any number of gods, religious and otherwise, to put shackles upon sleeping men.
>
> —Voltaire [François Marie Arouet] (1694–1778)

> Men never do evil so completely and cheerfully as when they do it from a religious conviction.
>
> —Blaise Pascal (1623–1662)

> No morality can be founded on authority, even if the authority were divine.
>
> —Alfred J. Ayer (1910–1989)

Lying, cheating, and resorting to corruption and deception in order to amass riches and gain power at the expense of others are all examples of exploitation and are contrary to a humanist approach to life in society. Lying, or deception of any kind, is inimical to humanist morality.

Not to lie is an obligation that applies to individuals in their daily life, but it applies even more so to people in positions of authority. Indeed, the most insidious corruption in a democracy occurs when

79

elected officials are untruthful. Then confidence and trust are destroyed, and so is the moral fiber of the nation. Such public corruption is often accompanied by the corruption that feeds all the others: the corruption of the media. When the government and the media are both corrupted, all the other forms of corruption follow.

In daily human interactions, economic or social, there is no exploitation when exchanges or transfers between people are voluntary and mutually rewarding. However, when these exchanges or transfers are made under duress or through lies, deception, or misrepresentation, they are tantamount to exploitation because they arise from a situation of abuse, oppression, corruption, or manipulation.

Indeed, people can be exploited either consciously or unknowingly. They can be taken advantage of and manipulated when they are lied to and when they are duped or deceived into not receiving their due. Most instances of human exploitation occur in the realm of economic life. But exploitation can also be psychological, social, political, sexual, or religious. In most instances, such exploitation is the result of hubris and greed and comes from a lack of humility and a wrong perspective on what is important in life.

THE ECONOMIC EXPLOITATION OF WORKERS

Economic opportunity for all means that people have access to employment without discrimination and are justly rewarded according to their productivity. In a well-organized society, the state uses its taxation powers to finance the supply of social capital and social goods—legal institutions, roads, ports and airports, schools and hospitals, and so on. Private goods are the responsibility of private producers. Economic free enterprise, indeed, means that people can save, accumulate capital, invent, innovate, and start new enterprises or expand existing producing facilities. The more a country is endowed with productive capital in the form of factories, machines, and technology, the more employment opportunities there are and the higher the wages and incomes.

What is to be avoided is a situation of absolute monopoly, either on the side of employers or on the side of workers. If owners of capital and the companies that manage such capital are few and possess monopolized power, they can impose unfair or unjust working conditions on their employees. There are two remedies to such a situation of potential exploitation: either the government establishes in advance the minimum working conditions that all employers must meet, or the workers must have a legal right to organize collectively and to bargain on an equal footing with employers.

When there is competition in the marketplace for goods or services, there is an automatic limit imposed on the terms of agreement between employers and employees, derived from the requirement of financial solvency for the producing entity. A company that goes into bankruptcy cannot both provide employment and cease to pay wages and benefits. Logically, however, when there is no competition in a certain market—for example, in the supply of certain public services such as fire or police protection—employers and employees are theoretically in a position to exploit the buyers of their services (the taxpayers) by unduly raising profits, wages, and prices. In such situations, the need to avoid the exploitation of consumers and taxpayers by private entities or individuals requires the establishment of rules of arbitration. In all other cases, the free functioning of markets can take care of most conflicts between employers and employees and result in fair solutions.

SEXUAL EXPLOITATION

Humanist ethics is a useful guide in matters of love and sex. In general, human love and consensual sex between adults is both natural and an important source of happiness and contentment. It is only when sex is exploitive and degrading that it becomes bad. In particular, sexual exploitation of children, the weak, and the vulnerable is reprehensible and punishable. The sexual exploitation and degradation of women is also unethical. Similarly, people who enter into living or marriage contracts have an obligation to respect their fidelity vows. These are general humanist principles that allow for natural human interactions and commitments without connotations of exploitation or degradation. Through proper education, people may learn to develop their sexuality in positive ways. Proper education of the young regarding love and sex, both by parents and at school, is a prerequisite for developing healthy and moral attitudes toward this important aspect of the human experience.[1]

FINANCIAL EXPLOITATION AND HUMAN GULLIBILITY IN RELIGIOUS MATTERS

Martin Luther, the founder of Protestantism who fought the abuses and the sale of indulgences by Catholic Church officials,[2] once said that people place their trust in the god of their choice. Indeed, the choice of a god is actually the choice of a philosophy, the choice of a vision of the world. Nowadays, many Americans seem to have literally adopted the motto "In gold we trust," as they flock to adopt the new gospel of prosperity. The new theology of "God wants you to get rich" is prevalent among the 10 million–strong Pentecostal wing of American Christianity.[3]

American televangelism seems to be one of the fastest growing moneymaking machines for those who have access to a camera and a microphone. Televangelists have no qualms selling prosperity theology to the poorest members of society, promising them miraculous material success if they part with ten percent of their meager incomes. This is an example of a conflict between religion and morality. In fact, in these circumstances religion becomes an instrument of exploitation and domination.[4]

Indeed, TV-based prosperity preachers are raking in money by the ton, profiting from a sort of religious pyramid scheme by placing themselves as the receivers between the givers and the hypothetical god, supposedly the source of material prosperity. Such money-making preachers have turned the original Christian message "For what profit is it to a man, if he gains the whole world, and loses his own soul?" on its head, and they have invented a new national (American) religion which says instead: "If you are not rich, you are not with God!"[5]

Such a flawed social theory has heralded a period of moral decay that is threatening the very foundations of a democratic and civilized society. In the United States in the 1980s, for example, the Republican administration of Ronald Reagan introduced the notion of "trickle down" economics and made it politically and socially acceptable. In the early twenty-first century, opportunistic televangelists made economic greed religiously acceptable.[6]

This new materialist religion clothed in religious garb is dangerous because it can be used to condone get-rich-quick schemes, which are tantamount to exploitation.[7] Some may be more prone than others to deduce from such teachings that they can become rich quickly, while remaining moral. Implicitly, indeed, it could be thought that cheating and stealing to become rich is acceptable because this is supposed to please God, which is more like mammon in this case. This is another of those hoaxes that unscrupulous religious entrepreneurial characters have invented over the years to separate the gullible from their money, with no redeeming social value whatsoever.

Obviously one cannot pretend to be opposed to materialism and, at the same time, worship the accumulation of riches by any means. Crooks and cheats may then delude themselves into thinking that the money and resources coming into their hands are "the consequence of God putting them there," as one religious American embezzler is reported to have said in his defense.[8]

Exploitation, corruption, and moral bankruptcy take many forms. Whatever form they take, however, they are usually the end result of an insatiable lust for money, power, and privilege, above and beyond any common decency. Benjamin Franklin for one, feared the US Constitution would in time "fail...because of the corruption of the people, in a general sense." President Abraham Lincoln feared that corruption in high places would follow as "all wealth is aggregated in a few hands and the Republic is destroyed." History shows that economic exploitation and political corruption often go hand in hand. Both should be opposed and condemned.

To sum up, we can say that all forms of exploitation of human beings, gullible or not, are contrary to a humanistic code of ethics. In particular, persons in authority should resist the temptation to scare people in order to better control them and to sell them protection, security, and false reassurance.

SIX

NO SUPERSTITION

SIXTH HUMANIST PRINCIPLE:
RELY ON REASON, LOGIC, AND SCIENCE TO UNDERSTAND THE
UNIVERSE AND TO SOLVE LIFE'S PROBLEMS.

In the fullness of time, educated people will believe there is no soul independent from the body, and hence no life after death.

—Francis Crick, Nobel laureate

The concepts of the "soul," of the "spirit," of an "immortal soul" have been invented in order to despise the body, to make it sick—"holy"— and to supremely neglect everything that deserves to be taken seriously in life, like all things connected with food, lodging, intellectual exercise, treatment of the sick, cleanliness, and the climate!

—Friedrich Nietzsche (1844–1900)

I think all the great religions of the world—Buddhism, Hinduism, Christianity, Islam, and Communism—[are] both untrue and harmful. . . . I am as firmly convinced that religions do harm as I am that they are untrue.

—Bertrand Russell (1872–1970)

T he first question is whether there exists a supernatural world, besides or beyond our natural and physical world, in which the known natural laws of physics do not apply. This is a fundamental question because most religious systems of thought are based on the belief that there exists some higher, unseen, and all-powerful entity who has control over every human's destiny and to whom all humans must owe allegiance, obedience, reverence, and worship.

In a cosmic perspective, humans are like ephemeral flowers: they are born, grow, mature, and ultimately fade away. What distinguishes people is what they do with their potential during their existence. Like flowers, some produce delectable perfume, some poison the atmosphere, and others are barren. As humans, we come from matter present in the Universe when we are born, and we merge with the rest of the Universe when we are dead, leaving our deeds and memories behind. The existence of deities or similar entities remains a theory that has never been proven or tested successfully. There is, indeed, no proof of the existence of a supernatural world, except as it exists in some people's minds. It is a dangerous fiction.[1]

The claim to or pretension of a supernatural world inhabited by supernatural entities such as gods, demons, angels, ghosts, and so on, is at best a harmless illusion, and at worst a scam and a cruel hoax perpetrated on the most susceptible and gullible humans, often among the least literate and least enlightened segments of society. Religions may go on pretending that humans are not evolved animals but rather fallen angels; however, this remains an unproven pretension with no scientific basis. Nevertheless, many adults have difficulty leaving behind their obsession with the supernatural and fall victim to superstitions and religious theories of all kinds. For some, it is a childish trait that remains with them all their life. Indeed, it is the strength of organized religious systems to encounter generation after generation of distraught and bewildered people to whom they can peddle their mythical fabrications. Hallucinating or cunning religious entrepreneurs have no qualms about taking advantage of such human weaknesses. They do it for the sake of money, influence, and power, and for some, through self-deception. Some hear voices and are delusional but nevertheless become immensely rich and powerful. People retain their services and give them money for the same reason they buy magic powder or snake oil to soothe their fears. They take a chance... just in case, treading in the footsteps of French philosopher Blaise Pascal.

Paranoid delusions start with false premises.[2] Indeed, the Swiss psychiatrist Eugene Bleuler defined paranoia as the "construction, from false premises, of a logically developed and in its various parts logically connected, unshakable delusional system without any demonstrable disturbance affecting any of the other mental functions and therefore, also without any symptoms of deterioration if one ignores the paranoiac's complete lack of insight into his own delusional system."[3] Thus people, and that includes religious people, can become delusional when they hold strong beliefs that are not justified by available evidence and that are not discarded despite invalidating evidence.[4]

THE ECONOMICS AND SOCIOLOGY OF RELIGIOUS ORGANIZATIONS

More than two hundred years ago, the Scottish economist Adam Smith delved intensively into the economics of religion and morality. In his celebrated book, *The Theory of Moral Sentiments*, Smith asked the question "Why are humans moral?" He answered by theorizing that the beginnings of morality are innate, in the sense that our connection to other human beings makes us sensitive to their needs and sentiments. (This is the fundamental emotional response called empathy.) Morality is in our nature, deeply embedded in our genes. "Man, who subsists only in society," has a natural inclination to reciprocate to others in order to survive. It is thus in people's self-interest to be moral—it is a prerequisite for survival.[5]

For Adam Smith, legitimate self-interest is an engine of economic activity and is not synonymous with selfishness and greed, quite the contrary. It is rather a psychological need to serve society and win its favor. Self-interest is a moral sentiment. In *The Wealth of Nations*, Smith wrote, "It is not from the benevolence of the butcher, the brewer, or the baker that we expect our dinner, but from their regard to their own interest. We address ourselves, not to their humanity but to their self-love, and never talk to them of our necessities but of their advantages." In other words, an economy does not function out of charity or benevolence, but is spurred by the legitimate self-interest of its participants and the pursuit of mutually beneficial cooperation.

It should surprise no one that Adam Smith also wrote that self-interest motivates religious producers just as it does secular producers, and that competition among religious organizations would "make religion free from every mixture of absurdity, imposture, or fanaticism."[6] Many religious entrepreneurs pursue legitimate interests and are useful to society. This does not preclude greed and cupidity from seeping into this activity as in any other human activity. Indeed, the advent of modern communication techniques has opened up new opportunities for snake oil peddlers and other types of demagogues and charlatans. Radio and television, in particular, being powerful although passive media, are well suited to religious propaganda, indoctrination, and fund-raising schemes of all sorts.[7]

HOMO MORALIS VERSUS *HOMO ECONOMICUS*

Ever since Smith, economists have rejected the idea that selfishness and unchecked greed on the one hand, and self-interest properly understood in the other, are synonymous. Indeed, since we need other human beings to survive and prosper, this makes us naturally sensitive to their needs and sentiments.

However, could there be a conflict between a high level of individual moral responsibility when one acts within a group, and a lower level of individual moral responsibility when one pursues financial success within the economic system? In Smith's view, when people exert themselves to the utmost in order to achieve their own egotistical financial ends, such as the acquisition of a farm or a house, they do good not only to themselves but also to the whole community or nation in which they live. This is done through the division of labor and the economic specialization that arise from the process of competition.

Nevertheless, it is probably easier for one to be indifferent to the social consequences of one's actions within the anonymity of the marketplace than in the case of other more intimate interpersonal interactions. This does not mean that there exists an ethics for ordinary life and another for economic activity. The same principles apply to both activities. This is because wealth is not the criteria of real success, but happiness is. And nobody can truly be happy while hurting others or being dishonest. Those who violate the basic humanist rules of moral duty in the accumulation of wealth or power in or out of the marketplace are hurting themselves as much as they hurt others.

THE RELIGIOUS MARKET FOR CERTAINTIES AND SUPERSTITIONS

Why is it, then, that in this supposedly advanced modern age, irrationality and superstitions of all kinds, religious or otherwise, still hold sway over people? Why is it that ignorance and superstition are so prevalent? The answer has to be found in the fundamental human condition. It seems that people have a natural tendency to believe in mythology, astrology, fiction, and magic. They crave happy endings and easy answers to complicated questions. Indeed, when faced with a complicated question, many prefer a simple answer, even if it is false, to an articulate answer that is scientifically true but complicated. It is not surprising, therefore, that there is a market for things frivolous and marvelous.

One country where superstitions of all sorts wield a strong power over people's daily lives is India. A superstition is a blind faith in supernatural forces; it is an irrational belief about the relation between certain actions and later occurrences. In India, for example, after much criticism of the caste system by Mahatma Gandhi, discrimination, including against the lowest caste, the Untouchables (the Dalits), was officially abolished. Since independence in 1947, it is a crime under the Indian Constitution to discriminate along the rigid caste system. However, the forces of traditions, of superstitions, and of religious beliefs have worked to keep in place the segmentation of society. Especially in rural India, superstitions are prevalent in nearly every aspect of life, for choosing the date and hour of weddings, of funerals, for cabinet appointments, swearing-in ceremonies, even for the correct spelling of names. People blame their karma for everything that goes badly in their lives. In this sense, superstitions are an escape from thinking and a liberation from the obligation to look for the links between causes and effects. Superstitious people do not take responsibility for their own actions because, in their minds, everything seems to be predetermined.[8]

Humans live in an uncertain and probabilistic world, not in a certain and deterministic one. What will happen in the future, to them, to society, and to the Universe might be predicted, but cannot be known with certainty. People can either face up to this reality, try to orient it and even change it, or they can escape into the fantasy of fatalism, determinism, self-deceit and helplessness. Unfortunately perhaps for us, we live in a world of rational probability rather than absolute certitude. Most people accept the fact that we live in an uncertain world, even though they yearn for certainty. Thus, people buy insurance and try in general to remove traces of uncertainty from their lives. This is a completely rational behavior.

Religious movements are in the market of certainty—absolute certainties. They sell insurance on an afterlife and even promise immortality, even though it is irrational to believe in such exaggerated claims, which are so obviously contrary to the reality that has been observed over millennia. That is fundamentally why religious beliefs belong to the realm of dreams and fantasy rather than to the world of reality.[9] They deal with what people would like reality to be—for example, to be immortal—rather than with the reality they observe around them: human mortality.[10]

For some, this is irresistible, just like the hope to win big at the casino, even if the odds are stacked against them. (Although, at the casinos, at least some people do win!) But, as the saying goes, it's better to own a casino than to play in one. Some religious entrepreneurs have long understood this basic principle, and they have aggressively opened glorified stores to sell transcendental, mystical, and mythical goodies, all designed to escape from the harsh rational reality and alleviate the mind of its uncertainties. Thus, religions and their elusive and unverifiable promises. In fact, religions belong to the realm of primitive myths and provide very little to the understanding of the real Universe in which we live. Nevertheless, religions still retain a lot of economic appeal. They are the best of trades: low costs and high returns.

ORGANIZED RELIGIONS AS
SOCIAL AND POLITICAL SUPPORT NETWORKS

The most successful religious enterprises are those that sell the comfort of metaphysical certainty, propose supernatural explanations to
natural events, give the promise of some form of eternal life after
death, and offer a daily network of protection and support. The producers of religion in the faith market—churches, synagogues,
mosques, and others—compete among themselves as to which branch
offers the best cost-benefit package to people frightened and terrified
by death and by the unknown, and who are anxious for moral comfort,
guidance, and social support.[11] In this sense, organized religions fulfill
psychological and social needs, create bonds and social alliances, and
help individuals cope with life's vicissitudes, uncertainties, and challenges. In certain countries, churches and mosques are disguised
political and social organizations, very much involved in the power
structure of their societies. One joins a church or a mosque just as one
joins a political party.

On the demand side, we can say that people join organized religions or sects in order to derive some spiritual, social, or economic
benefits, or any kind of support, at a relatively low cost. For some,
religions provide easy and simple answers to personal existential
questions: Where do we come from? What is our destiny? What is the
meaning of life? What is life's relevance and in relation to what? How
should we behave toward other humans? What makes our existence
good? Why do we age rather than remain young forever? Why do we
have to die? What happens after death?

For some people, visiting religious sites and attending religious
services are convenient ways to find time for meditation and intro-
spection about life, its questions and its challenges. Immersing themselves in a religious environment may be the only opportunity they
have to escape the chores of daily life and contemplate a bigger picture. For many, religious teachings may be the only chance they have
to enter the world of philosophical thinking and reflection. In this
narrow sense, religious thinking is a form of mental activity and education and has positive effects.

It remains that religious leanings are primarily emotional in nature, not rational. Blind faith has nothing to do with critical thinking, but a lot to do with human emotions and primitive instincts. It is a legacy of the past, when man's old brain was expanding and sought explanations for the surrounding mysteries of life.[12] Blind faith (a conviction that cannot be shaken by contrary evidence) is a flawed inheritance from the past, when people had a piteous lack of knowledge about nature and the Universe. This does not mean that human emotions are not useful in people's quest to find happiness. To be happy, indeed, is to be satisfied with what one has, even though there are conditions, such as poverty or the loss of youth, vigor, or health, under which it is difficult to be content with one's lot.

Thus, some individuals feel emotionally secure and happy in accepting what leaders, religious or otherwise, tell them to believe. Some can become addicted to the habit of being told what to do and in receiving orders. To obey without questioning is best illustrated in a soldier's training, when an automatic response to commands is required. Some religious training adopts the same technique of requiring blind obedience and total self-negation. For instance, Ignacio de Loyola, the founder of the Jesuit order the Society of Jesus, was initially a Basque soldier. He transposed his military training into a vision of training an "army for Christ" by requiring an absolute vow of obedience from his disciples (*perinde ac cadaver*).

For most, however, metaphysical considerations about life and ideas of rewards in a mysterious and hypothetical afterlife have very little to do with their joining an organized religion and a lot to do with their emotional, material, and physical needs for survival and for protection. This is Emile Durkeim's collective feeling of security that people gain from living in a group. This does not mean that people are irrational in joining an organized religion. Far from it. There are very tangible net benefits in joining and belonging to any organization, and this includes religious organizations.

In practice, organized religions are also potent forces in many societies because they unite people around common rites. People recognize themselves in such common and routine rites, be they weekly group gatherings, or the usual rites for marriage, birth, child rearing, death, and so on. Such rites are an integral part of community life. That is the reason why people view organized religions as useful social institutions.[13] Therefore, for many, being religious is essentially about joining and belonging. The development of emotional belonging and the need for emotional connection with others and of social interactions among humans may have played a large role in the emergence of organized religions.[14]

Many churches, temples, or mosques are fundamentally social support organizations. More often than not, they are a mixture of disguised religious country clubs and religious political parties, with their own social and political agendas. Just as some people join political parties, social clubs, or any other support group for the psychological, emotional, social, and economic benefits they derive from such membership, so do people join churches and organized religious systems to find an identity, either social or political, or to share a unifying cause. For them, religious organizations become just so many political rallying points.

In a given society, there often exist strong pressures to conform and to band together. Nonjoiners are frowned upon, and the social and economic pressure for them to conform is enormous. In many societies, indeed, there is a stigma attached to the fact of not being seen as religious. Therefore, many people go along and resign themselves, not really believing in what is being pushed upon them.

Nevertheless, it happens sometimes that an entire nation writes and rallies around its official religion as a sign of social and political solidarity. As French sociologist Durkeim observed, "religion is the standard of the clan." The first allegiance of the citizens is to their church, temple, or mosque and not to their country. In fact, this may be the central reason why many civil wars have pitted one religious group against another within the same nation. When this is the case, religious organizations are much more than so many social clubs.

By joining an organized religious group, one becomes *de facto* member of a coalition, clan, tribe, or village; one may gain some social status, a sense of identity, purpose, and empowerment; and one may reap other tangible benefits. Joining and belonging offer a supportive social structure to the isolated individual. The religious tribe includes as a reward frequent reinforcement of one's self-worth by his or her peers. The member can find personal security and then relax inside the group or clan because he is emotionally (and in some cases physically and financially) protected by a supportive group of people who share the same beliefs and the same values.

On the other hand, those who are outside the totalitarian-like organization can be excluded and can easily fall prey to the proselytizing zeal of the insiders, and sometimes be demonized, persecuted, or placed in servitude. Indeed, for some, religion can serve as a rallying tribal insignia. They can easily convince themselves that the fate of all mankind coincides with the narrow interests of their own group. This could foster the prejudice that other people—the outsiders—are bad, inferior, or even subhuman. This is the sad historical legacy of organized groups and of organized religions.[15] The more absolutist and exclusive their system of beliefs, the more prone the members of such organizations are to commit irrational acts, including resorting to violence, in reaction to any perceived threat to their beliefs. Indeed, no organization other than organized religions can better mobilize large groups of people into congregations and turn them into mind-numbed automatons. Chapter 8 will delve further into how group behavior and group power can become antisocial and immoral when they become exclusive and fanatical.

In England and in the United States, for instance, there historically has been a tendency for the rich, the educated, the conservative, and the powerful to congregate within the Anglican, Episcopalian, or Presbyterian Churches, or in Jewish temples. The poor, the least educated, and the underdogs in general tend to congregate within the Methodist, Baptist, and Pentecostal Churches. To a certain extent also, in the Muslim word, Sunni Islam has traditionally been the religion of the wealthy and those in power, while Shia Islam has traditionally been the religion of the poor and the weak. In India, the social stratification of organized religion is even more pronounced; there is a socio-religious caste system in which the rich, such as the Brahmins, belong to Hinduism, while the poor, such as the Dalits, join Buddhism, Sikhism, and, increasingly, Islam. It is a fact that many religions have been invented over time as vehicles for social dissatisfaction and political dissidence. In this sense, religions have played a very important social and political role in people's search for equality and human dignity.

Therefore, the fact that religious organizations advance dubious propositions based on weird and utopian beliefs—which sometimes can serve as social narcotics, as tranquilizers for existential angst or, as Karl Marx put it, supply "the opiate of the masses"—does not mean that the psychological, emotional, social, or economic interests of the adhering person are nonexistent. In fact, the logical or rational consistency of an organization has little or nothing to do with the tangible benefits that a person derives by joining it. The sociable character of religions draws many. For some, just as with fake professional wrestling, religion is a form of entertainment and a low-cost distraction. In some countries, mosques and churches are not only centers of entertainment, they are the only providers of entertainment, certainly the only free entertainment in town. There, storytelling, sermons, and speeches by gifted orators attract attention and admiration.

For all these reasons, joining a religious organization can be a very rational decision, even though the official teachings of such an organization are rationally flawed and fundamentally illogical. If a person can be provided with some basic moral rules and be treated in a hospital, receive an education in a church-run enterprise at a low cost, or make friends and acquaintances, this could be enough to make adhesion attractive and rewarding. It is the same thing when one enhances the chances for gainful employment or any financial benefits by voluntarily joining a church or a club, or a secret society for that matter. In small and close-knit communities, the social pressure to join a religious organization may be overwhelming.

On the supply side, one might also expect that the producers and sellers of religious services will often be motivated by perceived tangible rewards in the real world (standing, power, security . . .), not in an imaginary afterlife. In the words of German economist-sociologist Max Weber, "The most elementary forms of behavior motivated by religious or magical factors are oriented to this world."[16]

There is an inescapable reality: throughout history, religions have been convenient nationalistic rallying points for ethnic groups. The development of different religions among different nationalities is a testimony to different needs and to the importance of organized religions as social and political institutions. Indeed, religions are institutions that can create a strong sense of belonging and cohesion within a group, a coalition, or a society, and that can help people to present a united front to the outside world.[17] At the national level, as opposed to the individual level, religion is a phenomenon that elites have often used to cement national and social cohesion. In the past, it has been a convenient substitute for the education of the masses because of the simplicity of the codes of conduct that religions are able to dictate to individuals who could not be reached and influenced otherwise.[18]

Evolutionary biologists suggest that an inclination by ancient humans to follow witch doctors, sorcerers, or other leaders who claimed divine support could have had tangible social and political benefits. Adherence to religion and a will to follow such leaders turned the tribes of early cavemen into more cohesive bands, increased their chances of survival, and, if need be, enabled them to kill off their rivals more easily. The question remains whether humankind can afford to adhere to such a primitive approach to living and to human cooperation.

FEAR AND CREDULITY

The human mind has difficulty comprehending intangible notions such as infinity and eternity. Living in a finite physical world, people cannot easily understand how all physical matters are caught in a revolving circularity of perpetual change. In the Universe, the law of the conservation of energy prevails; and, as French chemist Antoine Lavoisier, the father of modern chemistry, is credited with postulating, "nothing is lost, nothing is created," but everything is continuously rearranged and transformed, in very, very long cycles.

Humans have difficulty positioning themselves in this large and ever-changing Universe. Their fear of the unknown, of the immensity of the unknown, and of the inexplicable, is understandable. This has been and continues to be the founding impulse for all superstitions and for all religious systems of thought. In particular, the fear of death, the fear of falling into oblivion, is the source of many of mankind's mental inventions to cope with the uncertainties of life. Religion is one of those safety valves that serve to relieve the emotional distress that humans experience when confronting the idea of their unavoidable death. Many people are terrified at the thought. They much prefer to be duped and made intellectually comfortable than to confront the harsh reality. That is why it can be said that the fear of death is the greatest ally of religion.

It is a fact that death is a requirement of nature and every living thing in this physical Universe (bacteria, trees, birds, mammals . . .) has a limited life span. The human body is no exception. It is a marvelous ambulatory machine, but, as with any machine, it is subjected to wear and tear. Over time, it can be cured and repaired. However, it cannot survive forever. To be born and to die is the natural cycle of every living thing on this planet. It is a law of nature that upon death, the molecules that make up an individual organism disperse into the Earth's ecosystem. Even stars are born, consume their energy, and end up transformed into something else. In this sense, the only difference between species is their life spans. Some, like humans and elephants, can live one hundred years or more.[19] Some, like the mayfly, live only a day or two.

Humans do not easily accept the reality of death and of physical disappearance or transformation. It goes against the basic survival instinct. In fact, the human mind yearns to negate the objective reality of death. At birth, a person is not conscious of the passage to a new world of reality. But death is a foreseeable event that everyone knows is coming. The exit from the living physical world to the inanimate one can be postponed, but it can never be avoided. Death is a great leap into nothingness. We all come from nothingness, and we must all necessarily return to nothingness. That is why time seems to be man's greatest enemy. It can never be overcome and vanquished. But it is perfectly natural to cling to life and to refuse annihilation. Indeed, to live is to want to survive. Hope in the future is endemic, even if life itself is finite. The instinct of survival is the basic natural commitment. Nevertheless, man sees death as the ultimate danger and even as a supreme insult. But nature is not absurd, as some existentialist thinkers pretend; it may be random and unpredictable, but its laws apply to all living things.

It remains that death, the terror of death, and its uncertainty are the principal reasons why humankind has developed the coping mechanism of religious superstitions. The mixture of fear and ignorance creates a fertile ground where the most outlandish fantasies can be cultivated. In most cultures, the passage from life to death is surrounded by a series of rituals and ceremonies, in order to wrap it in mysterious and intuitive meanings and to tame an unavoidably harsh reality.[20] The invention of another, imaginary world and of an everlasting life after physical death was precisely aimed at soothing man's fear of death and keeping alive a false and irrational hope. Especially as a person's mental and physical capabilities decline with age, there is an increasing thirst for remedies that can calm the fear of death and even a yearning for some sort of eternal existence. Religious superstitions and quackery fulfill that need. It is mainly because humanity as a whole has never accepted death that superstitions and beliefs in unreal worlds flourish and perpetuate themselves, in the face of all the evidence to the contrary.

That the unsubstantiated and counterintuitive idea that there is life after death has endured for so long is a demonstration, first, that the human mind has an infinite capability to invent metaphysical and artificial beliefs in order to live through the tragedies that beset earthly life, and second, that religious entrepreneurs can easily take advantage of the situation, for very long periods of time. Indeed, peddlers of snake oil have always been around. However, they are never as successful as when they clothe themselves in religious garb. If this were only an innocuous demonstration of wishful thinking on the part of the weak and the gullible, it would be irrelevant. But since entire systems of thought and power are based on such fallacies, and because of its social and political consequences, one has to take such myths and fairy tales very seriously. The wide acceptance of superstitions may not create infinite life, but it sure can give power and wealth to those who promote them.

For centuries, kings, emperors, and popes have rested their legitimacy not on the will of the people but on the shaky and extravagant idea that their authority was bequeathed upon them by anonymous and abstract deities who, in turn, were supposed to be the final dispensers of eternal bliss to obedient and deferential followers, reserving a life of eternal suffering to the others. In prescientific times, there was no human community that did not have its sorcerer, a sort of intermediary between the real and the imaginary worlds. He was expected to use his magic powers to intercede with the abstract spirits to cure diseases or call for rain during droughts.

Indeed, very young children, old people, and sick people are more prone to resort to wishful thinking or to prayers. Praying is the easy way—or the lazy way—to solve one's problems, just by magic. A prayer is nothing more than an internal conversation with oneself or with an imaginary outside entity to obtain strength, guidance, and good fortune in one's actions or endeavors, and, sometimes, to wish the reverse for one's enemies. Indeed, as Mark Twain once observed, it happens that people sometimes pray with the "intent [of invoking] a curse upon a neighbor at the same time."[21]

Prayers have a psychic and cultural origin, and they represent an attempt or a short cut to solve problems by harnessing the mysterious powers of a benevolent Universe in one's favor. For instance, when people say "Do you have faith in God?" what they imply is "Do you believe there is a force somewhere which works in your favor," or it could imply "Do you have faith in your fate, in your good luck, in yourselves." Thus, for good people, praying to a deity is one way to have their own sentiments reflected, like in a mirror, into a wishful reality. If some people ask that a deity perform wicked deeds ("smite my enemies"), this is because they have wicked ideas or purposes, and praying is merely a way of having their own vile thoughts thrown back at them. Praying can therefore be good for good people, but can be bad for bad people, since prayers are just the reflection of one's thoughts and intentions.[22]

A true story may help understand why praying to divinities is no substitute for thinking and acting, and, as the dictum says, "God helps those who help themselves."

In March of 1891 Captain William D. Collier, the founder of a small Florida town, undertook a hundred-mile journey with his three young sons in his new sailboat, the *Speedwell.* There were a few other passengers aboard, including a young protestant minister. Suddenly, about sixteen miles from their destination of Key West in the Florida Keys, a strong squall started blowing. Captain Collier immediately locked his sons and the other passengers below the deck for their protection, telling only the young minister to remain on deck to help him. The captain shouted to the man to take a nearby axe and cut the shroud lines, in order to quickly lower the sails and render the ship safe. But the minister had other intentions. Instead of cutting the lines as ordered, he fell on his knees and began to pray. The result was that the ship capsized and all the passengers below deck perished. Captain Collier lost his faith in religion and never set foot in a church again.[23]

Too often, when people should be thinking and acting, they close their minds instead and start praying for a miracle, that is to say, for a fortuitous turn of events that may or may not come.[24]

REAL VERSUS IMAGINARY WORLDS

Since people live in the real physical world, where time and space constraints rule and where the laws of physics, biology, and economics prevail, some prayers can seem to be answered just by the randomness of human and physical events. Others can provoke a *placebo effect* in the brain that gives one the impression that his or her condition has improved and that can yield a real improvement. In general, however, people who want to avoid disasters and tragedies follow the physical, biological, and economic laws of this world and do not base their actions on the false hope that some magical supernatural force will somehow come to their rescue. Nevertheless, prayers are probably the least harmful of all superstitions since, in many cases, they are inconsequential, and, in some circumstances, they may be helpful as a means of self-improvement.

However, let us not confuse the invisible and the supernatural; the two are quite different. Many things are invisible. For example, the functioning of the human brain—or of any animal's brain for that matter—

is invisible, but it is entirely natural. Dreams and prayers to imaginary gods may be irrational, but they are naturally produced. On the other hand, to claim that when a human dies, he or she can resurrect or live eternally, that would be supernatural. Nothing in the Universe is above nature. Therefore, there is nothing intrinsically supernatural.

This does not mean that organized religions are not useful institutions, even if their claims to intercede between the natural and the supernatural are bogus. Historically, indeed, they have been very instrumental in raising humanity above the law of the jungle. Moreover, one of the greatest contributions of organized religions in every society has been to provide rituals and rites of passage for deaths and burials, and for other important existential events, thus reinforcing the social cohesion of society.[25] This has been a task generally assigned to sorcerers and priests in most human groups.

In the wonderful world of religious imagination, the fear of death is thus tamed with ideas of a continuous ethereal life after one's physical life, sometimes accompanied by the promises of a future reincarnation or resurrection. Armed with such illusionary wishes, the human mind can be persuaded that death is not the end of a marvelous voyage, but is the continuation of life in a different form. Some can even be persuaded that their physical life is only a preparation for a future eternal life. In this sense, the role of organized religions has been to anesthetize the human mind against reality and the fear of death. Astute entrepreneurs invented religions, couched in elaborate systems of irrational beliefs and religious thoughts about the supernatural, in order to profit and exploit humankind's natural fear of death.

American psychologist Ernest Becker, for example, claimed that it has been scientifically proven that the only way for man to deal with his fate, to achieve his innate heroic need, is to transcend his mortality and give his life up to something greater than the physical, call it god or whatever you wish. In other words, a person must adopt a fetishist religious illusion in order to cope with life's challenges. Otherwise, he risks anxiety or even a mental disorder. Religion then becomes a refuge or a way to camouflage the insupportable reality of death. Thus, for many, religion is an escape into fantasy, that is to say, into a world of alternative nonexistent realities that are sustained solely by a general belief or by the power of propaganda. They become religious because they believe it is the only way to give their lives some hope and meaning. In the face of the inescapable collective human reality called death, and with the assumed impossibility to tame it, Becker invites human beings to drink the hemlock with Socratic courage and turn religious. As Jean-Paul Sartre said, "There is no exit" (*C'est sans issue*). Humanity is stuck and can do nothing about it. This is a true philosophy of despair, and even of impotence and resignation.[26]

RELIGIOUS THINKING, REASON AND RATIONALITY

In the matter of religion and superstitions in general, it is often the case that for those who believe, no justification is necessary, and that for those who don't, no justification can suffice. When they are rational, people normally calculate the cost-benefit ratio of their choices and decisions. Such thinking is predictable. However, religion-based thinking is not rational; it is based on emotions and faith. Therefore, choices and decisions made under religious influence can be most unpredictable and costly.

This is because religion emerges out of emotions and feelings rather than from rational thinking. In this sense, religion belongs to the world of magical thinking, of fantasy and of wishful thinking. It is, to a certain extent, an escape from reality. By definition, the religious mind can find peace because there is no need to search for truth, since all the answers are provided in one big ready-made scoop. There is no need to face reality, to check facts and to be rational. One may merely drown oneself in an absolute and hermetic ideology. What's more, in the world of actions, simple certainty can free the most extremist among religious followers from self-doubt, and for some, from any personal responsibility or from the need to rely on one's personal conscience.

Armed with such metaphysical certitude, for example, some leaders of a fundamentalist persuasion may be inclined to think that they are infallible, that they are omnipotent, and that, somehow, they are endowed with a special mission that cannot be constrained by the surrounding reality—by institutions, by law, or even by normal morality. In a word, they may think of themselves as ideological dictators.[27]

What distinguishes humans from other mammals is surely not bodily functions; it is rather the power of reason, the capability to use the brain to discover the laws of nature and to apply them to improve human conditions on this planet. That is what it means to be human. But there can be two interpretations of rationality: to be rational is commonly meant to act objectively in conformity with reality, facts, and logic and to organize human affairs accordingly, employing the means to obtain desired ends in a demonstrably causal and efficient way. Someone can be said to be rational if he or she makes decisions according to empirical truth and facts. For instance, a farmer anxious to increase crop yield will prepare the soil adequately through tilling, fertilizing, and watering, according to the rules of experience and the art of farming. This is an objective and rational chain of causality. If, however, the farmer does nothing of the sort but relies instead on incantations to spirits or gods to produce a good crop, through magical or supernatural means, such behavior would qualify as being irrational. It is within this type of rationality, that is, a proven means-end scheme, that German economist-sociologist Max Weber wrote about a capitalist society relying on increasingly rational forms of organizations and, especially, on bureaucracy.[28]

There is also a narrower, more restrictive, and more subjective interpretation of rationality. A person can be said to be rational if he or she makes choices according to personal wishes or perceived self-interest, even though such choices can be demonstrated to be misguided and groundless.[29] The way some people use the latter version of self-interested rationality can easily turn into a tautology. Some rational choice economists of religion, for whom decisions made on a religious or superstitious basis are presumed to be *self-interested rational*, make this case. Since these choices are derived from some sort of personal cost-benefit calculation, they assume them to be rational. I would call this reasoning the circularity, or tautology, of the rational choice economics of religion. The syllogism goes this way: decisions made according to the cost-benefit approach are rational; individual religious decisions are made according to a cost-benefit approach of one's personal interests; therefore, choices made from religious beliefs are presumed to be rational.

According to this subjective view of rationality, the person who commits suicide is rational because he deems the escape from life's problems more valuable than the loss of life itself. An alcoholic is also thought to be rational because he believes that the marginal benefits in pleasure derived from drinking are higher than the marginal costs incurred to financial and physical well-being. The same applies to smokers, to consumers of hard drugs, and so on. Even sociopaths who have neither empathy for others nor any shame whatsoever can be considered rationally self-interested because they would refrain from hurting other human beings only if they calculate that the personal costs to themselves exceed the personal benefits they derive from harming others.

Are these behaviors rational and logical, even if the person involved is intelligent and of sound mind? Young children are not irrational to believe in Santa Claus. As they mature, however, most would admit that it would be irrational, or at the very least, non-rational for them to still believe in Santa Claus and to base their daily life decisions on something that does not exist. In this expanded sense, everything a person does could be deemed rational. But then, in this subjective sense, the term rational loses all practical and objective meaning. Some benchmarks of what can normally be considered rational must be established in order to judge if certain behaviors are rational or not.

People could rationally believe in flying saucers, or that there exist super intelligent extraterrestrial beings that can magically cure them of diseases, even though such beliefs have never been proven to be true. Beliefs of this nature can be said to be a conviction with a very low probability of being true. For instance, if people in a cinema are watching a movie in which some rain is falling, after hearing the sound of thunder, some may conclude that it is also raining outside. Unless they walk out to check if it is really the case, their belief that it is raining outside remains an incomplete notion with some doubt as to its verified truth. The belief some have that they will keep living forever after their physical death belongs to ideas with a low probability of being true, since such a claim has never been verified conclusively.

It is rational, of course, to promote such beliefs, especially if the persons involved derive an income, power, or some personal satisfaction through such a promotion. However, if they refuse life-saving treatments because of their fantasy thinking, very few people would consider such behavior to be rational and sound. Even a fool could be said to be rational according to this extended definition of rationality, since it could be shown that his decisions are derived from a crude cost-benefit analysis. To accept that proposition is to say that there is never any crazy or delusional behavior. This is patently untrue. And what is true of individuals is even more true of crowds. Crowds can turn mad at the drop of a hat. The madness of crowds is a recurrent phenomenon, in many domains, not the least of which can be observed in the political arena or in religious affairs.

It can be said that people are not always strictly rational because, depending upon circumstances, their raw emotions can temporarily overcome their capacity to reason. This does not mean that a person is deranged or emotionally disturbed; it only means that sometimes people follow their instincts and their emotions more than reason and common sense. We know that the right side of the human brain is the locus of emotions and feeling, while the left side is the realm of reasoning and thinking.[30] Dreaming or letting emotions take over surrounding reality and normal rational thinking does not make a person irrational and incapable of maximizing behavior, but this could be an indication that the person derives more enjoyment from dreams than from the satisfactions obtained from a less glamorous reality.

In this sense, religions and superstitions belong more to the realm of dreams and emotions than to the objective reality of existence. After all, this is why people buy lottery tickets, even though the chances of being a winner are infinitesimal. Most people make the right calculation, however, equating the marginal cost of a lottery ticket with the expected marginal value of the prize, and do not quit their jobs. Some pathological gamblers do, however, quit their jobs and ruin themselves and their families by gambling. One group of gamblers is rational, the other is not.

In the realms of religion and of superstition, a bit of each does no harm, and may, like dreams, increase happiness. However, if people start hearing voices that tell them to go around killing people and stealing their lands and properties, all for religious reasons or other hallucinatory impulses, then nobody would argue that such persons are rational. One cannot be rational and delusional at the same time.

In many societies, the interpretation of dreams is big business. And, just as for religion, this can be a cultural trait. Dreams are nothing more than the biochemical process of clearing out one day's activity in preparation for another day, so the human body is refreshed and ready to meet new demands and challenges. They usually happen in the late and light stages of sleep called REM sleep, just before waking.[31] The human brain runs on biochemistry and the activities of thinking and dreaming cannot occur without a concomitant activity in the brain. The human body is a whole, and one cannot realistically separate the activity of thinking from the physical human brain.

It is a far cry from this normal physical brain activity to ascribing some magical predictive capability to dreams. Some see in dreams premonitions about the future. They interpret good dreams as good omens, and they fear that bad dreams portend ill. Others believe that spirits from another world visit them in their sleep. Since the same dream is open to different readings, it follows that the interpretation of dreams is a subjective activity rather than a rational or logical one. Dreams are the result of natural brain chemistry and are manifestations of the subconscious. They help processing information that the conscious brain may have overlooked. As such, dreams play an important role in people's lives. Traditional religion can also be useful, provided one knows what it is good for. However, to look to religion for absolute truth is irrational and, almost always, leads to an exploitation of human credulity.

MONISM AND DUALISM: THE MIND-BODY SPLIT

When the Greek philosophers Plato and Aristotle introduced the erroneous idea that a human being was composed of two independent entities—a physical body and a spiritual (immortal) soul—they launched western philosophical thinking on an erroneous and tragic path. Such a mistake is much less prevalent in Asiatic philosophies. In the West, until very recently, there persisted the curious idea of a dichotomy between the mind and the body, as if they could ever exist separately.

Organized religions picked up on Plato's and Aristotle's dualist reasoning that people's intelligence, conscience, or mind did not identify with, or could not be explained in terms of, their physical body. They developed a philosophy and a set of moral codes beginning with the idea that people's mind or soul was immortal and that physical death did not end its functioning. Other philosophers, such as the Algerian Augustine of Hippo and the seventeenth-century French philosopher René Descartes, expanded on the Platonic fallacy of the separation of the mind and the body. Thus they contributed to firmly fixing in Western culture the idea that somehow the human body is less noble than the mind because the former is physical and mortal while the latter, in their view, is immaterial and immortal.

For some religious people, only humans have what is called a soul, which is a sort of immaterial spirit endowed with an eternal life of its own. Recent developments in evolutionary biology and in neurology indicate instead that human consciousness and all mental activities are perfectly real and are products of the functioning of the physical human brain. And, what is more, there is a transition from the animal brain to the human brain, but it is gradual and not unconnected. Indeed, the human brain functions pretty much like the brain of any other mammal, except that it is more complex. Scientists have identified the physical places in the brain which are the seat of human feelings and from which moral sense emerges, not just in people but also in other animals as well. The idea is thus growing that what has historically been called by religions the soul of an individual is analogous to the conscience found in many other animals. What is called moral reasoning in humans is the result of physical traits that have evolved over millennia, along with everything else. As one editorialist put it, "With all deference to the sensibilities of religious people, the idea that man was created in the image of God can surely be put aside."[32]

It is obvious that such discoveries have profound consequences for establishing the basis for human moral systems and for framing one's worldview. For example, René Descartes' famous quote, "I think, therefore I am" must be reversed and should read instead, "I am, therefore I think." Such a philosophical turnaround can have seismic consequences. It would indicate, for example, that the metaphysical foundations upon which many religions have built their moral codes are wrong and are in serious danger of crumbling. This does not mean that all religious moral rules are to be discarded. Far from it. Only that the basis and rationale to extol them have been wrong and are in dire need of being reassessed.

The fact that the idea of the dualism of mind and body is one of the oldest and most widespread philosophical and religious theories does not mean that it is true. Rather the reverse is the case. However, so much has been invested in this theory that those who hold it will hesitate to abandon it.[33] The reason is simple: accepting new fundamental knowledge about human nature would be risking the collapse of their entire religious house of cards.

NEUROSCIENCE AND THE EXPLANATION OF SPIRITUALITY AND RELIGION

Neuroscience is the study of the animal nervous system, including the human brain. It posits that like any other kind of activity, such as linguistic production, spirituality originates from a very specific area of the human brain.[34] The more certain areas of the brain are stimulated, the more religious a person seems to be.[35] These results have contributed to establishing that spirituality and religious thinking are a natural phenomenon that is related to the natural functioning of the human brain. Intellectual activity, meditation, and spiritual experiences do exist, but they are the product of the human brain and are an integral part of the physical reality in which we live. When the atoms of the human brain disintegrate, nothing remains of the immaterial phenomena produced by the active brain—neither spirit, nor conscience, nor soul has an independent existence.

In the coming decades and centuries, the world will have to come to terms with that reality and adapt philosophical thinking and moral codes in consequence. The world can no longer afford to proceed on such false philosophical premises. This is a new moral paradigm.

SCIENCE AND THE SCIENTIFIC METHOD

Science is the rational and logical study of reality. Reality exists. And scientists study the natural and the physical world, as well as the social world, through observation and experimentation. It is a philosophy of discovery of the unknown in order to push back the frontiers of human ignorance. It is a cumulative process, as new knowledge leads to new questions and new insights. It is a most rewarding human enterprise, and, to a certain extent, the acquisition of scientific knowledge carries its own reward.

Mathematics, chemistry, physics, all have useful laws that allow us to understand the surrounding nature and survive in our physical Universe. In mathematics, two plus two equals four, not five or ten. In chemistry, the correct mixture of oxygen and hydrogen produces water, not wine or milk. In physics, the proper design of an airplane enables it to fly. When confirmed by observation or experiments, scientific laws do exist, and they are not a matter of opinion or intuition.

Fundamentally, scientists look for answers and explanations to questions about nature that can be tested by experiment and observation in the material world. But according to the rules of science, it is well understood and accepted that all scientific knowledge is provisional and can be overturned or modified when better answers or better explanations are discovered. In fact, science emphasizes doubt and questioning, rather than faith in dogmas or in authoritative dicta. That is why scientific knowledge is rarely definitive or absolute, even though it is very useful in solving life's problems. This is not the case with religions.

Religions rely more on mystery, enigma, revelation, intuition, and tradition to find answers to questions related to human existence, and not principally on reason, logic, induction, and observation. Virtually all religions and sects have some sort of revealed sacred text that serves as the supreme source of truth and that describes the beliefs and practices of their followers. Some religious people believe every word found in their sacred texts; they are fundamentalists, absolutists, or integrists, who orient their lives within the framework of a tightly religious and ordained worldview that leaves little room for interpretation or for contrary evidence. They find peace of mind, reassurance, and intellectual protection in being told what others have proclaimed.

To this mindset, facts are not important, compared to the tranquility that any such revealed and permanent truth offers. For example, these people can believe that Earth was created some 6,000 years ago, despite that science has proven this false. No matter; strongly religious persons are impervious to facts. What matters is the metaphysical certitude that such a belief brings into their life. They reject science and scientific knowledge, especially when they conflict with their revealed truths. They are comfortable with a mythical view of the world. They reject reason and favor blind faith, and, if the occasion arises, they would not hesitate to trade democracy for some form of theocracy. Other religious people are more open-minded, and they complement their religious "truths" with other more rational sources of knowledge to arrive at their worldview; they are relativists, realists, or pragmatists. For them, sacred texts do not need to be interpreted literally but should be understood in a figurative sense, and seen as didactic stories, legends, parables, metaphors, propaganda myths, allegories, and fables that underline moral, social, and political messages.[36] The vast majority of ordinarily religious people belong to the latter category. They are moderate and tolerant, whatever their religious faith may be. Most religious people do not refuse scientific knowledge even when it contradicts the rigid dicta found in their sacred book.

Science encourages people to ask questions. It looks to the future.

It is always open to new ideas and new intuitions. Scientific knowledge is cumulative. The history of many civilizations shows that scientific knowledge is synonymous with human progress and prosperity, and where ultra conservatives are sympathetic to religion, progressives tend to rely more readily on science and scientific thinking to organize human affairs. Scientific endeavor is a force for change; it challenges existing knowledge, especially if it is found inadequate for solving real problems. Science is the greatest achievement of humankind. It has raised humanity's stock of knowledge and standard of living like nothing else. Science, the universal product of reason and logic, is what distinguishes *Homo sapiens* from other species of mammals on Earth.

Scientific truth is also universal by nature and so evidently useful that it does not need to be imposed on people. For example, if one wants to build an airplane, the laws of aerodynamics do not need to be forced upon the builder: without following them, the plane will not fly.

There are many natural phenomena that humans have not yet been able to explain. For example, is the Universe finite in time or eternal? Is it possible that it has no beginning and no end, and that it evolves into different forms over time? Even though there are many interesting theories to explain this reality, the answer remains, for the time being, unknown, or at best, only partially understood. But to answer these as yet unexplained questions with magical-like explanations is an abdication that does not advance human knowledge and civilization. It's better and more productive to keep pressing for rational and scientific explanations of natural phenomena, through trial and error, hypotheses and theories, testing them empirically against the evidence and, in the process, discovering and understanding the natural laws of the Universe.

Jumping to mystical religious explanations in order to make sense of perfectly natural phenomena, such as the workings of the Universe or the evolution of living forms on Earth, is a sign of intellectual laziness or of a lack of curiosity. The epitaph of a Vermont humanist perfectly describes the true relative contributions of science and religion to humanity: "Science has never killed or persecuted a single person for doubting or denying its teachings, and most of these teachings have been true; but religion has murdered millions for doubting or denying her dogmas, and most of these dogmas have been false."

When antiscientific religious people climb to power, they often feel threatened by the freedom of thought required in scientific research. This doesn't mean that there could not be scientific progress; scientists can still attempt to make contributions to the understanding of nature even in a religious environment. However, they are rarely encouraged and rewarded for doing so and, on the contrary, can be submitted to censorship and exclusion, if not persecution or worse.[37]

This does not mean that all religions are systematically and insurmountably hostile to scientific knowledge and are *ipso facto* sources of fatalism and opposed to change. The Roman Catholic Church, for one, more recently can be said to have been instrumental in the development of modern science, rather than an obstacle to it. Indeed, while relying on its view of an Earth-centered Universe—rational, orderly and harmonious, even if this could not be proven from experience— the Catholic Church reluctantly came to accept the scientific study of natural laws, even if some of these laws turned out to be in direct contradiction to its religious teachings. Other religions have been less receptive to freedom of scientific inquiry, and this could be one explanation why Western civilization has been more open to science during the last five or six centuries than other great civilizations have been.[38]

For example, even today Islam remains profoundly anchored in the traditions of a seventh-century tribal society. It denies the right to freedom of conscience and of religion, refuses the principle of religious tolerance, and tramples the principle of the equality of the sexes, while rejecting the democratic principle of the separation of church and state. Islamic countries need not search very far to discover the causes of their relative economic backwardness; they need only to look at their official religion and its devastating effects on work, education, research, saving, and investment. All this despite their enormous oil wealth.[39]

On the whole, throughout history, when religions did not actually stifle science, scientific progress occurred in spite of religions, but rarely because of them. Populations that have adopted the scientific view of the world have progressed and prospered. Populations that have retained a primitive religious view of the world have declined or stagnated. Science is probably the single greatest factor that has permitted Western civilization to move ahead of all others and is the reason it is imitated, to different degrees, by all progressive people around the world.

This does not mean that Western culture is perfect and is readily exportable. Far from it. In fact, Western culture is a double-edged sword. In its reliance on individual freedom and ingeniousness, and on scientific knowledge, as derived from the ancient Greek philosophy and philosophers of the Renaissance and of the Enlightenment, it is a culture to be emulated by all because it is an engine for progress and liberty. However, because of its biblical roots, it may have a proclivity toward violence. In fact, during the twentieth century, those countries that have inflicted the largest number of unwarranted deaths and committed the worst atrocities against humankind were nominally Christian countries or proponents of a Judeo-Christian ethic.[40]

RELIGIOUS BELIEFS AND SUPERSTITIONS SURROUNDING NATURAL AND RANDOM EVENTS

In religious as in other human affairs, if blind faith is necessary for a proposition to be accepted, this means that such a proposition cannot be accepted on its own merits. This should immediately raise suspicions because a rational human mind requires explanations and justifications before accepting assertions and propositions.

Some people believe that world events are not random and accidental, but are predetermined by a supernatural power. However, disasters, calamities, horrors, diseases, and human suffering and misery in general are not easy for them to explain and reconcile with their belief in a just, omnipotent, and beneficent god. For the most gullible and paranoid among them, earthquakes, floods, plagues, epidemics, and famine are manifestations of divine punishments for human misdeeds sent by an occult force. Religious opportunists take full advantage of such instances of human misfortune to offer false comfort to people traumatized by such events. They stand ready to advance explanations of why their god had allowed such wickedness to rain upon their heads. They say people suffer because they deserve to suffer, and their austere god is only reluctantly punishing them, just as parents admonish their children, because they have sinned. Just like the snake oil salesmen of another time, religious entrepreneurs see benefit in tragedy and use cataclysms and other natural disasters as stepping-stones to expand their following and their personal power.

After the terrorist attacks of September 11, 2001, two prominent American fundamentalist televangelists, the late Jerry Falwell of the Moral Majority and Pat Robertson of the Christian Coalition, opined that Americans had only themselves to blame for the calamity. They declared on Fox News that the attacks were God's punishment for the secular character of American society. Falwell claimed, "God continues to lift the curtain and allow the enemies of America to give us probably what we deserve," and Robertson replied, "Well, I totally concur."[41] Robertson went at it again in early 2006 when seventy-seven-year-old Israeli Prime Minister Ariel Sharon suffered a stroke. For the fundamentalist preacher, God himself undoubtedly conjured up Sharon's illness. Sharon's stroke was not a disease like any other. Instead, in Robertson's mind, it was nothing less than divine retribution for the politician's decision to vacate some occupied Palestinian lands.[42] That is surely recuperation of a natural phenomenon for religious and political purposes on a grand scale.

Other religious minds attempt to be more rational by creating a convenient division of responsibility for natural events between a good god—theirs—and a bad god, the devil. All the nice things happening in the Universe are ascribed to the good god, while all the worldly catastrophes are assumed to be the work of a bad god, a fallen angel. They become obsessed with the problem of evil, and since they cannot logically ascribe bad intentions to their merciful god, they pretend the miserable state of humanity must be the result of the devil's actions. This was the fundamental superstitious hypothesis of the Manicheans, disciples of Manes in the third century, and of the Cathars[43] or Albigensians, in the twelfth and thirteenth centuries in southern France.

With more subtlety, some simply deny that their god, while supreme and omnipotent and the only force to have shaped and ordered the world in accordance with his exact intentions, is responsible in any way, shape, or form for the suffering, the death, and the misery that is humanity's lot. Such sorrows have no ultimate meaning at all, but these people ascribe the responsibility for these afflictions to a mythical human couple: Adam and Eve. According to them, our natural physical world is not perfect because of the first humans' original sin. Their god has nothing to do with natural calamities and human suffering. Thus, the flawed human race is accused of having brought its miseries upon itself and is, therefore, entirely responsible for its shortcomings.

The obvious question here is why would a just and benevolent god condemn the whole human race because of the acts of two persons (Genesis 3:16–23, Romans 5:15)? This does not make much sense. In all this, the god of religion has the starring role, since he is assumed to have made sure that a perfect world will exist one day, except it will be after everybody is dead and reborn in a vaporous place called Paradise.

Such religious fabrication is necessary to solve the thorny theological problem of evil in this earthly world. Indeed, if an all-powerful, all-knowing, and supremely good deity is responsible for the creation of the physical world, then why is this supposedly god-created world not perfect, but rather full of imperfections and injustices? The question of the coexistence of an all-powerful entity and evil in the world has never been answered satisfactorily by any religion. This is well illustrated in St Augustine's dilemma: "Either God cannot prevent evil, or he will not. —If he cannot, he is not all-powerful;—if he will not, he is not all good."

The German philosopher Gottfried Leibniz also tried to reconcile religion and scientific knowledge and thought he had the answer in his essay *Theodicity*. For Leibniz, since he assumed that religion could not be discarded, the only logical answer was that we must be living in the best of all possible worlds that the heavens could deliver. Leibniz's metaphysical belief was the object of a devastating satire in Voltaire's *Candide*, in which the protagonists face disaster upon disaster, but nevertheless cling to the myth that they live in "the best of all possible worlds."[44] As British philosopher Bertrand Russell said, "No man who believes that all is for the best in this suffering world can keep his ethical values unimpaired, since he is always having to find excuses for pain and misery."[45]

Religious mythology can't resist a rational and logical analysis. It is a sum of irrational intellectual inventions used to account for anything that science has not yet been able to explain. For those who engage professionally in its promotion, it is a subversive attempt to obtain personal and political power, as well as financial riches, by persuading psychologically fragile and gullible souls that they are immortal and will, someday, be eternally happy. When they are presented as absolute and definite truths, these myths anesthetize the brain and freeze the human mind in a perpetual state of disempowerment. Such myths are themselves very powerful, however, since they can destroy civilizations and bury scientific knowledge for centuries.

Such a catastrophe befell the Arab world during the seventh century when one of the most advanced civilizations of the times was subjugated and destroyed by the rise of a proselytizing and absolutist religion: Islam. A similar tragedy could well befall the United States in the coming years, if the movement toward religious fundamentalism succeeds in censoring scientific discourse and shackling scientific research.[46]

SCIENCE, RELIGIONS AND ETHICS

Science is a tool crafted by humans. It can be used for good or for bad. It is by definition amoral, in the sense that it does not deal with normative issues, only with objective ones. Science has brought much good to humanity, but its findings have also been used to build increasingly deadlier chemical and nuclear armaments. In the wrong hands, scientific discoveries can harm human progress and not enhance it. This is its main weakness, not that this weakness is intrinsic to science, but rather that scientific discoveries can be misused for immoral ends.

Organized religions, on the other hand, are strongly preoccupied with morality, with how people behave and how they treat others. This has been the main contribution of religions, since they have been relied upon to civilize primitive peoples and to provide them with spiritual and moral values. Thus, on the question of ethics, religions are less concerned about objective truths but rather concentrate on what people believe and how such beliefs affect their behavior. For example, by inspiring the fear of eternal damnation in the minds of people, religions have contributed to softening the sharpest edges of an otherwise primitive human character.

That is why organized religions cannot be discarded on the sole basis of the truthfulness and logic of their teachings, unless their moral teachings (Bible, Qur'an, Torah) are also replaced by a superior moral code. The fear of gods and devils may be anachronistically old-fashioned and an insult to human intelligence, but such beliefs have had positive societal influences in the past and continue to provide some moral guidance to many people. It is, therefore, not enough to demonstrate the weak logical foundations of religions; it is also important not to throw the baby out with the bath water. Indeed, there is an obligation to advance moral rules that are at least as good as, and preferably superior to, those taught by religious systems we wish to replace.

THE SEPARATION OF CHURCH AND STATE

The fundamental principle of a secular and humanist society is the separation between religion and partisan politics. In a well-functioning democracy, people are free to listen to different arguments and free to agree without fear of retribution; they are also free to listen and disagree without being subjected to exclusion. This is one of the greatest contributions of the US Constitution.

There is a US law that states that a tax-exempt religious organization cannot get involved in partisan politics without losing its privileged tax-exempt status.[47] Organizations risk loosing their tax-exempt status if they "participate in, or intervene in...any political campaign on behalf of any candidate for political office." Unfortunately, this law is rarely applied. When it is, it is done on a partisan and ideological basis.

Humanist Rites of Passage

For social, emotional, and spiritual reasons, many people wish to congregate on a regular basis with others to meditate and communicate. In particular, they want to celebrate the most important events in their lives (birth, marriage, death, and other life milestones), surrounded by their friends and loved ones, performing ceremonies that are more than a simple legal formality. This is perfectly natural and rewarding. As we pointed out, these civilizing rituals are perhaps one of the greatest contributions of organized religions to mankind.

However, not everyone wants to involve traditional religion or disputed ideas of abstract deities in such exercises. What can be done? The answer consists in organizing secular ceremonies or gatherings, either on a regular basis or on the occasion of special events. More and more organizations do exist that stand ready to provide such humanist rites of passage. But a largely accessible humanist social structure is yet to be built.[48]

SEVEN

CONSERVATION

SEVENTH HUMANIST PRINCIPLE:
CONSERVE AND IMPROVE EARTH'S
NATURAL ENVIRONMENT—LAND, SOIL, WATER,
AIR, AND SPACE—AS HUMANKIND'S COMMON HERITAGE.

> We do not inherit the Earth from our ancestors, we borrow it from our children.
>
> —Native American proverb

> A human being is part of the whole, called by us "Universe," a part limited in time and space. Our task must be to . . . embrace all living creatures and the whole [of] nature in its beauty.
>
> —Albert Einstein (1879–1955)

> Take the skeleton of a man. Tilt the pelvis, shorten the femur, legs, and arms, elongate the feet and hands, fuse the phalanges, elongate the jaws while shortening the frontal bone, and finally elongate the spine, and the skeleton will cease to represent the remains of a man and will be the skeleton of a horse.
>
> —Buffon [George-Louis Leclerc de] (1707–1788)

The Earth's natural environment—land, soil, air, water, and space—forms a unifying whole that sustains human life and all living organisms. Whether we like it or not, humans are a significant part of the Earth's environment, and this means that we can do something to preserve it. We have to pay attention to the environment and to the global life-support system. We need more scientific understanding of the Earth's complex ecosystem and more enlightened international collaboration to face the new challenges that global pollution presents. But the general principle is clear: Earth's current inhabitants have no right to leave a damaged and depreciated environment to future generations. We must conserve, avoid waste, and refrain from polluting the Earth's natural environment. The Earth is the only planet we have, at least for the foreseeable future, and we should behave accordingly.[1]

When using the Earth's resources, we must abide by the fundamental economic rule of using resources. For each economic decision, a positive balance must be established between the marginal social benefits derived from the decision, be they be private or public, with the marginal social costs incurred, also encompassing the private and public sides, in order to maximize the total social good over time. This means that pollution of the environment and the overuse of resources should be taken expressly into consideration in measuring the total social costs of any economic activity.[2] Cleaning costs and replacement costs must then be added to the private costs of production to arrive at the final price paid by buyers and consumers. In particular, the price of fossil fuel for energy consumption, a main contributor to atmospheric pollution, should reflect the damage it is causing to the environment. Thus, in this spirit of efficiency, the prices paid should reflect the true costs of producing a product. In general, this implies that all costs, both private and public, should be covered by market prices. When this is not the case, governments have a social responsibility to correct the anomaly.

The idea here is that the use of the environment is not free, that some restraint should be exercised, and that pollution and replacement costs have to be factored into the total costs of production and into the prices of goods consumed. What it also means is that for the environment to be preserved, we must make a virtue of self-restraint, moderation, and self-sacrifice.[3]

THE ENVIRONMENT AND HUMANIST VALUES

Billions of years ago, humans did not exist. Radioactive dating shows Earth itself, formed from space debris, to be about 4.55 billion years old. It was about 3,800 million years ago that Earth's atmosphere began to form. The stage was set for the beginning of life on our planet. It was 245 million years ago that dinosaurs roamed the Earth, until their complete disappearance in a mass extinction 65 million years ago. The first humans appeared two million years ago.

When placed in perspective, human life on Earth is relatively recent, even though a few million years may seem a very long period to time-constrained humans. Human civilization is even much younger. The last six or seven thousand years marked a rapid rise in human civilization—a relatively recent phenomenon. Nothing guarantees that human progress will be linear and positive in the future or that a catastrophic regression could not occur.

Billions of years from now, odds are that there will be no humans on Earth. Since our star, the Sun, is scheduled to vaporize and implode in approximately five billion years, this would appear to establish a maximum finite span for life on Earth.[4] Numerous other natural catastrophes, such as major climate changes, are likely to present themselves much earlier and hasten this ultimate fate.

Humankind exists in a finite world, both in space and in time. The unfolding drama of human life on planet Earth goes on, but in what contexts and for how long? The natural environment of humankind is constantly changing. Life is an ongoing struggle for survival. For all living organisms, nature is a given to which they must adapt or disappear. However, humans have the capacity to change nature at the margin, and they have the mental and moral capability to change themselves and their behavior. In this sense, human beings are unique among living animals. Each person has a singular destiny, partly due to circumstances beyond his or her control, but also partly due to personal choices and actions. We are all the sum of our decisions.

Humans are part of the Universe, but this does not mean that the Universe did not exist or will not exist in the absence of human beings, or any other living things for that matter.[5] Indeed, the evidence seems to indicate that matter and energy in the Universe are continually changing form in a long, eternally repeated cycle of creation and destruction, going from Big Bang to Big Bang. The last Big Bang, when numerous galaxies collided and collapsed into a Big Crunch, is estimated to have happened 13.7 billion years ago. Astronomer Lyman Spitzer first proposed this theory of the Universe in 1955, and specialists at NASA, working with the orbital space observatory FUSE,[6] confirmed it in 1999. Astrophysicists are now trying to evaluate when the previous Big Bang happened. In theory, there could have been trillions and trillions of Big Bangs before, each one being preceded by an unimaginably immense void of burned-out stars, occurring about every 100 billion years, and there will likely be trillions and trillions of Big Bangs in the future. —It is only from a human perspective that we can subjectively envision being the center of the Universe; objectively, we are not and never have been.

Man's ideas about the Universe have evolved over time as human knowledge expanded. Primitive man used to think that the Earth was the center of the Universe and that the stars moved around it. When it was discovered, at the time of Galileo Galilei (1564–1642), that Earth was only one of the planets that circle around the Sun, people thought that the Sun was the center of the Universe. Understandably, some people thought the Sun was a god, providing essential warmth and energy.[7]

As far as the Universe is concerned, humans have no more meaning than a colony of ants or a black hole. A sense of genuine humility and of pragmatic realism is a prerequisite for humans to understand the human condition. The key to humanity's long-term survival is in our inner selves and our adherence to a humanistic morality of survival.

Of course, the idea that humankind is at the center of the Universe is an old (erroneous) idea. It is mainly derived from religious teachings. For those who base their faith in the Bible, they learn that their god gave humans total dominion over all other species: "And God blessed them, and God said unto them, Be fruitful, and multiply, and replenish the Earth, and subdue it: and have dominion over the fish of the sea, and over the fowl of the air, and over every living thing that moveth upon the Earth." (Genesis 1:28) This is the source of the myth that humankind is at the center of the Universe.

Once this useless myth is discarded, human responsibility and obligations are much greater, both for mankind's survival and development and for the preservation of the living environment. The fact that humans have survived in such great numbers—more than six and a half billion individuals, and counting—is no guarantee that they will survive as a species in the future. It is in this sense that humankind may be in need of a new morality that meets the new requirements for survival and progress. Humankind has the means to destroy itself through cataclysmic wars or through an inability to adapt to a changing natural environment. Humans have the means to destroy the planet and perhaps not the wisdom and intelligence not to do it.

THE CATASTROPHES THAT WE CAUSE AND THOSE BEYOND OUR CONTROL

Life on Earth has gone through dramatic disruptions. In particular, there have been two near extinctions of life. Around 65 million years ago, the order of dinosaurs was completely exterminated. The most plausible scientific explanation for this devastating event is that a giant a comet collided with our planet, killing half of all species then living on Earth. Indeed, dinosaurs appeared on planet Earth about 230 million years ago. They were a great biological success, surviving for some 165 million years. By contrast, human beings (from the genus *Homo* that includes modern humans and their close relatives) have been around on planet Earth for only between 1.6 and 1.9 million years. All human subspecies, except *Homo sapiens* (modern humans), are now extinct. And *Homo sapiens* has been around for only between 200,000 and 250,000 years.

One might wonder if we humans are not the dinosaurs of the modern age, destined also to disappear one day from the surface of the Earth. Indeed, because of our neglect of the environment and because of our wars, we humans may become the dinosaurs of our era. Earth can last without humans, but humans cannot survive without planet Earth.

Far less known is a similar but much greater catastrophe that took place at the end of the Permian, 250 million years ago. Then, 90 percent of life was destroyed, including saber-toothed reptiles and their rhinoceros-sized prey on land, as well as vast numbers of fish and other species in the sea.[8] In both instances, a huge comet hit Earth. The first comet, 250 million years ago, had a diameter of about 48.3 km and landed in Antarctica. The second comet to hit the Earth, 65 million years ago, was smaller, with a diameter of 9.6 km, and it landed in the Yucatan peninsula of Mexico. The devastation of life from these two comets was such that it left the planet with only about 4 to 10 percent of its previous species. These two near extinctions of life on Earth had major consequences for Earth's biodiversity. The lesson drawn from these two devastating catastrophes is adapt or disappear. Adaptation is the first law of survival for living organisms.[9]

If Earth were to be hit by a massive meteorite, the resulting pollution of the atmosphere could curtail agriculture and food production for years, leading to widespread starvation. But it is less the fear of meteors and more the shock of climate change that may represent humanity's most formidable challenge. Not long ago, entire peoples had to adapt and suffer under climate changes. This was the case for the Greenland Norse settlers, who were wiped out by the Little Ice Age that began in the fourteenth century. Also, climate changes played an important role in the disappearance of Central America's Mayan civilization around 950 CE.[10] Sudden changes in climate have occurred in the past and will most likely happen again in the future, with unsettling results. There are, indeed, natural cycles in climate changes with warm periods followed by colder periods, over which humans have little or no control.

THE PARADOX OF POLLUTION AND CLIMATE CHANGE

Earth's climate seems to be following long and short cycles over time under the influence of various factors. One important factor is sunspot cycles, another is changes in the Earth's own axis in relation to the Sun, and yet another is related to fundamental shifts in atmospheric circulation. Climatologists have discovered, for example, that Earth's climate went through a period of abrupt warming about 14,700 years ago, with a 22° (Fahrenheit) spike in temperature within only about fifty years. Then, around 12,900 years ago, there was an Ice Age that lasted about 1,200 years. This was followed by a second period of climate warming with a 22° increase within just about sixty years.[11] Much closer to us, the Earth warmed greatly between 1915 and 1940, cooled between 1940 and 1975, and then warmed significantly again between 1975 and today. There is nowadays growing and compelling evidence that the Earth's surface is getting warmer. For example, it is warmer today than it was a century ago, and sea surface temperatures are running about 1.8° to 3.6° above the past hundred-year average.[12]

Many scientists believe the current trend of global warming is one of the greatest environmental threats facing humanity, next to a man-made nuclear cataclysm. Permafrost in Siberia, Alaska, and Canada is melting, as is the case with Arctic and Antarctic ice. In particular, climate warming is accelerating the melting of the West Antarctic Ice Sheet (anchored in the ocean below sea level) and of the Greenland Ice Cap. The resulting rise in sea level over the next century could threaten major coastal communities all over the world.[13] Moreover, this ice melting has the consequence of lowering the planet's albedo ratio[14] and thus contributing further to global warming in a vicious cycle of cumulative effects.

If the current scientific consensus is correct, as global warming drastically alters the climate all over the world, the economic and social implications for modern civilization are very serious, even though all its damaging effects remain to be fully ascertained. Future food production, for example, may be fundamentally affected in some regions of the globe. Indeed, even in areas that will remain habitable, traditional crops may not grow as well or as fast because climatic conditions will be either too hot, too wet, too dry, or too cold.

Because so many forces influence Earth's climate, there is still some uncertainty about the relative importance of each set of causes behind the current observable climate warming. For example, some scientists estimate that part of the trend in Earth's warming could be caused by natural factors acting within a very long climate cycle, such as a recurring closer proximity of Earth to the Sun, (our heat and energy source).[15] The remaining observed warming could be attributed to human-made pollution, such as the release of carbon dioxide gas (CO_2) in the atmosphere.[16] Carbon dioxide is an important form of greenhouse gases and is a by-product of fossil energy consumption. Carbon dioxide is removed from the atmosphere by trees and plants through the photosynthesis process. Carbon dioxide absorbs Earth's infrared radiation and reradiates part of it back to the Earth, thus causing warming. Such a greenhouse effect is beneficial for humanity. Indeed, without it, the infrared radiation from the Sun would escape into space and Earth would be about 50° cooler than it is. Therefore, life as we know it is critically dependent on the greenhouse effect. The damage comes from too much of a greenhouse effect, which results in global warming.

As we have seen, there were other periods in more or less recent history when global warming occurred. During the last two millennia, there was the Roman Empire warm period (200 BCE–500 CE), the medieval warm period (900–1300 CE) and the current warming period (1850–present). Such periods have been prosperous times, and human populations did not seem to have suffered markedly from the warming of the climate, and could even have benefited from it. In other periods, when the climate was cooling, people fared less well and suffered difficult times. Such were the cases with the Dark Ages (500–900 CE) and what is known as the Little Ice Age (1300–1850 CE).

It can be argued that previous warming periods were much less severe than the one in which we seem to be living presently. This time, it appears that human-made pollution of the atmosphere is having more serious effects on Earth's climate and on its ecological system.[17]

There are two types of air pollution and this poses a terrible dilemma to humanity. On the one hand, human activities over the past 150 years, such as the burning of fossil fuel (coal, oil, natural gas, etc.), all connected with the Industrial Revolution, have contributed to creating the phenomenon known as global warming, which is mainly caused by the release of invisible greenhouse gases into the atmosphere. On the other hand, and this is paradoxical, the same man-made air pollutants caused by fossil fuel use—which result in the visible layers of smog in the atmosphere of large cities—turn clouds into giant mirrors that reflect more of the Sun's rays back into space, thus insulating the Earth. This last phenomenon creates a contrary effect known as global dimming, whereby less heat and energy from the Sun reach the Earth. And as a result of Earth receiving less sunlight because of visible pollution, there is a global cooling effect on land and the oceans.

But the dimming effect has other disastrous consequences. It tends to affect weather patterns and rainfalls in different regions around the globe, thus causing droughts and famine in some areas, and heavy rains and floods in other areas. This has been clearly observed in the Northern Hemisphere mid-latitudes.[18] For example, it has been postulated that global dimming may have caused the failure of the monsoon in sub-Saharan Africa during the 1970s and 1980s.[19]

Earth's climate seems to be caught in a sort of tug-of-war between two competing atmospheric effects: one kind of visible pollution prevents sunlight from reaching the Earth, while another one, the invisible pollution, prevents heat radiation from the Earth from escaping into space. The global cooling effects of air pollution with visible particles thus tend to mask somewhat the stronger global warming effects of invisible greenhouse gases.[20]

This poses a potentially difficult dilemma to humanity regarding the fight against both types of atmospheric pollution. Indeed, if there were less visible pollution in the air at the same time that greenhouse gas emissions continue to increase, a reduction in global dimming would tend to exacerbate global warming. That would translate into the quick melting of glaciers and a catastrophic rise in the level of oceans. Thus, paradoxically, a rapid solution to global dimming may lead to more pronounced increases in the Earth's temperature. The ice caps at the Earth's poles would melt at a faster rate and the level of oceans would rise faster, with all the consequences that such occurrences would entail for low, sea-level inhabited regions and for the global ecological system.

It would seem that humanity has no choice but to reduce, and eventually eliminate, both the visible and invisible causes of air pollution. Indeed, the obvious but difficult solution consists in reducing and eliminating simultaneously both visible pollution (particles) and invisible pollution (greenhouse gases). This will be the mounting challenge facing humanity in the coming years and decades. If this challenge is not met, humanity may pay a steep price for polluting the atmosphere.[21]

THE NEED TO FIRST CONTROL POPULATION GROWTH

However, all efforts to thwart the degradation and destruction of the Earth's ecosystem could prove to be ineffective if concrete steps are not first taken to reduce population growth. Indeed, in the poorest places on the planet—in Africa, in the Middle East and in Asia— population growth is exploding. That is why it is expected that by 2050, if the current rate of human reproduction remains the same, there will be between 8 billion and 10 billion people living on planet Earth. Such a population explosion will necessarily translate into an expanding need for energy, housing, food, and other resources. The need to fight pollution and prevent climate changes will thus be frustrated. Indeed, the concrete solution to a host of problems is tied to the success or failure in preventing the global demographic catastrophe that is in the making.[22]

HUMANS IN THE NATURAL ENVIRONMENT

Humans are products of the natural environment. Without a sustaining natural environment, there is no human life. As for all mammals, every human has a biological starting point in time as well as a biological ending point. The beginning of life occurs at fertilization, when a spermatozoa and an ovum, each carrying 23 chromosomes, join to form a fertilized egg. The end of life occurs when the brain ceases to function. The fertilized egg contains the complex genetic make-up of a new human being, such as sex, color of eyes, hair color, skin tone, susceptibility to certain diseases, and so on. All this information is written on a double helical genetic ribbon called the DNA molecule (*d*eoxyribo*n*ucleic *a*cid).[23]

One of the great scientific advances of our times was the unraveling of the DNA chain for humans and other mammals. The first surprise was the discovery that the genetic code (DNA) of a chimpanzee is from 96 to almost 99 percent the same as the DNA of a human being. Humans and chimpanzees have evolved separately since splitting off from a common remote ancestor about 6 million years ago. Even more astounding is the discovery that there is only a 10 percent difference between human DNA and the DNA of a flu virus.

This leads to the extraordinary conclusion that all animals, and all living things, have a common biological ancestor, going as far back as three and a half billion years ago, when life first appeared on this planet. That common ancestor was almost certainly a one-celled organism, formed near an underwater volcanic steam vent, near enough to the surface for sunlight to participate in the process of interaction with minerals in the water and oxygen in the atmosphere. The key differences between the species are mostly subtleties that are related to patterns of gene activity and how proteins interact during the very long process of evolution.[24]

Humans are more advanced than other related animals because, in the past, our lineage experienced beneficial genetic mutations. Such advancements occurred, for example, when human ancestors began walking upright, instead of walking on all fours. Also, a mammoth improvement took place when the human brain increased in size, providing for more intelligence power, and allowing for the development of better language and hunting skills. Our distant ancestors were thus better equipped to compete for survival and were able to eclipse competitors.[25]

As we move toward modern humans, research has permitted the identification of minute variations over time in the human female mitochondrial DNA (which is passed only through females) and in the human male Y chromosomes. Y chromosome data are passed only through males.

Every living person today has a small part of the DNA of a woman who lived some 200,000 years ago.[26] Also, about the same period, some important genetic mutations occurred in humans' ancestors. These mutations resulted in the appearance of the first *Homo sapiens*, an ancestor of the modern human.[27] Why are humans talking animals, while close relatives, such as chimpanzees or gorillas, have not developed a spoken language? A particular gene present in all mammals, called FOXP2, appears to have gone through some critical mutations in early humans and is likely to be linked to spoken language. Mutations of this gene, through fine developments of the mouth and larynx, allowed our ancestors, some 200,000 years ago, to utter a wider range of sounds that served as the foundation of human language.[28]

Human intelligence and human consciousness also took a step forward when other important genetic mutations occurred, between 50,000 and 80,000 years ago. This time it concerned genes present in the male Y chromosome. Such genetic mutations affected various aspects of brain function and increased human cognitive and neurological capabilities.[29] This is also around the time when modern humans experienced culturally what Jared Diamond and others characterize as a Great Leap Forward. For example, humans began to bury their dead with care, made clothing out of hides, developed sophisticated hunting and fishing techniques, and made cave paintings.[30]

With more intelligence came more knowledge, and with more knowledge people were able to design more complex and better technological, economic, and social systems and make better tools for food production. As a consequence, population increased dramatically, as humans learned to use the resources of the environment more efficiently.[31] Greater population and more competition among groups—and possibly new environmental challenges—led early humans to move out of Africa and disperse throughout Europe, Asia, and Australasia. That is why it can be said that "humans have spread globally, but have evolved locally."[32] After migrating from Africa, some 50,000 to 60,000 years ago, humans continued to evolve through a random process, as they faced different challenges in various continents, overcame new diseases and new climates, and adapted to new food supplies and to different societal demands.

Even though all contemporary human beings living today carry the same genetic baggage, they have evolved differently as they colonized different continents. But the genetics of all humans comes from a common human ancestor. Indeed, the genetic code of this common ancestor is practically identical to the one found today in all human beings, without exception, whatever their race or culture.[33] As a result of these discoveries, we know that human beings are genetically highly homogenous, even if they are physically and culturally different and even if each population is adapting to a different environment.[34] Genetically, therefore, it can be said that humans form one large, common, human family.

CREATIONISM AND EVOLUTION

Some people do not like or accept the idea that humans have evolved over a very long time from ancient species. They rather prefer to cling to the myth that humans are the descendents of invisible gods and angels who have created them and made them kings of planet Earth. This may be a useful self-serving myth, but it is contrary to all scientific knowledge. There is an expression for such reasoning: magical thinking. This is the world of small children who make believe and imagine various fantasies. It is also a world where superstitions and religions of all sorts prosper.

Religions and science belong to two different worlds. Science establishes that humans are incidental elements in the Universe, while religions arbitrarily place them at the center. Science, as a positive source of human knowledge, attempts to explain and prove things with logic, rational analysis, and the observation of reality and experimentation. Religions, on the other hand, attempt to propose and impose preconceived, imagined, and arbitrary views of the world that are often in violation of logic and facts and that therefore are of little assistance in learning about the real functioning of our world. In the normative field of ethics and morality, which is more a question of judgment, science has less to say, except that if humans want to survive in this harsh environment, they must adopt rules of behavior that are effective and productive. Thus, if religion wants to play a role in designing moral codes of conduct for humans, it cannot establish this morality on false, absolutist views of the world that contradict the physical laws of the Universe.

Scientific discoveries have shown creationism to be a fabrication.[35] The Bible is very misleading on this issue. For example, there are two conflicting versions of creation in Genesis. In one version, God is said to have created plants and animals before man. In another version, man is supposed to have come before the plants and animals![36] Plants and animals, such as the dinosaurs, existed long before man—in fact, millions of years before. All living creatures on Earth share a common ancestor, and their evolution is determined by purely natural mechanisms, not supernatural ones. All species existing today, including *Homo sapiens*, evolved from earlier species. In this sense, we must recognize that humans are an advanced species of animals—nothing more, nothing less. Scientific knowledge, derived from fossil and chemical evidence, is now advanced enough to elucidate many of the questions related to the appearance of life on this planet, and this is without resorting to magical divine intervention.[37]

There is a strong push toward obscurantism and a refusal of scientific knowledge in certain groups in the United States today. This could tarnish its favorable international reputation earned by the US Constitution, which was inspired by humanist values.[38] In particular, one political tactic of extremist religious groups in the United States is to claim that creationism has scientific value. They call their faith-inspired ideas about creation the intelligent design theory. According to this theory, advanced with the aim of using the terminology of science for propaganda purposes, life is presumed to be too specifically complex (complex structures with specific functions, such as DNA) as well as being irreducibly complex (reduce a complex structure, such as the eye, by one part and it loses its functionality) to have evolved through only natural forces. They then deduct that a supernatural force—an intelligent designer or a god—must have created life and everything else.

A theory that cannot ever be proven (because it does not rest on evidence but on an unsubstantiated and authoritative assertion) is a tautology that belongs to the realm of faith, not of science. Intelligent design is such a theory that has no scientific value. It doesn't contribute any new information about the functioning of the world.

In all human societies, systems of thought are related to power. That is why errors and falsehoods can remain in circulation for so long after they have been demonstrated to be false. For example, during the Middle Ages, there was a general belief that living organisms can arise not only from parents, but also spontaneously, from inorganic and organic matter, independent of any parent.

This theory of spontaneous generation is now considered a quaint and weird idea, but it did dominate the view of theologians and natural scientists alike for a very long time, even after empirical experiments had demonstrated the falsity of the notion. Ever since Darwin's work in the nineteenth century, we know that complex life has evolved from simple, microscopic life forms and has progressed over vast periods of time.[39] It remains that during the Christian and totalitarian Middle Ages, secular philosophy was considered heretical and even illegal. Intellectually, this was truly a Dark Age and a period of intellectual and moral regression.

Galileo, and especially Darwin, changed all that. Darwin's famous "warm little pond" may have been an incomplete picture, but it demonstrated a break with established notions.[40] Complex life evolved from simple life, not "fully blown from a soiled shirt" through spontaneous generation. Only in the twentieth century did technology and the discovery of unanticipated life forms in extreme conditions allow a look at the chemical basis of life before complexity could emerge.[41]

Today, most scientists accept the idea that all life on Earth arose from a single ancestor, that all species are mutable, and that geographic and temporal changes in species' compositions are driven by a similar mechanism of organic change: evolution, diversification, and natural selection. Similarly, geneticists believe that modern humans, no matter how different they may seem, are biologically extremely similar. Our DNA betrays the fact that we are all descended from a small group of modern humans who lived in Eastern Africa some 60,000 years ago.[42]

EIGHT

VIOLENCE, WAR, AND PEACE

EIGHTH HUMANIST PRINCIPLE:
RESOLVE DIFFERENCES AND CONFLICTS COOPERATIVELY,
WITHOUT RESORTING TO WAR OR VIOLENCE.

War, like murder, will one day number among those extraordinary atrocities which revolt and shame nature, and drape opprobrium over the countries and centuries whose annals they sully.

—Marquis de Condorcet (1743–1794),
French philosopher

Of all the enemies to public liberty, war is perhaps the most to be dreaded, because it compromises and develops the germ of every other. No nation could preserve its freedom in the midst of continual warfare.

—James Madison (1751–1836),
Fourth US president

The lowest standards of ethics of which a right-thinking man can possibly conceive is taught to the common soldier whose trade is to shoot his fellow men. In youth he may have learned the command, "Thou shalt not kill," but the ruler takes the boy just as he enters manhood and teaches him that his highest duty is to shoot a bullet through his neighbor's heart—and this, unmoved by passion or feeling or hatred, and without the least regard to right or wrong, but simply because his ruler gives the word.

—Clarence Darrow (1857–1938),
American lawyer

Most people would like to see wars become as obsolete as slavery or duels, that is to say a legacy of less civilized times. Moreover, in today's conflicts, 90 percent of victims are civilians. This makes waging war an even more barbaric practice that needs to be eradicated from human customs.[1] Unfortunately, humanity is still saddled with the curse of war. In fact, there have been 118 interstate wars during the last two centuries.[2]

The sources of human violence and brutality toward other humans remain the object of numerous areas of research and speculation.[3] Are humans more prone to violence and to being more morally irresponsible when acting in isolation or when acting within a group? Why was the twentieth century one of the most violent in human history while, paradoxically, human civilization is supposed to have progressed over time? Is moral progress keeping pace with advances in technology, or is there a widening gap between the two? What would be the consequences for human survival if technology advances but morality regresses?

As Hungarian-born American psychologist Ervin Staub put it, "The widespread hope and belief that human beings had become increasingly 'civilized' was shattered by the events of the Second World War, particularly the systematic, deliberate extermination of six million Jews by Hitler's Third Reich." Why then are moral progress and institutional progress so slow, as compared to scientific and technological progress?

To answer these questions, we must realize that human conflicts are more often than not the consequences of diverging interests among people and among nations during the normal course of human interaction and of the lack of an institutional framework to settle such conflicts peacefully. That is the fundamental reason why we need a combination of moral systems and of judicial systems to deal with conflicts of interest and to prevent society from plunging into wars, anarchy, or chaos.

While both systems apply to individuals and to groups, it can be argued that freely accepted moral systems work best for individuals who are naturally inclined to follow spontaneously the reciprocity and empathy principles of human conduct, and judicial systems and institutions are more a necessary requirement for group behavior, in order to regulate intergroup competition. Indeed, empathy is the opposite of violence; it is a deep feeling of brotherhood with equality. In short, empathy is respect for others, their person, their assets, and their rights. However, it is not excluded that some individuals can lose this ability to be empathetic and practice moral judgment when acting within a group or within a coalition of individuals.

Bouts of collective madness have been observed in many otherwise advanced societies, and they are often related to how belonging to certain groups can push individuals in the wrong direction. Not that all groups have the potential to steer people toward immoral or anti-social behavior. Group adhesion can often be an effective means for individuals to promote their legitimate social and economic interests and even serve at times to resist oppression. Belonging to a labor union, a political party, or a social club may fall into this category. However, whether political or religious, groups that require members to leave their capacity for critical judgment at the door are particularly susceptible to exerting a negative influence on people. And groups that breed suspicion and hatred toward others are the most pernicious of all.

A blatant example of group madness under a wicked leadership was the mass suicide of Jonestown, on November 18, 1978. On that fateful day, Reverend James Warren Jones, a deranged preacher of the People's Temple Christian Church in Jonestown, Guyana (South America), led 914 people, including 276 children, to commit a mass suicide by consuming a soft drink laced with cyanide and sedatives. The clergyman had cast such a spell on his congregation, and the members of his church had so completely abdicated their capacity for intellectual and moral judgment, that he could persuade them that the end of the world was imminent and that they should all die together. They were convinced that they would leave this planet for a better world and a life of bliss.[4]

Several famous studies have confirmed that, in certain circumstances and under certain demagogic leaders, otherwise normal individuals acting within a group can turn violent against other people more easily than if they were acting alone and could freely exercise their own moral judgment.[5] The classic 1971 Stanford prison experiment, for example, carried out by psychologist Philip G. Zimbardo and his colleagues, demonstrated vividly how it is easy for otherwise nonpathological individuals to behave violently against others when they hold a position of power within a group.[6] This is because the moral constraints that normally operate upon people when they act as individuals are somewhat dimmed when they act within a group. What these studies show is that every human being has the potential to turn into a moral monster, given the right circumstances and the right situational influences.[7]

For instance, it has been observed throughout history that fanatical and extremist individuals, acting within a fundamentalist religious group, can turn into violent persecutors, especially if such religion-inspired violence can be used to promote a particular political agenda. Indeed, fanatics of all stripes seem more inclined to commit atrocities than are otherwise normal people, when they believe they are acting nobly to promote a faith or to serve a god. Such actions are all the more probable when confronted by a threatening enemy, whom they can easily demonize from their own religious perspective.

It may be that fundamentalist religions—because they impose strict dogmas and require blind obedience from their followers, and because they advance what they consider to be immutable truths that are open to self-serving mutable interpretations—can easily slip from their core mission of doing social good and become conduits for violence and brutality. Most religious people prefer to ignore religions' violent practical legacy and choose instead to focus on their theoretical moral underpinnings. This explains why some thinking people, such as physicist Freeman Dyson from Princeton University, still view religion as having important societal value.[8] In Dyson's words, "My own prejudice, looking at religion from the inside, leads me to conclude that the good vastly outweighs the evil. . . . Without religion, the life of the country would be greatly impoverished."[9] But more astute and skeptic observers, such as Nobel physicist Steven Weinberg, arrive at a different bottom line. As Weinberg aptly put it, in general, good people behave well and bad people behave badly, but it takes religion to make good people do evil.[10]

FUNDAMENTALIST RELIGIONS AND MORAL JUDGEMENT

For centuries, religious fundamentalism and zealous patriotism have often reinforced each other as implacable forces of murder and destruction. Indeed, the two biggest curses of humanity have been proselytizing political religions and chauvinistic wars. Often, religions *per se* are not a direct cause of war; rather, they can provide justifications and tools that warmongers use to wage war. Because they encourage in-group morality and foster xenophobia and exclusion between groups, the ancient religious creeds have been one of the principal causes of divisiveness, dissentions, strife, and wars between peoples. Indeed, proselytizing religions and wars of aggression have often been interrelated, one feeding upon the other.

In this early part of the twenty-first century, religion still plays an important role in many armed conflicts. It seems that today, as in the past, those who say they are protected by God want to wage war on those who say they are protected by Allah, who, in turn, want to wage war on those who say they are protected by Yahweh. It is a fact that too many religious people seem to have a holy book in one hand and a bomb in the other. Contemporary examples where there is ongoing civil unrest and bloodshed between religious faiths are numerous. We only have to consider the Israeli-Palestinian conflict between Jews and Muslims,[11] the Sudanese conflict where fanatical Arab Muslims are killing militant black Christians, the conflicts between Maronites and Shi'ites in Lebanon, the conflict between Sunnis and Shi'ites in Iraq, and the conflict between Muslims and Christians in Kosovo.

It also seems that when religious fundamentalism takes hold in a given country, it is often the forerunner of aggressive political fascism, as was the case in Germany, Austria, and Italy, during the twentieth century. It can also portend imperialism, as in Britain and France in the nineteenth century and in America at the beginning of the twentieth century and during this early part of the twenty-first century.[12] This is because the marriage of fundamentalist religion and politics tends to weaken and corrupt both society in general and its public institutions. As for the link between state-sponsored violence and extremist religion, it is due to the fact that in the minds of religious zealots, war and aggression are not last resorts and self-defense activities but can be seen as the tools of best resort to attain piously cloaked politico-religious goals.

Wars are usually the result of decisions made by a ruler or members of a ruling class who live off those who pay taxes and sustain the economy with their ingeniousness and production. For this parasitical minority and its allies, wars can be very profitable in serving their interests. Wars can even be profitable to the majority if a war leads to the annexation of territories and brings with it the loot of more land, more gold, more oil, and more resources in general. They even have the political advantage of mobilizing the masses against an outside enemy, thus distracting the attention of the people from any domestic morass. That is why I say that wars are for warlike, gambling, leaders who bet their citizens' lives to fulfill their megalomaniac dreams of grandeur.

In general, we can say that the glorification of war and the waging of war are sure signs of a barbarous and decadent society, whether or not it is religious. Wars are cruel and inhuman schemes designed to enrich the few and impoverish the many. Those who supply the war machines profit enormously from wars. The victims of war are those who are killed or maimed, those whose property is destroyed, or those who are left paying taxes to cover war debts. Wars of aggression are the most barbarous of all human endeavors and are more often than not the instruments of insane tyrants who hear voices. Those in power who initiate wars of aggression are war criminals and they should be subjected to the full authority of the Nuremberg Charter and to the United Nations Charter. That is why this eighth humanist principle rejects all wars of aggression.

RELIGIOUS MORALITY, WAR, AND FEAR

A clear indication of the moral bankruptcy of many religions is their condoning the killing of innocent people.[13] Contrary to modern international law, which makes it a crime to carry out indiscriminate attacks against a civilian population, Jewish religious law, for one, still permits the slaughter of non-Jewish civilians in wartime. The Israeli Yesha Rabbinical Council recently reiterated this ancient Judaist religious rule. Here is what they have to say about killing children, women, and the elderly, in times of military conflicts: "According to Jewish law, during a time of battle and war, there is no such term as 'innocents' of the enemy. All of the discussions on Christian morality are weakening the spirit of the army and the nation and are costing us in the blood of our soldiers and civilians."[14]

Islamists are not any more advanced than the Judaists in regard to their immoral and violent views concerning the admissibility of targeting and killing innocent civilians in times of war. For example, the deeply religious terrorist Osama bin Laden issued a *fatwa* after the terrorist acts of September 11, 2001, in order to explain the Islamic rationale behind the killing of thousands of innocent people: "It is allowed for Muslims to kill protected ones among unbelievers in the event of an attack against them in which it is not possible to differentiate the protected ones from the combatants or from the strongholds. It is permissible to kill them incidentally and unintentionally according to the saying of the Prophet."[15]

Such religions—Judaism and Islam—establish vengeance and retribution as *modus operandi*. And, since one side is always one revenge behind, this is a recipe for perpetual conflict and perpetual war. Even among Christians, those who dwell intensely on the Old Testament rather than on the New Testament can be inclined to seek revenge to correct perceived wrongs.

Why can some religious minds become so cruel and dangerous? It is because they see everything in black and white. There is no compromise possible between their moral certitude and the ideas or interests that diverge from theirs. Religious thinking can be used to justify the use of force to destroy evil, as represented by people who do not think like the members of their own sect or religion. Indeed, the opponents are irremediably demonized and dehumanized in order to wage holy wars against them and, if need be, to kill them and their families. History is littered with religious massacres.

The explanation for all these crimes against humanity can be traced back to the propensity of some devious characters to think in absolute moral terms. They use this twisted morality to justify collective punishment against entire populations—a crime that we thought our civilized world had made illegal, but which has a tendency, like a tough weed, to regularly spring back to the surface. When the deep-seated humanist morality present in every human being is suppressed under a veil of religious hypocrisy, anything is possible, including the greatest atrocities against humankind.

When organized religions do not succeed in creating a hell on Earth through religious strife and absolutist wars, they rely on the century-tested fear of hell in an afterlife to terrorize the minds of those who fall under their spell. Most monotheist religions impose their intransigence and maintain their dominance over people though the reliance on a form of religious terror: the fear of spending an eternity in hell. By keeping their followers in a constant state of fright, religions can manipulate individuals more easily and orient them in what their leaders consider to be the right direction.[16]

The doctrine of hell found in the monotheistic religions of Christianity and Islam is presented as an ultimate sanction of eternal punishment and everlasting banishment for those who do not adhere to their ethics. It is extremely troubling and can be seen as unduly threatening, cruel, and unjust. Why would a just god condemn any human being to eternal suffering? Why the need to threaten people with the admonition "Believe or you will burn in hell for eternity!" If religious moral edicts are so beneficial to humanity, why should their observance be based on a doctrine of fear and of unforgiving cruelty? The readiness with which religious zealots have used torture and cruelty toward other people may find its origin and justification in this religious concept of eternal retribution for those who choose to be independent of their doctrines. Why have they launched religious wars and crusades? Why did they torture people during the Inquisition? Why did they burn women as witches? The notion of hell found in many passages of the New Testament encourages contempt, intolerance, and hate toward those who follow other religions. It has inspired countless crimes, religious persecutions, and wars. Because of this, it is an ideology of fear and cruelty, and as such, is profoundly regressive.[17]

INTERGROUP AND INTERNATIONAL VIOLENCE

Religiosity is often a form of aggressive nationalism in religious disguise. It sometimes encourages entire countries or nationalities to claim to have abstract deities on their side and, consequently, to be above all the others. Therein lies the source of countless wars and conflicts. It has left a long and terrible trail of bloodshed and suffering throughout history.

Much man-made suffering can be directly attributed to religion. The most savage and cruel perpetrators of sadistic and brutal violence against other human beings have often been those who foolishly believed that they were acting under divine authority. Such people could then claim moral legitimacy for their acts of violence and exonerate themselves from any personal responsibility. They justified their cruelty by the convenient myth of divine mandate and hid their wickedness under a shroud of false righteousness. It doesn't matter if the killers and murderers are ordinary individuals or heads of state: they are madmen and criminals, even when they absolve themselves of any moral blame. It is a great human tragedy that when people become captivated by a messianic ideology, whatever it is, they also acquire the capacity to become murderers.

As the great French Enlightenment philosopher Voltaire wrote, "Those who can make you believe absurdities can make you commit atrocities." The celebrated American essayist Mark Twain created an immortal parody about people who pray to deities before committing atrocities, when he wrote his War Prayer: "O Lord our God, help us to tear their soldiers to bloody shreds with our shells; help us to cover their smiling fields with the pale forms of their patriot dead; help us to drown the thunder of the guns with the shrieks of their wounded."[18]

Why are the most religious people often violent, even though, paradoxically, most religions condemn violence? The answer comes from their deep mistrust of human beings. For extremist religious people, human lives do not matter because the human condition itself is inherently evil, and people are condemned to suffer eternal and everlasting punishment in hell...unless they can somehow be redeemed though the intermediary of a religious hierarchy. For

Christians, for example, human beings are assumed to be born saddled with an original sin that predisposes them to evil and sin. With such a frame of mind, it is not surprising that some may think that human lives in general do not count for much.

There are, indeed, few human endeavors where religious hypocrisy is more rampant than on the question of organized violence and wars. It is a sorry indictment of organized religions that most of them have, at best, an ambiguous record regarding human conflicts. In principle, religions should be against murder and killing. In practice, more often than not, they have tended to condone and even exacerbate wars, rather than mitigating them. As Irish author Jonathan Swift wrote, "We have enough religion to make us hate, but not enough to make us love one another."

Throughout history, priests and other religious sycophants have accompanied armies of conquest. The purpose and usefulness of these sorcerers was to soothe consciences and justify mass killings. The Islamic empire in the Arabic peninsula, the Spanish empire in South America, the French empire in Africa, the British Empire around the world, and even today the American empire in the Middle East, all are examples of human brutality condoned and even encouraged by religious people and religious organizations.

Christianity and Islam, two of the three religions rooted in the Abrahamic tradition, are perhaps the most ambivalent toward state violence and wars. They have demonstrated time and again that killing and murdering infidels or simple enemies can be acceptable if such cruelties advance their conquests. This is understandable, since religious views of the world tend naturally toward absolutist issues and divisions rather than toward encouraging political negotiation and compromise. They accept in practice the saying that the end justifies the means, if it is for the greatest glory of their deity as well as their more earthly ambitions. In that spirit, many basic religious texts are filled with violence and hatred toward the others, fostering aggressive attitudes based on the childish belief that "my god is stronger than yours."[19]

In the Bible, for instance, the word "enemy" appears frequently, as does the word "war." The Hebrew Bible contains numerous incantations to war and to killing other human beings.[20] Suffice it to decree that an enemy is evil, or the devil, and religion condones his or her murder. That was a good propaganda ploy in an age when tribal wars were endemic.[21] One should also remember that the Bible is a composite book, written and edited by many authors, at different times. It is full of contradictions and inconsistencies, and often several versions of the same event.[22]

These old religious books are a reflection of the social and political context prevailing at the time they were written. Nevertheless, when religious people take literally and at face value every exhortation they find in these holy books—commandments that must be accepted without criticism, without doubts or questions—they can easily transfer into their own times conflicts and wars that belong to another age. Supposed holy books, and the Bible in particular, put forward very unethical standards of conduct. That is why such ambivalent religious morality regarding human violence and human cruelty toward other human beings must be replaced by the more universal humanist principle of not doing harm to others, period.

CRIMINALS IN POWER AND MILITARY MURDERS

A fully scientific explanation of the pathological origins of evil in human societies would require that we explain how it is that criminal and mentally ill persons sometimes succeed in reaching the pinnacle of authority. To the distress of the citizenry, indeed, it can happen that deranged or psychopathic personalities reach positions of power. Psychopaths have no ethics, no morality, and can lie with great facility. This could give them an advantage in the political arena when others follow customary rules of decency. The fields of psychiatry and psychology can help us understand why certain persons in authority can have no conscience whatsoever and be incapable of guilt, even when they commit the worst crimes. They live in a valueless world, even though they are sometimes hypocritically religious or seem to be inebriated with patriotic zeal. Such people often feel contempt for the suffering of others and have no qualms imposing such suffering themselves.

Polish psychologist Andrew M. Lobaczewski, who practiced under Communist rule, analyzed in great detail the phenomenon of evil and violence by pathological individuals.[23] His research was carried out in several Eastern European countries. In his clinical work, Lobaczewski noticed a high correlation between acts of violence and other acts we would label as bad, and pathologies of various types in the perpetrators that could be identified in a clinical setting. An overwhelming majority of these acts were carried out by people with pathological tendencies. Lobaczewski explains in great detail how people suffering with different forms of pathology work together in the political arena to subvert social movements, in order to impose what he calls a *pathocracy*. The dynamics of this pathocracy are the same, regardless of the ideology that served as the original banner of the movement, which is why we see the same dynamics at play under communist rule, fascist rule, and, in some instances, democratic rule.

It is a frightening thing that pathology among people in power can have disastrous effects on their country and on the rest of the world. (Hitler, Stalin, and Mao come to mind.) What science reveals, moreover, is the dangerous negative selection that can take place within a government when psychopaths are in charge: these defective personalities tend to surround themselves with like-minded persons who share their own pathologically determined worldview. When that happens, the damage done is cumulative.[24] A related application of such a fruitful analysis would be to identify to what extent psychopaths and sadists join volunteer armies, as compared to their minute representation in the overall population.

What about religious hallucinations that some perturbed minds seem to experience from time to time? The Oxford Advanced Dictionary defines hallucination as "the fact of seeming to see or hear things that are not really there." When people claim to have extrabody experiences or to have seen the heavens, they confuse malfunctions in their brains with reality. When they hear voices in their heads and think they are receiving messages from heaven, their behavior is consistent with a seriously deranged personality and a pathological condition. They could possibly become very dangerous. For such a mind, indeed, killing other human beings might become a sort of irrational duty.

Things become much worse if a madman who hears voices and suffers from delusional hallucinations is in a position of authority. Who could prevent him from thinking that he is like a god, or that he is acting according to his god's call and god's glory?

The rationales for killing, murdering, torturing, and sexually abusing other human beings vary from one individual to another, but none is more pervasive than using military orders to excuse evil actions. Indeed, what can be disconcerting is how easy it is for ordinary people to commit atrocities when it is possible for them to pass the blame for such acts onto orders received or to some outside authority. American author Hannah Arendt used the phrase "the banality of evil" to describe this phenomenon, documenting how easy it is for supposedly "normal" people to become barbarous killers when they dress in a uniform and abandon their moral autonomy.[25]

PUBLIC MORALITY AND THE JUST WAR TRADITION[26]

People with a religious bent sometimes refer to the ancient and medieval concept of Just War or righteous war when they want to justify an offensive and aggressive war. Crafted at a time when the technology of violence was much less advanced than today, the concept of Just War pertains to justifying war along Christian moral principles.[27] In reality, the Christian Just War concept is an improvement upon the Hebrew Bible's approach to Holy War[28] and is the equivalent of the Muslim concept of jihad.[29]

Since war's central objective is to inflict suffering and death on other people, and since religions purposefully forbid doing to others what one does not want to be done to oneself [or as in St. Paul's writings, one must not render evil for evil but overcome it with good (Romans 12:17, 21)], it is not easy to justify war and military murder in the name of religion. Nevertheless, especially after the church became identified with the Roman Empire, some religious scholars attempted to devise pragmatic arguments to justify wars under certain conditions, from then on considering religion as a stalwart supporter of public authority.[30]

Although the Just War tradition can be traced back to Aristotle and Cicero, Aurelius Augustinus—better known as St. Augustine of Hippo—was the originator of the Christian Just War Theory. He contended that there was a difference between individual morality and public morality. For the individual, even in cases of self-defense of one's life or property, there was never a justification for killing one's neighbor. For a government, however, the Christian morality was more elastic when it meant killing other human beings. State killing became acceptable to Christian doctrine, even though individual morality continued to forbid such inhuman acts.

But by splitting morality in two, St. Augustine opened a Pandora's box: from a religion of the weak and dispossessed, Christianity became a religion of state power, and it has remained so for centuries. Augustine rendered a tragic service to Christianity, and even more so to humanity as a whole, when he proposed to exempt politics from the constraints of Christian ethics. Countless wars and killings could have been avoided if the Christian faith had stuck to its fundamental ethics.

Nevertheless, in Augustine's thinking, if Christianity were to become an integral part of the Roman Empire and gain influence, it had to cease being a pacifist religion opposed to all wars and killings. Augustine, following the ideas of Paul of Tarsus, believed that the rulers of nations have an obligation to maintain peace, and to do so, they may rely on different means, including war and killing, under certain circumstances. It must be said, however, that for Augustine, there were very few instances when one nation is justified in militarily attacking another. A government, and therefore its citizens, can wage war only when it is absolutely necessary to defend the nation's peace against serious injury.

In general, the Just War Theory for waging offensive wars of aggression characterizes a war between two sovereign nations as being "just" if it meets three main classical criteria:

- The war must be waged with the *right intention* and for good reasons; that is to say, it cannot be undertaken for revenge or for economic gain and to acquire territories or riches, but to restore peace, and not be carried out for the sake of pursuing a victory won by violence.

- The war must be authorized and declared by a *legitimate authority*, that is, an emperor or a king. Today, when considerations of international peace and good order are paramount, only an international authority, either an international organization or an international court of justice can authorize war.
- The war must be undertaken for a *just cause*. It must satisfy the principle of proportionality between the force used and the injury suffered, as well as of discrimination between aims and means in order to defend the nation's peace. A nation must not use excessive force to protect itself against serious injury. Military force may be used only to correct a grave threat, where the basic rights of a whole population are at stake.

During the Middle Ages, scholastic philosophers such as Thomas Aquinas, Francisco Suarez, and Francisco de Vitoria, further developed the Just War Theory, not on the basis of the teachings of Jesus, but based on natural law. For them, a war of self-defense needed "no special moral justification." However, an offensive war of aggression should be viewed only as essentially a defensive measure and must be justified by two additional principles, besides the three main criteria already outlined:

- The war must be fought as a *last resort*, after all avenues of peaceful negotiations have been exhausted.
- The war must be carried out in a *proper manner*, without killing innocent people indiscriminately.

Nowadays, with the awesome destructive power of modern weapons, especially nuclear weapons, such principles of Just War can be judged as irrelevant, and they cannot be invoked to launch aggressive wars. It is obvious that the use of nuclear weapons, tactical or otherwise, is morally prohibited under any circumstances because they are designed to kill innocent people indiscriminately. The same applies to neutron bombs.[31] Even the so-called smart bombs that certain US military people boast about are morally indefensible and unjust. According to the Pentagon itself, such smart bombs miss their targets more often than they hit them.[32]

Such is also the case with cluster bombs.[33] At least 5 percent of them explode days or weeks after impact, and are often picked up by civilians, especially unsuspecting children. The same can be said about land mines that kill more noncombatants than combatants. The moral conclusion is clear. Sophisticated modern weapons have rendered warfare obsolete because it is no longer waged between armies, but against civilian populations.[34] Political thinkers who say aggressive wars are justified in theory and in practice are misguided. There cannot be a Just War under modern conditions. In the aftermath of World War II, Pope Pius XII declared, "the enormous violence of modern warfare means that it can no longer be regarded as a reasonable, proportionate means for settling conflicts."

Pope John XXIII (1881–1963), in his encyclical *Pacem in Terris* (1963), also condemned wars of aggression when he stated, "Therefore in this age of ours, which prides itself on its atomic power, it is irrational to think that war is a proper way to obtain justice for violated rights." For this humanist pope, war is not a legitimate instrument of justice, and it must be rejected as a viable modern political option. Some form of legitimate global government should replace it, sooner or later.

Regarding the 2003 war against Iraq,[35] Pope John Paul II took it upon himself to send a special emissary, Cardinal Pio Laghi, to meet with then President George W. Bush and to tell him that his planned aggressive and unprovoked war against Iraq did not meet the criteria of a just war. It would therefore be immoral.[36] In a letter pleading against war, Pope John Paul II asked Bush "to spare humanity another dramatic conflict."[37] However, Ari Fleischer, then White House Press Secretary, said that his boss wouldn't be influenced by the Pope. National Security Advisor Condoleezza Rice went even further and declared that she could not understand how anyone could consider a war against Iraq immoral.[38]

One can safely say, therefore, that the Just War Theory has been completely eliminated from religious or, for that matter, from humanist and secular morality. This tool of moral analysis is outdated and out of step with the advent of nuclear weapons. What is left is the moral concept of self-defense and defensive wars, but then, only when there is proportionality between the needs to secure a country's peace and the means for doing so.

Regarding the general notion of wars of aggression, nations, peoples, and governments should always do their utmost to avoid three deadly political and social diseases that lead to such wars: *militarism* above and beyond self-defense requirements, *attitudes and policies that are based on revenge and aggressiveness* found in Old Testament Christianity or Judaism, and *hegemony and the will to power* that led to imperialism and colonialism. Countries or nations that caught such political diseases in the past paid a high price in terms of sufferings, miseries, and national guilt.

Nothing exemplifies better the profound immorality of contemporary warfare than the increased reliance on high technology to kill people. And one country, the United States, is at the forefront of such a development. It seems that when individuals drop bombs on people from a fighter jet at an altitude of 35,000 feet, they experience less guilt than when they have to shoot other human beings at close range. But now, one can be 8,000 miles away, sitting in front of a computer, joysticks in both hands, and as in some sort of gruesome video game, use remote-controlled, unmanned drones to drop laser-guided, highly explosive bombs on buildings and people.

That is what the new technology of military killing allows: killing at a distance. The new development is the so-called MQ-9 Reaper (named after Death's grim skeleton and its scythe), which is an efficient remote-controlled killing machine. At a military base forty miles outside of Las Vegas, Nevada, computer-savvy soldiers sit in the "cockpit" of these heavily armed robot aircraft loaded with guided Hellfire missiles and bombs, facing a 17-inch monitor screen, and kill people on the ground, thousands of miles away in the Middle East, just as easily as if they were physically there. The commands to kill are sent through secure satellite links. Then, after a day's work of killing people that they have never met, they can stop to get a hamburger at the local joint, or go back to their family, attend church, or go talk to a chaplain afterward, for relaxation or guilt removal.

Wars and political dominance will thus become easier to carry out and implement, and this could all be done anonymously and at a safe distance. This is the grim and immoral picture of the future, the killing of faceless people far away.[39]

RELIGIOUS TERRORISM

Religious zeal, mixed with politics and ambitions, has produced a lot of violence throughout history and even today. For instance, when people blow themselves up in public places with the express purpose of killing and terrorizing other innocent people, they usually do it on the pretext that they act on orders from God or Allah or some other divinity. They most often use religious scriptures to justify or explain their violent acts, an indication that they are not guided by their own conscience but by some outside force. This is called religious terrorism or "Holy Terror."[40]

Indeed, it is a sign of our times that the religious imperative for terrorism is on the rise and is behind much murderous terrorist activity. It is a reflection of the increased merging of religion and politics, where religious indoctrination is mixed with political activism. From the nationalistic religion-based Jewish yeshivot (Orthodox Talmudic seminaries) to the well-financed Wahhabi madrassas (extremist Koranic schools), young pupils, usually boys, are taught a mind-set of intolerance and hatred of others, all dressed up in religious mythology. Such schools are privileged sites for indoctrination and recruitment of politico-religious terrorists. They are not only found in countries that are ruled by religious totalitarianism, such as Shiite Iran or Sunni and Wahhabi Saudi Arabia, but are present in most large European and North American cities. They represent a major threat to civilization in this nuclear age.

The fundamental question of the religious foundation of certain forms of violence and terrorism is the most pressing issue of the twenty-first century. The world cannot tolerate for very long being subject to blackmail and having its prosperity and freedom threatened by such degenerate religious behavior. It is no surprise that terrorist leaders use the mask of religion to demonize their enemies and to cloak their cruelties and atrocities in pious justification. The cover of religion to justify terrorism and the killing of innocent people also has the advantage of making it easier to recruit martyrs and fanatics, if not utterly deranged people, who would not be as easily mobilized for a purely political cause. That may be one reason why today's religious-based terrorism is more deadly than the nationalist-based terrorism of forty or fifty years ago.

ISLAM AND VIOLENCE

Islam was born in war and grew the same way. From the time of Muhammad, the sword and military conquest were the main tools that fueled Muslim expansion. Islam, at least at the beginning, was far from a "religion of peace." It was fundamentally a militarist movement that initiated offensive wars against peaceful nations and territories in order to impose its faith by force, to seize riches, and to expand its dominion.

Muhammad began the first violent movement in Medina, after the declaration of a jihad against what he called "infidels." The Jews who refused to convert to Islam were driven from the land or murdered. Approximately fifteen years later, Muhammad marched on Mecca with an army of twenty thousand men, and after that, against the Assyrians, the Armenians, and the Copts in Egypt. Those who converted to Islam were spared. Those who refused to convert were beheaded.

After 622, Islam inspired a century of Arab conquest. Islamic armies swept from Syria to Spain. King Charles Martel of France, grandfather of Charlemagne, finally stopped them outside Paris, at the battle of Tours, in 732. This series of violent wars was in direct response to Muhammad's call: "They will not invade you, but you are those who will invade them."[41] Economic advantages were at the center of these wars of dispossession, since stealing is openly condoned in the Qur'an: "Allah promises you much booty that you will capture" (48:20).

In theory, Islam teaches not to use revenge and not to rely on the ancient Babylonian (Hammurabi Code) and Jewish precept of "a tooth for a tooth and an eye for an eye." Instead, it says: "Do not say, that if the people do good to us, we will do good to them; and if the people oppress us, we will oppress them; but determine that if people do you good, you will do good to them; and if they oppress you, you will not oppress them" (Islamic hadith). As far as theory prevails, it could even be said that Islam professes the individual right of freedom of religion and religious tolerance. One of the verses in the Qur'an says, "There is no compulsion in religion" (2:256).

However, we soon learn that the above verse does not apply to a Muslim but only to people of other faiths and convictions. And even for the latter, Islam can be less than tolerant and generous. For example, the Qur'an commands that non-Muslims, in a Muslim Sharia regime, "feel themselves subdued" in a state of *dhimmitude*, that is to say, in a political state of subservience (Surah 9:29). In practice, moreover, as though it were a vast hermetic and possessive sect, Islam does not permit a Muslim to revert or change religion. Indeed, in countries where Islam is the official religion, and where there exist official Sharia courts, one cannot choose to stop being a Muslim. The right of freedom from religion is thus denied. There is no such thing as freedom of conscience. It goes even further, reserving the draconian punishment of death to any Muslim who changes faith and joins another religion.

Muslims must abide by the basic tenet of Islam of *Believe or die* and may never apostatize.[42] There is only one religion in the world that imposes the death penalty on those who leave the religion, and that is Islam. In some fanatic countries, the death penalty is even imposed on those who do not join Islam. In 1983, for example, ten young female teachers of the Baha'i faith were executed by the Islamic Republic of Iran for refusing to convert. Islam is a most monopolizing political religion. As such, it is in essence inimical to the fundamental human right of freedom of conscience and of religion. Indeed, since officially Muslim countries in practice deny the fundamental right of conscience, making the act of leaving the Muslim faith a crime, they cannot presume to belong to the world of democratic countries. They remain basically totalitarian regimes.

There are few religions that are as intrusive as Islam. It is a religion that regulates a follower's everyday life through a whole set of absolute commandments, precepts, rituals, and hadiths (traditions), leaving very little to the discretion of the individual. Indeed, for the devout Muslim, every aspect of life becomes religious: personal life, family, social relationships, work, politics, and so on. There is a despotic, normative religious control of Muslims, who must submit to what the theological leaders establish to be their god's, Allah's, commandments. Very little is left for an individual's free will and self-improvement. All depends on an omnipotent, supernatural god—the past, the present, and the future are severely limited, leaving very little to an individual's own initiative. Worse, to attempt to discover things and learn about the surrounding Universe can be considered an insult to the divinities and a sort of sacrilege, since all the science that is needed is supposed to have been ascribed forever by Allah in holy scriptures.[43]

Certain Muslim countries under archaic despotic authorities have retained the equivalent of a religious Inquisition, prevalent in Catholic Europe from the twelfth to as late as the beginning of the nineteenth century. According to the nefarious practice of *takfir*, Muslim extremists can accuse fellow Muslims of religious heresy, in order to condemn their enemies and justify wanton violence against them.[44] Similarly, the Qur'an and its surahs (chapters) contain some very intolerant passages, such as: "O Prophet! Struggle against the unbelievers and hypocrites and be harsh with them" (Qur'an 9:73). About the disbelievers: "[K]ill them wherever you find them, and take not from among them a friend or a helper" (Qur'an 4:89). About Jews and Christians: "Fight against such of those to whom the Scriptures were given, as they believe neither in Allah nor the Last Day, who do not forbid what Allah and His Apostle have forbidden and do not embrace the true Faith, until they pay tribute out of hand and are utterly subdued" (Surah 9:29).

All interpretations of the Qur'an and *sunnah* (tradition) seem to be fluid and subjective. You can find in it theoretical religious tolerance as well as a license to kill.[45] There are no certainties here, only a moral hodgepodge. Thus, whether one is oriented toward peace or war, there are verses in the Qur'an to suit one's immediate needs for justification.[46] The Egyptian scholar Sayied Qutb, for instance, argues in his 1950 book of Qur'anic interpretation, entitled *Fe-zelal-al-Qur'an*, that a state of permanent war is normal between Muslims and non-Muslims, ignoring that the Qur'an dictates that its teachings be understood in full, not in bits and pieces (Surah 20:114). Others disagree with such narrow interpretations and distortions, and they deny such outlandish claims. But since Islam has no single supreme authority for interpreting its ancient holy book and hadiths, a certain state of religious and moral anarchy prevails, opening the door to any validation that one desires.

Even though there are passages in the Qur'an that forbid aggression, there are other passages in which an aggressive Islamic fundamentalist can find solace for his violence toward others, especially if they are not of his faith. On the one hand, Muslims are forbidden to be aggressors: "Fight for the sake of God against those who fight against you, but do not attack first; Allah does not love aggressors" (Surah 2:190). The Qur'an also prohibits war and hostility against any one who does not oppress people: "Let there be no hostility except to those who practice oppression" (Surah 2:193).

On the other hand, curiously, Allah seems to order Muslims to terrorize non-Muslims on his behalf: "Strike terror into the hearts of the enemies of Allah and your enemies" (Surah 8:60); or again, "Fight [kill] them [non-Muslims], and Allah will punish [torment] them by your hands, cover them with shame" (Surah 9:14); and, if this is not clear enough, one can get inspiration from the following verset: "I will instill terror into the hearts of the unbelievers, smite ye above their necks and smite all their finger-tips off them. It is not ye who slew them, it was Allah" (Surah 8:12, 17).

Islamist zealots could wage war against the so-called infidels and other non-Muslims, merely because such people do not accept the Muslim religion. Islam has often been a religion of conquest and intolerance.[47]

ISLAM AND SCIENTIFIC PROGRESS

Arab civilization was more advanced and more peaceful before Islam was widely accepted than after its imposition through violence, in the early

part of the seventh century. Arabs had participated fully in the rich
Greek, Assyrian, Persian, Chaldean, and Babylonian civilizations. We
owe them mathematical breakthroughs, such as the concept of zero
found in the Greek and Hindu decimal systems, and the Pythagorean
theorem in Babylonian mathematics. For centuries, Baghdad was the
intellectual and scientific center of the world, while Europe was still
mired in religious superstition.[48] It is a tribute to Arab advances in
astronomy, for example, that two-thirds of the stars have Arabic names,
even though the names of constellations derive from Greek and Latin.
The words algebra and algorithm are Arabic.

This all changed when Muslim zealots gained absolute political
power and began to profess that revelation, not science, was responsible for human progress. Around 1100, a dark age descended upon
the Arab world, for which their populations are still paying a high
price. Religious high priests attacked mathematics as being the work
of the devil, and proclaimed that with divine revelation there was no
more need for scientific investigation. Scientists were ostracized and
the entire intellectual foundation of their societies collapsed.

We have a clue about this lack of Islamic respect for science in
the following legend: It is reported that one of Muhammad's succes-
sors, the caliph Omar of Damascus, distinguished himself by having
centuries-old literary treasures destroyed by setting afire the large
Egyptian library of Alexandria, a wonder of the ancient world.
According to the legend, Caliph Omar is reported to have justified
his order to destroy the books in the library of Alexandria by saying
that they will either contradict the Qur'an, in which case they are
heresy, or they will agree with it, so are superfluous.[49]

Since many religions have theologies that stress divine revelation
over human reason, it is not surprising that religious extremists can be
opposed to intellectual progress, especially if such progress is perceived as a threat to their political power. Not surprisingly also, such
a bias against the human intellect and against scientific achievements
is bound to have a detrimental influence on the economic, social, and
political development of countries that embrace such an attitude.[50]
Censorship and the absence of intellectual freedom are the biggest
enemies of human progress.

During the ninth and tenth centuries, Islamic civilization redeemed itself somewhat by having many ancient scientific and philosophical tracts translated from Greek to Arabic. It is these translations that were imported into Europe and that played such a central role in bringing about the European Renaissance, from which Western civilization still draws most of its inspiration.

THE REJECTION OF WARMONGERING VIOLENCE AND THE INTRODUCTION OF THE RULE OF LAW

Violence is incompatible with humanism and is contrary to reason and the requirements of human survival. Neither religion nor any other ideology can be used as a pretext for bellicose behavior toward other human beings. Following this eighth humanistic principle, wars of aggression and organized violence should be outlawed once for all.

As British General John Frederick Maurice said, "if you want peace you must prepare for war—I now believe that if you prepare thoroughly for war you will get it." Indeed, history shows that countries that heavily arm themselves and prepare for war do get it. In the twentieth century, for example, Germany twice prepared for war, and got it. Imperial Japan also prepared for war, and got it. The reason is simple. Once a country is more heavily armed than what is necessary for its self-defense, some politicians are bound to get into power with the intention of using the extra military strength for self-aggrandizement, by undertaking imperialistic or colonialist adventures. This has happened again and again.

That is why the American founding fathers, in their wisdom, were deeply suspicious of large, permanent standing armies. In President George Washington's words, "Overgrown military establishments are under any form of government inauspicious to liberty, and are to be regarded as particularly hostile to republican liberty." One can also meditate upon another wise pronouncement by the first US president: "The Constitution vests the power of declaring war in Congress; therefore, no offensive expedition of importance can be undertaken until after they shall have deliberated upon the subject and authorized such a measure."

Armaments in the absence of morality or moral law are even more to be feared because they give rise to anarchy and disasters. Humanist morality and international law, not war, should be the main objective of humankind. Rejection of violence and force as an acceptable method to deal with human conflicts is the paramount sign of civilization. For it is violence and the law of the jungle that assimilate humans to beasts of prey; and it is reason, humanistic thinking, and the rule of law that set humans apart as a civilized species.

There is a rich literature on nonviolence and civil disobedience, and on the moral obligation to refuse to cooperate with evil forces. A classic promoter of nonviolence was the ancient Chinese Taoist philosopher Lao Tzu, for whom "Violence, even well intentioned, always falls upon oneself." American essayist Henry David Thoreau was also an eloquent and passionate advocate for peaceful civil disobedience. But the most effective model of passive resistance toward aggression was the Indian leader Mahatma Gandhi. Gandhi said, "I object to violence because when it appears to do good, the good is only temporary; the evil it does is permanent."

As humanists, we reject unprovoked violence on the part of individuals. We also denounce, as a moral imperative, wars of aggression or preventive wars. Even violence within the legal framework, such as personal and collective self-defense of one's life or property, must be strictly circumscribed and kept at an absolute minimum. Just as an individual is never justified to kill, even in situations of self-defense, when it can be avoided, no state or government can assume the right to kill or execute human beings. There is not one humanist morality for a person acting as an individual and a different one for a person acting within a government or a state. There are not two humanist moralities.

State-sponsored killing abroad or state-imposed capital punishment at home are both inimical to general humanist principles. Both war and capital punishment are inhuman and barbarous acts. In this sense, state-sponsored war killing and state-imposed capital punishment are in the same class of reprehensible acts. Capital punishment is a barbaric practice enshrined in vengeance and mass violence. Just as within most countries tribal warfare and cannibalism have been abolished, in civilized countries capital punishment will one day disappear. The fact that the United States is the only democratic country that has retained state-imposed capital punishment says much about its historical culture of violence.

In the twenty-first century, even more than in the disastrous twentieth century, thinking that war is a legitimate and efficient way to solve human conflicts is the height of folly and moral depravity. Nuclear armaments have made total war a crime against humanity and civilization. In particular, the large-scale massacre of helpless civilians, as witnessed during the twentieth century, has heralded in a new immoral age of barbarism and modern horror.[51] Even limited warfare is absurd and uncivilized because it inevitably involves civilians and widespread destruction. As sociologist Herbert Spencer once observed, the advance of mankind from barbarism to civilization occurred when the world shifted from a military to an industrial society. The fact that some countries today value their military superiority above all others is a sure sign of cultural regression. By reverting to the barbaric military way, these countries repudiate modern humanism and reject the principles of peace and freedom that are the foundation of a modern and complex industrial society. The fact that in these countries there is a concomitant resurgence of religion may provide a partial explanation.

FREE WILL AND HUMAN MORALITY

The ancient Greeks believed that the Universe was eternal and that neither man nor gods created it. They personified the laws of nature in cosmic deities, such as Zeus and Hera, but these imaginary gods were mostly symbolic and could not intervene in human affairs. Greek ethics was a product of rationalism and was based on philosophical and scientific knowledge.

As a third sacrifice for novices, Ignacius Loyola, founder of the Christian order of the Jesuits, required the sacrifice of the intellect in order to facilitate the jump to blind faith.[52] He knew that a person deprived of the capacity to think independently was rendered vulnerable to any indoctrination imaginable. This is the old technique of brainwashing that different totalitarian regimes have used over time to subjugate and dominate people.

To require that a person renounce human reason is to ask that person to cease being completely human, to abdicate the attributes of humanity, and to become an automate, a robot, a quasi beast. It is reason that distinguishes man from other animals. In our emotions and instincts, we are much closer to other mammals. The capacity to reason and our ability to question our senses make it possible for humans to exercise free will, to make conscious choices, and to develop a conscience. People's will power is not unlimited, however, because humans have both a conscious and an unconscious brain. Therefore, people's decisions are not always conscious, rational, and deliberate, but may also result from emotional impulses and intuitive subconscious decisions. Intuitions and emotions can assist reason in understanding a perceived complex reality. It's only when intuitions and emotions push reason completely aside that they may result in delusions, denials of reality, and even delirium and psychotic behaviors.

Therefore, because of their capacity to reason, humans have the power to imagine the consequences of their actions and have the intellectual power to control their impulses and their emotions. That is what makes humans responsible moral agents as compared to other species of animals, which are solely driven by instincts and deterministic behavior.[53]

We can say that when reason is completely sacrificed in favor of blind faith, emotion, or any other thought-control system, then everything becomes possible. This is because then one ceases to be personally responsible. There can be no liberty where there is no responsibility. Indeed, when a person's power of thinking is abandoned in favor of an external revelation, that person's mind becomes anesthetized and free will essentially disappears. Accountability yields to a state of moral irresponsibility. If the imposed moral system were theoretically perfect, good human actions would automatically follow. However, since religion-based moral systems are far from perfect, often ethnocentric and selective—blind obedience to such flawed moral dicta is likely to lead to profoundly immoral behavior and to human catastrophes.

This is possibly why throughout history, piously religious people within spiritual or political churches have been so scandalously cruel to others. It is because their actions have no personal moral consequences in certain circumstances. For example, on July 22, 1209, Dominican Arnold Amaury, Abbot of Citeaux and papal legate, a man of the cloth (and of the Book!), issued one of the most terrible orders ever proclaimed: "Kill them all; God will know his own!" Twenty thousand men, women, and children were massacred in the Southern French town of Béziers, during the Albigensian Crusade. Pope Innocent III had made a deal with the king of France and had launched a crusade against a Christian sect whose crime was not sharing his dogmas and doctrines, and, like other dictators and tyrants before and after him, his reaction was to kill them.[54]

Perhaps all religions should publicly declare which values in their old holy books are to be kept and which ones are to be rejected and placed in the historical trash bin of dangerous and antisocial ideas. Then they could avoid being accused of serving as the foundation for the hatred between nations and for the unfathomable evil of bloodshed among humans. As long as such repudiation of the most violent passages in these so-called holy books is not proclaimed and adhered to, a state of confusion will continue to prevail, and sick minds will continue to seek the moral justifications for their violent acts in these books. But then these religions will have to abandon the extreme claim that such books were written or inspired by a deity and are totally infallible.

NINE

DEMOCRACY

NINTH HUMANIST PRINCIPLE:
ORGANIZE PUBLIC AFFAIRS ACCORDING TO
INDIVIDUAL FREEDOM AND RESPONSIBILITY,
THROUGH POLITICAL AND ECONOMIC DEMOCRACY.

Democracy is impossible without some kind of secularist foundation.
—Thomas Sutcliffe, British commentator

I feel like God wants me to run for President. I can't explain it, but I sense my country is going to need me. Something is going to happen . . . I know it won't be easy on me or my family, but God wants me to do it.
—George W. Bush (*The Faith of George W. Bush*)

Only God who appointed me will remove me, not the MDC [Movement for Democratic Change, an opposition party], not the British.
—Robert Mugabe, Zimbabwean dictator, 2008

W hen people accept to live in society—and they have little choice to do otherwise—they are bound to reap various social benefits (personal and economic security, education, health services, etc.), but they also have social responsibilities. It is immoral to profit from society and its institutions and from the economic system and its markets (economic opportunities and rewards, respect of contracts, stability, etc.), and to act in a way that is contrary to the common good. Antisocial behavior that undermines social and eco-

163

nomic stability and efficiency is tantamount to freeloading on the rest of society and is contrary to humanist morality. However, not all political and economic systems guarantee the maximum net benefits to people in terms of individual freedom and economic opportunities. Experience has demonstrated that some systems are more conducive to individual happiness than others. Those systems that place the individual at the center of their functioning are the best. Those systems that oppress and exploit the individual are the worst.[1]

In the humanistic order of things, one of the worst political systems is undoubtedly totalitarian theocracy, which denies people control over their own affairs and even their own thinking. It is followed by totalitarian military dictatorship, which usually shows little respect for human life and individual freedom. The different forms of monarchy and aristocracy can be less objectionable, especially if they allow for some decentralization of power, although they are all based on authoritarianism and are far from the principle of government with the consent of the governed.

Democracy, in its various forms, especially representative democracy, remains the best and the most legitimate political system ever invented. However, in the words of the English historian James Anthony Froude, "A centralized democracy may be as tyrannical as an absolute monarch; and if the vigor of the nation is to continue unimpaired, each individual, each family, each district, must preserve as far as possible its independence, its self-completeness, its powers and its privilege to manage its own affairs and think its own thoughts."

Indeed, when the people lose their capacity to think and degenerate into an uncritical populace, they themselves can become nondemocratic and tyrannical, if they are not reigned in by a strong democratic constitution.[2] *One-person-one-vote* is the fundamental characteristic of representative democracy. However, the constitutional rights and the civil liberties of the individual must restrain majority rule, if mob rule and despotism of the number are to be avoided. In practice, this means that those who govern are at the service of the sovereign people, but individual rights and civil liberties must be pro-
~ted by a constitution and by independent courts of justice. This is
ram that is represented beautifully by the motto of the
ilution of 1789: *Liberty-Equality-Fraternity*.

A democracy without a strong, freedom-oriented constitution to preserve the rights of individuals and minorities carries with it the danger of oppression for some individuals or groups.[3] In a democratic republic, power is exercised under the constitution and is decentralized among various levels of government, all operating within a system of checks and balances in order to avoid the tyranny of the majority. Legislation should aim at creating a climate of equality of opportunity and of social justice without trampling upon the rights of the individual.[4]

Of course, without a functioning democracy, even the majority can suffer at the hands of the rulers. The general principle here, at least in theory, is that government should always be the servant of the people—never the contrary. Historically, dictators, kings, tyrants, and despots of all stripes have used the power of government over the governed to promote their own, selfish, personal interests and those of their entourage. They have waged wars from the warmth of their palaces and sent young people to die. They have enriched themselves and their cronies by plundering the public treasury and by allocating juicy defense contracts to themselves and to their friends. In other words, they have profited from the death and despair of others. This is the sour fruit of arbitrary power and tyranny. Only true democracy can prevent the exploitation through government of the majority by a minority.[5]

This was the fundamental principle proclaimed in 1776, when the United States broke away from the British Empire. Its founders swore to establish a democratic republic that would be the very opposite of an empire or an autocratic regime. They had a vision of "life, liberty and the pursuit of happiness" for all people, and they abhorred aggressive, despotic, and oppressive empires that trampled on peoples' rights and pursued narrow special interests at the expense of the public good. In the words of Thomas Jefferson, "The issue today is the same as it has been throughout all history, whether man shall be allowed to govern himself or be ruled by a small elite." In other words, men have always had to choose between despotism and democracy. They cannot both exist at the same time. When given the choice, people prefer to be free than to be slaves, unless they have been so brainwashed that they cannot take responsibility for themselves.

In practice, however, it would be somewhat utopian to expect that politicians will always strive to achieve the common good. For one thing, the population itself is often not sufficiently motivated to invest time and money to become well informed about the issues. This can open the door to misinformation, propaganda, and political manipulation on the part of the political class and its allies. What is more, political competition is usually much weaker than economic competition, since a few political enterprises—the political parties—tend to dominate the public agenda. Entrenched politicians are well placed to advance, with some impunity, the special interests of their backers at the expense of the public interest. Therefore, to counteract such tendencies, access to information regarding laws and projects must be encouraged, while competition among political parties and political movements should also be enhanced.

THE ERRONEOUS CONCEPT OF SOCIETY AS AN ORGANISM

There is no error more pernicious than treating human beings as cogs in a large social machine or, as the ideology of society as organism proposes, as simple cells within a bigger organism. This is an abusive analogy with the human body, where our cells have no importance outside their ability to serve our entire body. Similarly, people who subscribe to the ideology of society as organism profess that the individual does not count, except as a contributor to the welfare of the whole society. In such a mechanical and collectivist view of society, each individual can be discarded by a supreme authority and replaced by another one at will. Each individual's welfare does not really count, since the collectivist view of society envisages people as robots, to be used in the pursuit of the leaders' vision. Throughout history, there has been a continuing struggle pitting the People versus the Powerful. On the whole, unfortunately, it can safely be said that most of the time the powerful have had the upper hand.

The theory of society as organism underlies all collectivist autocratic political regimes, be they fascism, nazism, communism, or theocracy. In such nondemocratic systems, individual citizens have no intrinsic value outside their ability to serve the whole society. For instance, anyone can be forcibly enrolled in an army and sent abroad to kill and be killed, provided the supreme authority decides that this is good for the particular society. The government, as head of the social body, decides for the other atomized parts what is good and what is bad. The only morality allowed is the one proclaimed by the rulers of the day. In the twentieth century, these authorities had names: Lenin, Stalin, Mussolini, Hitler, Mao Tse-Tung, Khomeini, Hussein, Pol Pot, and so on. Without exception, these totalitarian leaders brought disaster to their countries. They were directly responsible for well over 100 million deaths. Throughout history, the ideology of totalitarianism, whether secular or religious, has resulted in the most numerous and cruelest crimes against humanity.[6]

The organic view of society is hostile to the basic principles of individual rights and democracy upon which Western civilization has been built over the last three centuries. The American Revolution of 1776 and the French Revolution of 1789 repudiated the organic view of society and replaced it with the democratic concept that each individual matters, independently of the government, and that the representative government rules with the consent of the citizens, who are by nature depository of all political power.[7] That is why the collectivist theory of government is fundamentally bad and antihumanist. Even in democracies, it can be expected that the people in power will attempt to resurrect this bankrupt theory. Democrats and humanists must maintain a constant vigilance.[8]

THE ERROR OF ANARCHISM

Anarchism is at the other extreme of social organization. It proclaims that an organized society is not required for the survival of the individual and that laws and governments can be dispensed with. Each individual is seen as an autonomous island, a society of one. Such extreme individualism is contrary to the fundamental need for people to live in a relatively stable, organized society. Every organized society needs a government and a legal framework to define property rights and to make sure that the economic and social system is not a chaotic no-man's land. Humans are social animals, and human interaction is a requirement for survival and development in a predictable way. That is why laws and rules are necessary in any well-functioning society.

The sheer number of humans on this planet—more than six and a half billion individuals—points to the need to collaborate with each other to secure social order and a sustainable economy. Voluntary social interrelations without a referee are a sure recipe for chaos and conflict. Anarchism must answer the basic problem of the free rider, that is the tendency for some individuals to seek to obtain something for nothing and thus exploit others. As such, anarchism is a utopian social scheme that rests on a faulty view of human nature.

The constitutional and representative form of democratic government fulfills the requirement that people in large societies must have a say in decisions that affect them. Only in very small groups of individuals can an entirely voluntary system of social interactions theoretically be accommodated. Even then, human conflicts are bound to arise, and laws and rules must be designed in advance to avoid destructive and antisocial behavior. It's an error to believe that all human instincts are socially positive. Devious behavior, such as the natural tendency of the strong to dominate and subjugate the weak, is part of human nature. In its purest form, anarchism is the rule of the jungle. It is precivilization.

An indication that extreme or flawed social philosophies can lead to undesirable situations is that anarchism can ultimately lead to communism and the communal and collective ownership of everything. The result is the negation of the sovereignty of the individual. One reason that the French philosopher Pierre-Joseph Proudhon is considered to be the father of modern anarchism is his declaration that "property is theft." But if private property is denied, ownership must be collectively and centrally held. And under what authority? Usually, this requires a totalitarian government. This is how anarchism ultimately leads to authoritarian collectivism, the antithesis of individual freedom. As the example of the 1917 Russian Revolution shows, when Anarchists and Bolsheviks collaborated in overthrowing the social order, disorganized anarchism was no match for structured totalitarianism. Proudhon was naive in his statement that "anarchy is order without power."[9]

Therefore, there is not much difference in theory and in practice between society as organism and the anarchist society: both lead to authoritarian collectivism and the abolition of individual freedom. Anarchism has the tendency to morph into a totalitarian central state and to foster the disappearance of markets and voluntary exchange— the exact opposite of what anarchists profess to want. As Proudhon himself concluded late in his life, private property must be seen as a necessary evil in order to counterbalance the power of the state.[10]

THEOCRATIC TOTALITARIANISM AS THE ENEMY OF DEMOCRACY

Democracy is a dynamic process; it is a way to organize the division of political power and the political interactions between individuals living in a given territory. Power can be decentralized among the population or centralized in the hands of a few people. Theocracies, kingdoms, and dictatorships are the opposite of democracy. They are static; they are centralized; and they are exploitive.

Let's consider theocracies, that is to say the government of a country by religious leaders. Theocracies are political and economic systems based not on the wishes and consent of the people, and not on mass production and mass consumption, but on the exploitation of the masses for the very few—parasites at the top of the social and religious orders. They don't concentrate on building useful economic structures and production facilities—such as roads, bridges, schools, and hospitals—but on erecting castles, mosques, churches, and other self-serving monuments. That is why they require recurring wars of aggression to plunder, pillage, and exploit more industrious lands. They end up being systems of poverty and of slavery, not systems of wealth creation and freedom.

Kings, despots, and tyrants of all kinds have often claimed that their usurped power over people was legitimate because it was given to them by some far away gods and did not originate from the people.

They found convenient allies in clergymen who confirmed that their earthly powers came from remote deities.

The apostle to the Gentiles, Paul (Saul) of Tarsus, taught that political rulers receive their legitimacy from God and therefore should always be obeyed: "The powers that be are ordained of God. Whosoever therefore resisteth the power, resisteth the ordinance of God: and they that resist shall receive to themselves damnation" (Romans 13:1–2). This is the favorite biblical quote (from around 64–65 CE) of conservative politicians and conservative Christian theologians who oppose democracy and who defend the divine source of power for autocratic rulers. They view democracy with the deepest suspicion, since elected governments are assumed to pursue the common good, and not the interests of a specific social caste or of a state-established religion. Above all, they resent that democratic governments are responsible to the people as final arbiters of government policies. They object to the principle that the state derives its power from the consent of the governed as proclaimed in the US and French constitutions ("We, the People"). They much prefer the ancient autocratic form of government, which is imposed on the people by authorities who serve as intermediaries between the deities and common mortals.

The three main monotheist religions are all antidemocratic, to different degrees, in the sense that they profess that political power derives from abstract deities and not from the sovereign people. The Bible, in particular, is very much on the side of theocracy, not democracy. Numerous biblical passages warn that people cannot and should not govern themselves but should leave that task to a god and its representatives (Jeremiah 10:23). According to the Bible, democracy is destined to fail and lead to bad results (Ecclesiastes 8:9 and Luke 21:25), thus implying that an authoritarian regime is somewhat preferable to a democratic one. This may be the reason why established religions throughout history have had a tendency to ally themselves with centralized political systems such as monarchist, imperial, or fascist regimes.

When democracy was in its infancy in Europe, the Catholic Church was among its worst enemies. For example, the church denounced the 1215 Magna Carta, the first written constitution in European history, which reduced the god-given absolute powers of kings over the people and which established the right of *habeas corpus*, the right not to be detained without a trial. In September 1215, Pope Innocent III, the same pope who ordered the massacre of Béziers in 1209, issued an edict condemning any democratic reform in England:

> [The Magna Carta] ... is not only shameful and base but also illegal and unjust. We refuse to overlook such shameless presumption which dishonors the Apostolic See, injures the king's right, shames the English nation, and endangers the crusade. Since the whole crusade would be undermined if concessions of this sort were extorted from a great prince who had taken the cross, we, on behalf of Almighty God, Father, Son and Holy Ghost, and by the authority of Saints Peter and Paul His apostles, utterly reject and condemn the settlement.... The Charter with all its undertakings and guarantees we declare to be null and void of all validity for ever.[11]

Similarly, neither the Qur'an nor the *hadiths* recognize nor accept democracy. If a country happens to have democratic institutions and a secular constitution, militant Islamist organizations will tend to oppose the very concept and existence of a secular civil society. For one thing, Islamic clerics are taught to reject the concept of free will and of individualism. For another, as for all religious fundamentalisms, Islamic fundamentalism adopts a literal (and not a metaphorical) reading of the religious texts.[12]

The Jewish Zionist approach to democracy, as applied today in Israel, is also biased against true democracy. Even though the state of Israel[13] is, on paper, a democratic republic that operates under a parliamentary system with universal suffrage, it is widely recognized that Palestinians living in this ethnic country, (approximately 20 percent of the population of Israel), have a second-class status, without equal rights. As former President Jimmy Carter said, "When Israel does occupy this [Palestinian] territory deep within the West Bank, and connects the 200-or-so settlements with each other, with a road, and then prohibits the Palestinians from using that road, or in many cases even crossing the road, this perpetrates even worse instances of apartness, or apartheid, than we witnessed even in South Africa."[14] It is perhaps more difficult for an ethnic or religious-based country to be a true democracy.

RELIGION AND THE THREAT TO DEMOCRACY

Some organized religions are more politically oriented than others in the sense that their leaders and followers vie for political power, sometimes absolute or totalitarian political power. Organized religion then becomes a screen for gaining political control over a population or territory. If successful, such political religions could inpose a political system of theocracy, that is to say a form of government in which a state is governed by officials who profess to be divinely guided. Other organized religions are more socially oriented. They are like social clubs where people with the same affinities meet to share common ideas and common services. Such so-called social religions are much less a threat to democracy than openly political religions.

The United States is the only Western-style democracy that has a strong, politically active, religious movement.[15] According to polls, a third of the population believes that the Bible is literally accurate and is not, as many think, a collection of unsubstantiated claims, Hebrew legends and myths, stories, parables, metaphors, and fables, written by a composite of authors over time, sometimes decades and even centuries after the events they describe.[16] Moreover, according to a poll conducted in July 2005 by the Pew Research Center, 42 percent of Americans totally reject biological evolution and natural selection. They believe instead the creationist fable that humans and other living things have existed only in their present forms. Only 26 percent of Americans believe that humans evolved by natural selection, even if virtually all scientists now accept this view. Such basic ignorance may be the reflection of a lack of education or blind religious faith, since 20 percent of Americans also think that the Sun revolves around the Earth, and not the reverse. This has been an established fact for more than four centuries![17]

More frightening yet is the belief held by many Americans that they will see the end of the world during their lifetime. Some religious denominations and cults in the United States adopt the religious model of fear and violence to promote obedience and conformity, and to gain power and riches.[18] Puritan preachers declare the accuracy of their visions as coming directly from God, who supposedly speaks to humankind from the pages of the Old and New Testaments.[19]

These self-proclaimed prophets foresee the imminent and unavoidable great battle of Armageddon, the fulfillment of John's prophecy in the book of Revelation.[20] The cataclysmic conflict between the forces of Good against the forces of Evil would climax in our lifetime with a global holocaust, most likely a man-made nuclear cataclysm.[21] Politicians sometimes take on these fabrications in order to make political capital. For instance, in 1971, Ronald Reagan, then governor of California and future Republican president of the United States, seemed to be embracing Armageddon theology when he declared, "Everything is falling into place. It can't be long now. Ezekiel says that fire and brimstone will be rained on the enemies of God's people. That must mean that they'll be destroyed by nuclear weapons." These are frightening words in the mouth of a populist politician, especially one in a country that has ten thousand nuclear bombs.[22]

Consider also that, in the world of religious fiction, the most successful works are those of two authors, Tim LaHaye and Jerry B. Jenkins, who published a series of apocalyptic evangelical novels called *Left Behind*. These authors and other pop prophets, as they have been called, propose religious fantasies that, because of their supernatural themes, are the adult equivalent of the popular children's series Harry Potter. The message of their books is simple: the world should be viewed in terms of black and white, good and evil, with us or against us.[23]

What can be most harmful about such religious novels is the strong dose of hate propaganda they spread against the United Nations, against anything resembling a system of international or supranational law, and even against Europe, if not against Muslims. For example, they hawk the ridiculous notion that the creation of the European Union, the "United States of Europe," and the establishment of the European currency, the Euro, are signs that the end of the world is near.[24] And since there is a verse in the Bible that says that those who bless Israel will in turn be blessed, these books develop the idea that for the Bible prophesies to be realized, it is necessary that Israel be strong and victorious and destroy its Muslim enemies. The call thus goes out to fundamentalists and evangelicals to do everything in their power to persuade the US government to defend Israel, all the time and in all circumstances.[25]

Such is the wind of religious folly that blows over the United States in this first part of the twenty-first century.[26]

RELIGION AND DEMOCRACY

The potentially destructive power inherent in the paranoid mentality of those who read and believe this literature is enormous, especially when they team up with powerful politicians, as is the case in the United States and, to a certain extent, in the United Kingdom. When politicians start accepting myths as truth and facts and begin seeing the world from a divine viewpoint, this creates a very dangerous situation indeed. This is particularly true if they believe that they have the responsibility to manifest God's power before the entire world and frame foreign policies in accordance with these views.

One only has to consider the devastating power of religious myths in the past: those behind the Crusades to liberate Jerusalem, initiated by Pope Urban II during the Middle Ages, or the massacre of the Cathar sect by Pope Innocent III in the twelfth and thirteenth centuries in Southern France or the Spanish Inquisition against Muslims and Jews under Thomas Torquemada in the fifteenth century or the inspiration of the Puritan divines (pastors) that led to the slaughter of the Pequot Indians of Connecticut in 1636–37.

As such, modern manifestations of paranoia would be of little consequence, were it not for the fact that, sometimes, persons imbued with fanatical evangelical religion succeed in climbing to power. In 2001, such a person, George W. Bush, became the US President and commander-in-chief of the most powerful war machine in the world. As president, Bush had the capacity to act in a manner described by the books of the *Left Behind* series. Indeed, in what measure were the

Bush administration's positions on the United Nations, the International Criminal Court, Israel, the Iraq war, or Europe, for example, influenced by his fundamentalist religious convictions and those of his advisors?[27]

The evident mixture of religion and politics and excessive religiosity in the public sphere are a most ominous recent development in American politics. For some decades now, there has been a close relationship between politics and American religious organizations. As such, it is a betrayal of the letter and the spirit of the US Constitution. The First Amendment of the US Constitution, often called the Establishment Clause, stipulates that Congress cannot make laws "respecting an establishment of religion, or prohibiting the free exercise thereof." The courts have interpreted this amendment as being a clear intention of the framers of the US Constitution that they did not want government to get involved in religious affairs. Indeed, to make things absolutely clear, President Thomas Jefferson, on New Year's Day 1802, explained in a widely circulated official letter that the Establishment Clause meant that there should be "a wall of separation between church and state,"—not a door—a wall.

President James Madison (1751–1836) made it even clearer, stating that there should be a total separation between church and state: "The number, the industry, and the morality of the priesthood, and the devotion of the people have been manifestly increased by the total separation of the Church from the State." Thus, for James Madison and other American founders, the separation of church and state was not only a requirement of political freedom, it was also a means to safeguard religion from being encroached upon by politics and politicians. More recently, another great American president, John F. Kennedy, eloquently laid out his philosophy of government when he declared, "I believe in an America where the separation of church and state is absolute—where no Catholic prelate would tell the President (should he be Catholic) how to act, and no Protestant minister would tell his parishioners for whom to vote—where no church or church school is granted any public funds or political preference—and where no man is denied public office merely because his religion differs from the President who might appoint him or the people who might elect him."[28]

The principles here are clear and limpid. They are the principles of equality, fairness, and freedom of conscience that require, in a democracy, that the public place be open to all citizens, whatever their personal beliefs or philosophies. This means that in a democratic constitutional order, there is no place for religious preference, religious discrimination, or religious intolerance of people according to their conscientious beliefs. All people should be treated equally and no religion-based litmus test should ever be applied and used as a criterion for anyone to get involved in public life or to be under the protection of the Constitution and of the law.

THE FIVE MAIN DANGERS TO DEMOCRACY

Democracy is not the cure for all of humanity's ills. The democratic system of government is not perfect and is prone to several diseases that could sometimes be fatal.[29] Above all, democracies must guard themselves against five main dangers.

Median Income versus Average Income and the Sense of Progress

The first obstacle to true democracy is too much income and wealth inequality. How do we know when there is too much inequality in a society? It is when the median income (the level of income above which 50 percent of income earners earn more, and below which 50 percent earn less) falls too much below the average income (total income divided by the working population).[30] This means that income distribution is very unequal and that there are more people who are relatively poor.

According to the rule of the median voter, a democracy can be unstable if the median income stays for too long below the average income. This is a sign that a minority of the population receives high incomes while the majority receives below-average incomes. This is usually a symptom that the middle class is small, a majority of the population is in relative poverty and a small percentage of the population lives in opulence. When the gap between rich and poor is widening, this is also a sign that democracy is in peril. That's the reason why democratic societies cannot tolerate for long that super-rich individuals appear to gain more than they contribute to society. Social justice and a fair economic system are prerequisites of a well-functioning democracy.

One of the greatest benefits of democracy is its capacity to bring about change—change of government, change of policies, change in the distribution of income and wealth, and so on—in order to avoid stagnation and immobility. In any society, the tendency is for a few to concentrate power and wealth in their hands, leaving the many in a situation of dependence and despondency. The right to vote and to engage in political activity changes the balance of power in a country and opens the door for the establishment of a government, in Lincoln's words, "of the people, by the people, and for the people." Moreover, too great a concentration of wealth inevitably brings forth corruption in government and concentration of the tools of propaganda in the hands of the powerful, which together constitute one of the greatest threats to democracy.

More generally, social interactions through markets create both tensions and benefits. Indeed, a market economy or capitalism functions primarily under the principle of competition, sometimes with win-win results between consumers and producers, but often with win-lose outcomes between producers. Similarly, a democratic political system of government is fundamentally based on social cooperation with win-win outcomes, even if different political parties compete for power. This is because economic benefits derived from economic competition and innovations are more equally shared within the entire population through government actions and policies. Therefore, we may say that democracy is necessary to capitalism, less the latter leads to a socially unacceptable concentration of wealth and power.

Debt, Under-Funded Public Expenditures, and Inflation

The second obstacle to democracy is the pitfall of excessive debt, especially external debt. Because of the rule of the median voter, there is a political incentive to raise public expenditures to unsustainable levels. When a majority of voters have an income that is below average, it is to be expected that these low-income earners will vote for politicians who promise benefits for which they do not have to pay the full cost personally. The high burden of taxes is then concentrated on a minority of taxpayers with sizeable taxable incomes.

Politicians, for their part, have an incentive not to raise unpopular taxes, while still providing public and social services. They may choose instead to finance government programs through borrowing and debt. Essentially, politicians want to have their cake and eat it too. If care is not taken, such long-term borrowing to finance current government expenditures may result in building up the public debt without necessarily increasing the stock of social capital. Future taxpayers will then be saddled with the burden of paying higher taxes to cover the interest on the bloated public debt. Economic growth will decline, economic underdevelopment will result and the population will end up with a lower standard of living. Short-term gains would have been bought at the expense of long-term pains.

But the most insidious of all taxes is the inflation tax, which reduces the purchasing power of money. This is a hidden tax on anybody holding a national currency, which is then devalued because a government issues too much of it, usually to finance the public expenditures side of the budget. Mild inflation (two or three percent per year) is no threat to democracy. But *high inflation* (when consumer prices increase by more than twenty percent per year) and its worst cousin, *hyperinflation* (when prices increase by more than fifty percent per month) undermine the very foundations of any democratic society. When a government must rely on inflation to finance its expenditures, it's a sure sign of social, political, and economic dislocation.

Sociopaths or Psychopaths in Power

The third danger that can beset a democracy is even more ominous. It happens when incurable psychopaths, deranged characters, or rabid demagogues accede to power and then, through hubris or design, resort to violence and wars of aggression against other nations, in order to consolidate their own domestic political power. Weak political leaders of strongly armed nations are particularly dangerous to world peace when they create a crisis in order to enhance their own personal political interests. It's relatively easy for demagogues, backed by complacent media, to rally popular support by invoking external threats and resorting to belligerent, nationalist rhetoric and patriotic slogans. Democracies are as likely as dictatorships to threaten world peace and wage wars. Indeed, even in democracies, there can be too many people who find themselves in a position to influence history, but who have not studied history and have never, therefore, learned from it.[31]

It's not easy for a democracy to protect itself from the rule of warmongering demagogues or sociopaths. When such people are in power, they will attempt to use the enormous resources of the government to concentrate absolute power into their own hands. They won't hesitate to corrupt the legislative and judicial branches of government to achieve their goals. The people then become vulnerable to intimidation and to harassment of all kinds by dictatorial-minded politicians, their acolytes, and other sycophants.

The destructive powers of such people can be enormous, and sometimes, irreparable. Even the best-crafted constitution is no rampart against the subjugation of the political process by a devious cabal sufficiently well financed and in charge of an efficient propaganda machine. Personal liberty and individual freedom, the hallmarks of democracy, can be stifled and eroded to a point where there remains little difference between a totalitarian regime and a perverted democratic regime.[32]

The Curse of State-Sponsored Propaganda

The fourth danger faced by democracy is the danger of political propaganda and disinformation.

Propaganda is defined as a specific type of message presentation directly aimed at influencing people's opinions, rather than impartially providing information. It's a branch of the public relations industry. More specifically, *political propaganda* is the art of conscious and intelligent manipulation of the attitudes and behavior of the electorate, in order to control the democratic process.

Political propaganda and state-induced indoctrination may well be the most serious threat citizens face in a democracy. Once the will of the citizenry has been perverted, democracy is denied. Because physical coercion is not allowed in a democracy, this makes it all the more necessary for people who are bent on influencing voters to rely on propaganda and the manipulation of mass media to change people's minds.

Why is political propaganda so dangerously effective? Essentially, because most people pay scant attention to public affairs, being totally absorbed in their daily personal struggles. Not having the time and the motivation to get informed on their own, they are easy prey for those who have a direct interest in propagating particular ideologies, points of view, and interpretations of reality. On numerous occasions, they swallow, hook, line, and sinker, what the government propagandists put forward, whether to justify a domestic policy or to win support for a foreign war. It is indeed the strength of political propaganda that it can reinforce predisposed biases and misconceptions and make them more acceptable to the unsuspecting individual. Those controlling propaganda machines—politicians and their backers in the dominant media—are in a position to impose their agendas and advance policies that serve their special interests. In the age of electronic media, those who control the providers of information—or disinformation—control the political process. And, in this day and age, they're the ones with the most money.

In totalitarian states, where the levers of power are in the hands of a state bureaucracy, politicians and bureaucrats control and impose censorship over the media. In countries where private wealth and incomes are highly concentrated, those who own the media set the tone and are in a position to dominate the public discourse, impose their political agenda and influence the population at election time. In both cases, it is the government elite or the moneyed elite who control the principal means of information.

One who knew something about political propaganda, Chancellor Adolf Hitler of Germany, summed up its enormous power when he said, "Through clever and constant application of propaganda, people can be made to see paradise as hell, and also the other way round, to consider the most wretched sort of life as paradise." In other words, clever propaganda, when unchecked by critical analysis or confronted with reality, can persuade people of just about anything.

In the United States, in particular, political propaganda took a turn for the worse in the 1980s, when rich, Far Right groups took over the control of most of the main corporate media, thanks to deregulations that served their special interests well. Political propagandist Richard A. Viguerie was one of the leaders in the concerted move to monopolize the media for conservative political purposes. He wrote a book explaining how this was done. Viguerie and his coauthor David Franke showed how conservative American political groups capitalized upon alternative media (direct mail, talk radio, cable news TV, and the Internet) to spread their message, win elections, and gain political power.[33]

Serge Chakotin's *Rape of the Masses* is a classic reference on the techniques of mass political propaganda and the theory of conditioned reflexes.[34] According to Chakotin, those who intend to impose a political ideology need not speak to people's minds, but rather tap the primary collective subconscious and emotions of the masses, which rest in a country's history and founding myths. In that way, "people can be forced to act in ways predetermined without their knowledge," unaware that they are the victim of a systematic manipulation. That is the strength of political propaganda; people are conditioned to think and act according to the preset agenda of the manipulators. Even in well-established democracies, many prefer to be lied to and made comfortable in their own mind, than to be told the truth and made uncomfortable. In reality, some people literally enjoy being lied to, if the lies fit their predetermined ideas and interests.[35]

Recent history illustrates brilliantly the force behind political propaganda, as reported by James Bovard. Polls indicated that after the terrorist attacks of September 11, 2001, only 3 percent of Americans thought that the country of Iraq or its president, Saddam Hussein, had anything to do with the attacks. This is understandable, since Osama bin Laden's al-Qaeda network took responsibility for the attacks and the terrorists came from Pakistan and Saudi Arabia, not from Iraq. However, after the Bush-Cheney administration started making a direct link between Saddam Hussein and 9/11, and the media became party to the operation by echoing their message, by February 2003 the percentage of Americans who believed Saddam Hussein was personally involved in the attacks jumped to 72 percent.[36] The fact that this was an outright lie did not matter; the propaganda results were real and Bush could proceed with his war of choice against Iraq while claiming public support.[37] This illustrates the power of the propaganda tool, which consists of playing upon people's fears.[38]

How can we protect ourselves against propaganda? The answer is to develop a broad culture, to exercise the capacity for critical thinking, and to rely on a multiplicity of sources of information. But in the end, the best antidote to political propaganda is an honest and open government.[39]

The Concentration of Media Ownership and Campaign Financing

Finally, the fifth and possibly the most deadly failure in a democracy occurs when the same narrow money interests control both the main media and the main political parties. When this happens, democracy is caught in a vise. It may be on its death throes and about to turn fascist, that is to say, to become a state run by a few and for the benefits of the few. At that point, plutocrats would be in a position to choose the politicians and take over the central function of government for their own narrow interests.[40] As President Franklin D. Roosevelt once said, "That, in its essence, is fascism—ownership of government by an individual, by a group, or by any other controlling private power."

Indeed, the unrestricted use of money in politics can turn a vibrant democracy into a decadent plutocracy just as surely as poisoning a well can destroy a village. It is inevitably a source of political corruption.

This is particularly a threat when corporate entities with a lot of cash can enter the public arena at will and politically crush individuals who oppose their narrow money interests. As a general democratic principle, it can be said that private corporations created by legislation are not moral agents—only breathing individuals are—only they can adopt moral standards of conduct and be a source of law. In a democracy, the citizens are the only legitimate source of law. It follows inexorably that private corporations, not being citizens, cannot be legitimate political actors.

THE RIGHT TO POLITICAL OPPOSITION AND TO CHANGE THE GOVERNMENT

British philosopher Thomas Hobbes wrote that the persecuted, instead of rebelling, "must expect their reward in heaven." The use of religion as a means to subdue the lower classes is an idea that has a long history. Essentially, it says that religious leaders have a duty to promise celestial happiness to the oppressed of this world, in compensation for their earthly sufferings. This is the old idea of religion as the opiate of the masses.

John Locke took the opposite stance and presented a refutation of the divine right of kings, arguing for the right of people to overthrow illegitimate governments.[41] Indeed, resistance to despotic authorities is a virtue and a moral act. From a humanist point of view, there are times and situations when human beings are subjected to injustice, tyranny, oppression, or slavery. That should be neither accepted nor tolerated. As free and independent human beings, people have the right to be heard and to be respected. And when their conscience can no longer tolerate abuse and despotism, they have the most fundamental right to resist and oppose. But when government falls into the hands of fools, despots, or tyrants who abolish freedom and democracy, and who align themselves with exploiters, people are in a quandary. What should be done? Acquiesce or protest? Resign or resist? Nonviolent protests should be the first line of defense.

However, passive resistance to injustice is sometimes not enough and a proactive approach becomes necessary. As Thomas Jefferson wrote: "The law is often the tyrant's will, and always so when it vio-

lates the right of an individual." The implication is that it may be necessary, in certain circumstances, to go around an unjust law imposed
by a tyrant and to oppose an illegitimate and oppressive government.
When one individual or a clique of individuals governs without the
consent of the people, when they suspend basic human rights or when
they usurp absolute powers and concentrate them in their own hands,
people have a right to rebel. If civil authorities forbid peaceful protest
or resistance or declare them illegal, such laws or regulations are *ipso
facto* null and void, because they are contrary to basic human morality.
People always retain their natural and inalienable right to rebel and to
reclaim their freedom each time oppressive, tyrannical, and despotic
powers negate them.

In this case, as former Canadian Prime Minister Wilfrid Laurier
put it, what is reprehensible "is not rebellion but the despotism which
induces the rebellion; what is hateful are not rebels but the men, who,
having the enjoyment of power, do not discharge the duties of power;
they are the men who, having the power to redress wrongs, refuse to
listen to the petitioners that are sent to them; they are the men who,
when they are asked for a loaf, give a stone."

THE IMPORTANCE OF ECONOMIC AND SOCIAL PROGRESS

In general, religiosity and religious activities are the least prevalent in
societies where people have a high standard of living, with ready
access to a wide variety of goods and services, including food,
housing, healthcare, education, and job opportunities. Conversely,
societies where economic progress is absent or stagnant and where life
is precarious because of widespread poverty, famine, corruption,
sickness, low education, and unemployment, are those where a high
degree of religiosity and religious superstition is endemic.[42]

There seems, indeed, to exist a *cycle of poverty*, whereby poverty
makes education less accessible, thus creating a breeding ground for
superstition, religiosity, obscurantism, dependence, ignorance, large
families, less capital and fewer investments, and fewer economic
opportunities in general, which in turn bequeath more poverty, and

so on. Many regions of Africa are caught up in such a vicious cycle of poverty.

The *cycle to prosperity* works the other way: prosperity generates more education, more knowledge, more economic opportunities, less superstition and religiosity, more enlightenment, more independence, smaller families, more capital and more economic initiatives and innovations, and thus more prosperity and more economic security. Europe is a continent where such a virtuous cycle is at play.[43]

Economic progress, economic opportunity, and economic development are as important as democracy and political freedom for human progress. For individuals and their families, access to education and to the means of survival is fundamental. I would argue that an efficient economic system must provide economic opportunity for all if freedom and liberty are to flourish.[44] However, when there exists a state of permanent warfare, economic decline is to be expected. Indeed, the main reason why the overall standard of living is stagnating in some countries, notably in the United States, is due to the high proportion of resources being directed toward the parasitic military-industrial establishment.

A WELL-FUNCTIONING ECONOMIC SYSTEM

A well-functioning economic system prohibits the use of physical force to get one's way and provides individuals with personal freedom and economic security. The freedom to pursue peaceful economic activities means that individuals can choose the occupations that best suit their talents and preferences and are free to spend or save their income as they like. In a well-organized society, social and economic cooperation leads to a harmonious division of labor with specific knowledge being applied to the most efficient way of producing goods and services. The larger the body of knowledge in a society and the more advanced the means of production, the higher the standard of living.

Economic freedom and economic opportunities require a social environment of economic competition between various producers

and investors to increase the supply of goods and services for the benefit of all. Indeed, with economic competition among producers and
freedom of movement of people and capital between industries, the
rate of return on capital investments tends to move toward an
economy-wide average. In industries where the rate of innovation
and creation of new products is higher, the rate of return on investments is above average for a while, but does tend to decline over time
as new producers enter the field and create more competition. In
slowing or stagnant industries, the rate of return on investments tends
to be lower than average, thus inducing savers and investors to move
their capital to other more profitable industries. This tends to raise the
rate of return even in the declining industries and move it toward the
average rate of return for the entire economy.

Workers profit when entrepreneurs and producers invest capital
in a particular production because this creates job opportunities and
leads to increased productivity through technological progress, and
because this in turn raises real wages and incomes. People as consumers have a wider range of goods and services to choose from and
the competition to produce the best and the most economical products results in lower prices, thus raising the purchasing power of
earned incomes.

However, under their regulatory obligations, governments have a
responsibility to curb excessive financial speculation that is not related
to real investment or to risk protection, and that is not geared to
improving productivity. Some financial speculation can be simply
seen as scams designed to transfer money from the poor to the rich, or
from the less-well-informed to the better-informed individuals. Such
antisocial speculation has no place in a well-functioning economy.
The recent explosion in speculative *hedge funds*, in exotic derivatives
located in tax-free havens, and in new banking practices that remove
the direct connection between the lender and the borrower, does not
contribute to the overall efficiency of the economy, but is rather a
source of financial and economic crises and dislocations.

Avoiding Excessive Concentration
of Wealth and Income

Economic competition and the continuous flow of capital investments and technological improvements are two powerful engines of economic progress in a well-functioning economic system. In such an economy, there is no need for a heavy-handed and centralized government-run system of economic planning because monetary prices provide the necessary signals and incentives for using resources efficiently, according to their relative rarity and desirability. The system of fluctuating prices brings forth information that allows producers and consumers alike to weigh the relative value of things and to make the most economical and productive decisions within their budget constraints.

Therefore, when competition prevails in all sectors of the economy, it is normal that innovators and investors reap the rewards of their efforts. A certain degree of wealth and income inequality is the natural outcome of free markets. However, some people may also attempt to design combines, schemes, or devices to exploit their market power without much contribution to the collective wealth. Oppressors, abusers, and exploiters have to be reigned in so that workers and consumers do not become the victims of market manipulations. State regulation of business practices to ensure the efficiency and fairness of markets is consistent with a well-functioning market economy.

The danger arises when tricksters succeed in subverting the political system through corruption or otherwise, and cheaters use the government itself for their own economic and financial advantage. This is a great calamity for a country because the people risk losing both democracy and economic opportunity. With the inexorable working of the principle of compound interest, wealth concentration in a society tends to intensify, until most wealth, economic power, and political power are concentrated in a few hands. Over time, this inevitably leads to the collapse of a society and its economy.

To escape from such a calamity, there must be economic opportunity for all, and a nation's tax system must be designed in such a way as to avoid undue concentration of wealth and income.

THE ATTITUDE OF RELIGIONS TOWARD
POVERTY AND ECONOMIC STAGNATION

As Dutch philosopher Johan Huizinga observed, "Christianity, [during the Middle Ages], had so deeply ingrained the idea of sacrifice as a way to personal and social perfection that it became impossible for a long time to follow the second path, that is, the one that leads to the conscious improvement and betterment of the world." There is a general tendency for religious systems of thought to neglect the present and the material requirements for survival in the real world in favor of mysterious theories of ethereal worlds, where everything is infinitely plentiful and where the laws of economics do not apply. In this frame of mind, the economic organization of the real world is at best a distraction, and at worst a malediction that humankind must endure before acceding to a better (imaginary) world. Perhaps this is why Kierkegaard wrote, "Christianity demands the crucifixion of the intellect."

It shouldn't be too surprising that countries where religious thinking and practice are omnipresent experience less economic and scientific progress than more secular societies.[45] Historically, most political religions, when they were in control, tended to favor the status quo, be it political or economic, with the objective of perpetuating the past rather than changing the present and preparing the future. This is because most religions tend to de-emphasize the economic side of human existence and are inclined to impose a rigid system of thought on all. When in control, it's natural for their leaders to regard with suspicion the activity of innovators who advance new ideas and propose new ways of doing things.

Unfortunately, there's only so much economic progress that a country can make by copying what's being done elsewhere or by marginally improving on what is already being done. Innovations are necessary for an economy to grow in a sustained way, and their implementation is conditional on attracting the necessary capital. Innovations are, by definition, the leaven of economic growth, and they can only flourish if a high degree of freedom of thought and freedom to innovate prevails. Institutional or ideological barriers to innovation and dynamism translate into barriers to economic development and economic prosperity.

For example, in Christian Western Europe during the late Middle Ages (1250–1500), bankers and doctors were often Jews. For one thing, the church did not permit loans bearing interest, thereby preventing the development of an efficient system of credit. Also, the church did not allow the dissection of cadavers, an essential practice for doctors hoping to make advances in medicine by studying the complex workings of the human body. These are two fundamental reasons why these highly rewarding professions long remained closed to Catholics in Christian Europe.

Even in the twenty-first century, some religious prescriptions are still genuine recipes for poverty and economic stagnation. For example, it's no accident that today most Muslim countries are underdeveloped. This is because Islam is a religion that imposes some behaviors that hinder economic progress. First case in point: Qur'anic inheritance laws. Such laws forbid a father from passing a business on to one single son, but rather require him to divvy up the legacy among all his children—daughters, however, are supposed to get only half portions. This makes it harder to develop large enterprises as instruments of economic innovation and development.

Second case in point: birth control and unsustainably high birth rates. Indeed, some Islamic countries have among the highest birth rates in the world, notably in some of the poorest countries of Africa. When such countries adhere to the most fundamentalist Islamic tenets on procreation, poverty becomes unavoidable. Thus, hadith literature says: "To better propagate the faith, the Islamic Oumah [community] must procreate," which makes it very difficult, if it is followed, to teach birth control techniques to women and prevent a disastrous population explosion.

Third case in point: interest income and capital accumulation. Just as in old Christian teachings, now largely repudiated, Qur'anic rules forbid the lending of money against the promise of interest payments. Even though ways have been found around this requirement in some Islamic countries, in Turkey and Malaysia for example, the central religious message remains that capital accumulation is to be viewed with suspicion. Unfortunately, capital accumulation and technological innovation have been the two main interrelated sources of economic prosperity since the Industrial Revolution of the mid-eighteenth century. A society constrained by its religious hang-ups is deprived of the fundamental tools of economic progress and will be left behind.[46] These are often the countries that have a chronic surplus population and that must rely on the safety valve of emigration to maintain domestic political stability. But then they only export their own problems to other countries. That is why the question of backward-looking religions is a world problem, not a local one.

Even now, in a country as advanced as the United States, religious people in the White House and in the US Congress have erected barriers to scientific research. They have created obstacles for scientists in their quest for using stem cells to discover cures for fatal diseases, such as Alzheimer's and different types of cancer.[47] But, as history shows, it takes time to discredit crackpot ideas applied to politics and used in making wrong policies. More often than not, simple logic or scientific analysis does not suffice to open up closed minds. Sometimes it's only after a disaster has occurred, and after much human misery, that mentalities change.

RELIGIONS AND ECONOMIC PROGRESS

With the notable exception of Calvinist Protestantism, most religious systems reject worldly affairs and frown upon the pursuit of profit, income, wealth, and economic possessions. The Christian Bible (New Testament) teaches, for example, "It is easier for a camel to go through the eye of a needle, than for a rich man to enter the kingdom of God" (Matthew 19:24, Mark 10:25, Luke 18:25). It is therefore difficult to contend that Christianity was behind the rise of the capitalist economic system, as some have argued, unless one stands ready to substantially twist the Christian message.[48] This message is one of deprivation, poverty, and self-imposed sacrifice, all accepted in order to be prepared for a better life in the hereafter. There is no admonition to pursue earthly prosperity, whether this takes the form of a higher income, better housing, improved health, or more advanced education.

Calvinism represented, in part, a revolt against the Catholic medieval condemnation of usury and, implicitly, of profit in general. This led German economist-sociologist Max Weber to develop the thesis that certain types of Protestantism, especially the austere Calvinistic form of Christianity, could have played a determining role in explaining why certain parts of Europe where this creed prevailed (Holland, England) experienced faster economic growth than other European regions where traditional Catholicism dominated (Spain, France).[49] Indeed, the Puritan ethic, contrary to other religious ethics, made economic success one of the measures of eternal salvation and even regarded a lack of worldly success as the consequence of a combination of laziness and divine disfavor.

In this ideological climate, according to Weber's thesis, European capitalism became more dynamic following the Reformation, after the adoption of the Protestant work ethic.[50] This new ethic induced people to work harder, to create enterprises, and to engage more actively in trade and commerce. Since Calvinism also discouraged consumption, the end result was a virtuous cycle of increased savings, faster accumulation of capital for productive investment and faster adoption of division of labor production technologies, which in turn raised labor productivity and led to increased output and more income growth. We thus cannot say that all religions are inimical to economic development and economic progress.

TEN

EDUCATION

TENTH HUMANIST PRINCIPLE:
DEVELOP ONE'S INTELLIGENCE AND TALENTS
THROUGH EDUCATION AND EFFORT,
IN ORDER TO REACH FULFILLMENT AND HAPPINESS,
FOR THE BETTERMENT OF HUMANITY
AND FUTURE GENERATIONS.

Human history becomes a race between education and catastrophe.

—H. G. Wells (1866–1946)

The evil that is in the world always comes of ignorance, and good intentions may do as much harm as malevolence, if they lack understanding. On the whole, men are more good than bad; that, however, isn't the real point. But they are more or less ignorant, and it is that we call vice or virtue; the most incorrigible vice being that of an ignorance which fancies it knows everything and therefore claims for itself the right to kill.

—Albert Camus (1913–1960), *The Plague*

Nature has set no term to the perfection of human faculties ... the perfectibility of man is truly indefinite.

—Marquis de Condorcet (1743–1794), French philosopher

The gift of learning, that is to say the opportunity to acquire information, knowledge, and wisdom, is the greatest of them all. That's why education, education, education, especially disciplined education, should be the fundamental priority of every society. Education is the key to freedom, progress, and prosperity. It is the surest protector of liberty. To be knowledgeable is to free; to be ignorant is

193

to be a slave. Education is the avenue of social progress and of self-enhancement. It's the most important among all social investments. Moreover, investment in education is the best way to fight poverty within any particular country, but also worldwide.

An Instrument of Liberty, Progress, and Prosperity

Learning is much more than formal education in schools, although attending classes and good teachers are an integral part of the learning experience. In particular, parents should instill in their children the love of learning, of reading, of being curious about the world, and teach them about the joy of intellectual achievement, besides teaching them the art of living a disciplined and moral life. To be sure, education is not only about the acquisition of knowledge; it must also emphasize the development of morals and a sense of personal discipline. Knowledge without morals and without discipline can easily become a threat to society. Children properly educated stand to reap all their lives the benefits that come from the seeds that have been sown in them at an early age.[1] Learning is thus an essential humanistic value.

Therefore, we say that humans are not intrinsically wicked, wretched, and lacking, as so many religions assume and proclaim them to be. Rather, humans are great beings, adept at learning and at accomplishing great things. They are capable of intelligence, kindness, compassion, solidarity and cooperation. They can be motivated to learn, and they are predisposed to improve themselves and use new information. It is not blind faith in abstract dogmas that produces freedom; knowledge brings victory over ignorance and creates the conditions for freedom. Knowledge empowers human beings and equips them with the tools of survival. By definition, those who rely on blind faith miss what is important in life.

Not everyone is born with a natural endowment of intelligence, strength, and beauty. But everyone can improve his or her lot through effort, education, and hard work. Each day, everyone should strive to learn something new. Indeed, the entire society benefits when people are educated and knowledgeable. In fact, education and knowledge are a large component of what we call human freedom. Education is also the best capital upon which to build an economy. Indeed, brainpower is a people's greatest resource.

The equality of opportunity to succeed in life is a basic democratic right. At birth, boys and girls should not be deprived of this opportunity by artificial obstacles erected by governments or other power structures. In practice, this means that education is a human right for all because education is a requirement for functioning in a modern society. That's why it's the responsibility of any government to promote the development of children's intelligence and talents. Free access to education for all children is a prerequisite for establishing a genuine equality of opportunity among people. Indeed, early, primary, and secondary education should be freely accessible. Similarly, no child who has the talents, merit, and motivation to study and learn should be denied access to a college education. Ever since the nineteenth century, free public education has been the foundation of most democratic societies, but it is not yet a universal value.

The lack of education is the source of many social ills and a cause of economic stagnation. This is essentially because ignorance breeds poverty and hopelessness in a society, whereas education and knowledge liberate and empower. The lack of education in a given population is not only socially and economically disastrous; it also has negative political consequences.

First, ignorance and poverty open the door to extremists and agitators. The more ignorant are the masses, the easier it is for dictators and demagogues to exploit the fertile ground of misery and consolidate their power. Second, it is in countries that invest the least in education and which have the lowest income per capita that one finds the highest proportion of people who are deeply engulfed in religion.

THE IMPORTANCE AND FUTURE OF THE INTERNET

In the twenty-first century, Internet-related services will become as ubiquitous as access to electricity and to television was in the twentieth century. The Internet is, indeed, a basic technological innovation that has democratized the access to unfiltered information worldwide and opened a panoply of new services. The field of education and research has been profoundly transformed by the use of computers. And through computers, the Internet is at the very center of the information revolution. Imagine that there are more than 100 million Web sites and the number is growing rapidly! For its wide range and profound consequences, the invention of the Internet may be as important for humanity and its development as the invention of the printing press by Johannes Gutenberg in 1440. It's not surprising that governments and corporations alike are following this explosion of free information with some trepidation, although for different reasons.

The principle that airwaves and cyberspace belong to all the people and are public property needs to be reaffirmed and solemnly proclaimed. People must be vigilant because in the past, powerful money interests have succeeded in persuading distracted or venal politicians to pass bad laws that are very much against the public interest. Laws guaranteeing freedom of access to the Internet and the information it carries are required, just as was the case with the invention of the telegraph in the nineteenth century. Democratic governments should consider favoring the creation of Internet service providers to further democratize access to the Internet. Indeed, the Internet is a basic economic and social infrastructure and should be viewed as a public utility, on the same level as electricity and the telephone.

RELIGIONS VERSUS KNOWLEDGE

To be truly free, people must be intellectually independent. When this is the case, it's more difficult for tyrants and other oppressors to fool and to subjugate them. The acquisition of knowledge empowers people. To what extent have religions slowed people's movement toward empowerment?

There is no doubt that religions have acted as a major brake on the progress of humanity over many centuries. Religions have kept people in ignorance as long as possible, promoting old superstitions instead of the acquisition of new, real knowledge. It was only when people with independent minds resorted to revolts or even revolutions against the theocratic constraints that scientific inquiries could be seriously undertaken.

Armed with the fanatical tool of divine inspiration, many religions, especially the monotheist religions, clung to the theological notion that all knowledge came from their god. Scientific inquiry was seen as an irreverent insult to the Almighty and an ungodly pursuit, shrouded in doubt and in contention with authority. Scientists in their university laboratories were not acclaimed for their knowledge in natural philosophy, mathematics and geometry, medicine and biology, anatomy, astronomy, physics, chemistry, or psychology, but were often perceived as subversive forces bent on contesting religious teachings and mocking the church's authority.

In seventeenth-century England, for example, Puritan ministers felt so threatened that they called for the destruction of Oxford University. As Galileo observed before his death, "of all the hatreds, there is none greater than ignorance against knowledge." It is amazing that it was only in the seventeenth century that scientists rediscovered that the brain is the center of the nervous system, and not the heart, as it had been falsely taught for many centuries by philosophers and religious leaders alike.[2]

The main reason for this prolonged ignorance was religion. As we previously noted, dissection was the surest way to learn about the functioning of the human body, but churches ruled that doctors and researchers were not to dissect human cadavers, deeming this activity sacrilegious to the works of God. Some religions had been teaching the resurrection of human bodies and the survival of souls in the afterlife, and in such a fantasy world, it would seem illogical and lacking in respect to tamper with cadavers in any way, even if it were the only way to learn how the human machine functions.

It is a wonder that people who would never accept to be treated by physicians using twelfth or fourteenth centuries' medical techniques nevertheless blindly accept to be led by religious ideas dating back to the seventh or twelfth centuries. The choice of the latter is as ridiculous and illogical as would be the choice of the former. It reflects a refusal to use new knowledge and an attachment to superstitions of another age.

CONCLUSION

Let us say, to conclude, that human brains, but also animal brains, to a certain extent, can be stimulated, cultivated, and improved through education, exercise, and training, above and beyond our basic natural senses. That is why it is so important that every child's brain be stimulated by an enriched educational environment and by the most beneficial experiences. It is in this sense that education for all is the true hope for humanity.[3]

ELEVEN

MORALITY IN EVERYDAY LIFE

REALITY TEST:
THE NECESSARY BUT LIMITED ROLE OF INSTITUTIONS,
CONSTITUTIONS, LAWS, TRIBUNALS, AND LAW ENFORCEMENT.

> Principle of liberty: Each person is to have an equal right to the most extensive basic liberty compatible with a similar liberty for others.
> —John Rawls (1921–2002), *A Theory of Justice*

> The only purpose for which power can be rightfully exercised over any member of a civilized community, against his will, is to prevent harm to others. His own good, either physical or moral, is not sufficient warrant.
> —John Stuart Mill (1806–1873)

> One must have a strong mind and a soft heart . . . The world is full of people who have a dry heart and a weak mind.
> —Jacques Maritain (1882–1973)

How can one be an optimistic and practical humanist without being naive and unrealistic? That is the challenge all of us who strive to improve things in the world inevitably must face. More specifically, in a future post-religion world, how can personal and collective moral behavior be encouraged without the mythical and ethereal inventions of paradise and hell?

Between the two extreme perspectives of British philosopher Thomas Hobbes, who held the view that man is essentially selfish, and of French philosopher Jean-Jacques Rousseau, for whom man is naturally good, there is place for a more nuanced and more realistic approach to human morality. To act in a moral way is to adhere to a social contract that sets rules for living in society. People profit from living in society, but they also have an obligation to fulfill their end of the contract by contributing to the common good. This requires both an education in basic morality and a legal framework to enforce the social contract for living together.

Most people are naturally inclined to be moral in their interactions with other human beings, but in certain circumstances, some people can act less morally than others. Between the idealism of utopian perfection and the human reality of weakness, sickness, greed, and cruelty, there is a gulf that has to be bridged. We have no other choice but to strive to close the gap between the kind of world we would want to live in and the real world we inherit at birth.

It is a fact that human behavior is not guided by reason alone, and certainly not by altruism alone. It can also be guided by instincts, emotions, and self-interest, and, as we saw in chapters 8 and 9, it can sometimes be pathological in nature. The human brain has many layers and the primitive part is geared for simple and immediate survival, irrespective of any moral dimensions. It is only after tens of thousands of years of evolution that humans have become moral animals capable of cooperation and able to live in society. It may have been the principal contribution of early forms of philosophy, religions, witchcraft practices, and superstitions of all kinds to have introduced the moral dimension to simple minds, in total awe and wonder before the daily dangers surrounding them.

The challenge today is to make people more moral, not only within their own group or even within their own country, but within humanity as a whole. For that to happen, people need to be less in-group oriented and must feel that they are truly part of the whole human race, a participant in the worldwide human family. Is the understanding that humanistic behavior produces peace, solidarity, and prosperity sufficient to ensure its voluntary practice? Is it evident that extreme egoism, xenophobia, and the law of the jungle generate their own punishments in the forms of guilt, anarchy, and lawlessness?

There are four types of inducements for one to be moral and act morally: (1) one's conscience, (2) the surrounding social pressure to behave morally within a group or community, (3) the teachings and systems of rewards and punishments provided by religions, and (4) the legal and institutional framework supplied by a legitimate government. In any case, some institutional framework is required to protect society from the freeloader problem that arises when the natural tendency for one to profit from the good behavior of others, while indulging oneself in bad behavior, takes over and risks plunging society into social chaos. Utopian anarchism, therefore, must be rejected in favor of a democratic political and social system, based on the rule of law and the rule of social justice.

Similarly, simple calls to respect moral values are not sufficient in large societies where a network of deviant and psychopathic individuals may wish to dominate and control others. As we saw in chapter 8, such individuals need to be counteracted effectively and prevented from reaching power. This requires a strong political constitution, based on humanist values, to protect individual rights against the encroachment of devious and unprincipled individuals in a position of authority.

In a global perspective, as we have demonstrated in chapter 9, humanity needs to establish constitutional democracy, both domestically and worldwide, in order to guarantee freedom, justice, and prosperity. Just as a domestic system of independent individuals of different means and power is unstable without a system of law and justice for all, so it is that an international system of independent nation-states of different sizes and varying influence is also basically unstable. Indeed, for such a world order to provide stability, freedom, and prosperity, it requires a worldwide system of enforceable rules that apply to all nations, whatever their size and influence. A better-managed world is a prerequisite for humanity to progress and survive in the coming centuries.

The fact that it will undoubtedly require many generations to reach this goal peacefully should not make one pessimistic and despondent about its ultimate achievement. A humanistic and democratic world is possible and may be the only hope for humanity to avoid self-destruction.

HUMANISTIC BEHAVIOR AND ITS CONSEQUENCES

For normal individuals, what are the motivations to be moral, and what rewards can be expected from following a code of humanistic rules of behavior?

First and foremost, there is both a selfish and an altruistic motive to be moral. The reciprocity principle, according to which one must treat others as one expects to be treated, establishes a fundamentally logical and enlightened selfish reason for being moral.[1] The empathy principle, which enables us to imagine being in someone else's place and seeing things from his point of view, establishes an unselfish reason to be moral. Together, they form the humanist Super Golden Rule in the code for global ethics. If one follows this rule of humanist morality, one does not need other incentives to act morally, and that includes the myth of afterlife rewards and punishments.

Second, there is also the intellectual satisfaction and the emotional benefit in knowing that one can be moral, have a general commitment to duty and do good because it is right, not because of some primitive legend about an after-death system of rewards or punishments, and not because it is against the law. It means doing the right thing because it's the right thing to do.

Third, there is the satisfaction that we can teach our children and grandchildren to adhere to a supreme system of ethics and build their characters with a moral code that is based on reason and facts, not on superstitions and fairy tales.[2]

And last, there is also the satisfaction of knowing that humanity will have the best chance to survive and flourish in the foreseeable future, for ourselves, for our children, and for the children of our children, if we adhere to a superior and universal code of ethics.

While some religious groups and other delusional people are waiting for—and even hoping for—the end of the world, when they do not actively work for its apocalyptic demise in the short term, modern humanists would rather be actively working for the long-haul survival of humanity on this planet. Modern humanism and its institutions can best ensure that humanity can progress in peace, freedom, and prosperity.

FREELY ACCEPTED MORALITY, FREELOADERS, AND CHEATERS

In theory and in an ideal world, all moral rules for living in society would be followed voluntarily by everyone, with no need for any form of coercion whatsoever. Everyone knows that this utopia is wishful thinking. Most people can learn to live by the rules, but there will always be a minority who choose to disregard the common good and try to take advantage, or who cannot resist their pathological tendencies toward antisocial behavior. Freeloaders and shirkers end up placing themselves above the rules, and their selfishness supersedes any human morality, humanistic or otherwise.

Experience teaches us that in any large group of people there is a normal distribution between the extremely kind and generous people and the extremely violent and self-centered individuals. As an approximation, let us assume that 10 percent of people are extraordinarily nice. Odds are that there are also 10 percent of people who are extraordinarily obnoxious and antisocial. It's a fair bet that the rest of the population would be distributed between these two extremes along a normal curve, the largest number to be found in the crowded middle.

Within democratic societies, while the rule of tolerance must be followed, we must also guard against the imbalance that can develop when some demand rights and privileges according to standard democratic principles, but would refuse such rights and privileges to others, according to religious totalitarian principles. Everybody should thus abide by the rules of the democratic constitution, without discrimination. Tolerance and respect of the individual and of his or her choices means that a society must recognize the rights and freedom of the individual. It doesn't mean, however, that an open, democratic, and just society has to accept officially the ideologies and beliefs of everyone, but rather that there must be equality of all citizens before the law.

Therefore, while it is true that the main precepts of humanist morality are innate in all human beings, some of the most advanced precepts, such as the empathy principle and the moral requirements of democratic living have to be learned. Specifically, there needs to be teaching and reinforcement of such basic humanist principles of living at an early age. This does not guarantee a perfect world, but it can prevent the worst incidences of bad behavior against humanity. That's why, locally, when someone doesn't want to follow basic moral rules of conduct, society has to devise a social mechanism of protection against his or her negative behavior. Killers, robbers, liars, torturers, cheaters, and psychopaths of all kinds have to be confronted, educated, treated and, if need be, brought to justice. Similarly, internationally, the world needs functioning global institutions that can facilitate global justice and global morality.

In the context of religious morality, punishment for bad behavior is twofold: a mythic eternal afterlife punishment and a temporal banishment from society. With humanistic morality, there cannot be question of a hypothetical afterlife system of justice; the only reality that counts is the physical reality of our world and the real reward of living a peaceful and rewarding life. This is the path we all should follow.

CONCLUSION

FOR A BETTER AND MORE MORAL FUTURE

The meaning of life is not to be discovered only after death in some hidden, mysterious realm; on the contrary, it can be found by eating the succulent fruit of the Tree of Life and by living in the here and now as fully and creatively as we can.
—Paul Kurtz, professor and humanist

The greatest derangement of the mind is to believe in something because one wishes it to be so.
—Louis Pasteur (1822–1895)

A mind once expanded can never return to its original dimensions.
—Anne Hathaway (1556–1623)

The ten basic humanist commandments espoused in this book constitute the general framework of a universal philosophy for all human beings. They can be used as a universal moral code that we believe to be superior to any existing religion-based moral standard.

Rational humanism offers such a superior universal moral code. When people say they believe in religion, they usually mean they believe in a moral standard for themselves, their children, and society in general. Obviously, most people prefer to live in a moral world than in an amoral or immoral one. However, although we should have respect for tradition and for religions in their philosophical aspect, for their ethical underpinnings, and for their historical contributions, they should no longer constitute the principle source of moral standards necessary for survival on this planet.

As we have demonstrated throughout this book, most religion-based moral codes are fundamentally flawed. First, because they are group selective in their application; second, because they often establish a disjunction between individual morality and public morality, the latter being less commanding than the former; and third, because they encourage exclusion and division between people, when they are not overtly xenophobic, sometimes going as far as to demonize others under the subversive notions of eternal heaven and eternal hell, which encourage violence, persecutions, and wars.

One is not obliged to subscribe to such flawed moral systems. There is an alternative to the absence of moral ethics and to the flawed or incomplete religion-based moral standards, and that is the code for global ethics derived from rational humanism. Children all over the world can be raised and taught within this universal humanist moral approach in order to live a more fruitful life. They can learn how to exercise better control over their selfish instincts and develop the art of caring and of living harmoniously with other people.[1]

Even though it would be futile to search for a perfect moral system, humanity has no other choice than to adopt the most civilized rules of private and collective behavior that can best guarantee its chances of survival. From the Super Golden Rule of humanist morality, it follows that people have a natural right to human dignity and equality, and this should be the fundamental principle governing relations between individuals and among nations. This is the first and most fundamental humanist rule of ethics.

It follows also that all people have a right to be respected in their physical integrity. This is the second humanist rule. No person, in any capacity, has the right to take anyone else's life. Similarly, a person's possessions—unless acquired unjustly—and means of survival are also to be respected.

Even though humans must live in society to survive, this does not mean that personal freedom has to be sacrificed in favor of social uniformity and general conformity. Provided that society's survival and functioning are not threatened in a substantial way, individuals, whether they belong to a minority or to the majority, have the fundamental right to develop their own thoughts, their own philosophies, their own opinions, their own beliefs, their own religions, and their own approaches to life and to living. Humanists should always show tolerance to other people and to their choices. This is the third humanist rule.

The marriage of reciprocity and empathy lies at the core of humanistic morality. To sympathize with others while expecting that others feel sympathy for ourselves is the foundation of human morality. Such an outlook on life translates into the fourth humanist rule, that we should all have a willingness to share and aid other people. Is also signifies that material and spiritual domination over others should be avoided. This is the fifth humanist rule.

True individual freedom and contentment are reached when each individual is able to think independently, without the crutch of absolutist religious dogmas. Real freedom comes from knowledge and the feeling that one can understand the Universe that surrounds us. That is the sixth humanist rule.

As the human population increases in numbers and as the Earth seems to be shrinking, new ways to live in harmony with each other and with the environment must be discovered. To conserve and respect the environment for us and for future generations has become a new requirement for survival. This is the seventh humanist rule.

However, even before humankind destroys the environment, it has the capacity for self-destruction, if a new universal morality is not soon adopted. Indeed, the spread and proliferation of inhumane nuclear armaments has created the greatest threat to survival that humankind has ever faced. According to the humanist way of thinking, humanity itself is a community of brothers and sisters, and to wage wars against each other is the epitome of immorality and stupidity. Wars must be avoided and outlawed. This is the eighth humanist rule.

Human progress requires a climate of freedom and liberty in order to flourish, and appropriate institutions must provide the necessary framework. Individual countries should be more than open-sky prisons. All power comes from the people and no one—neither secular nor religious—can usurp the right to govern without the express consent of the people. There is no other system better suited to realizing the joint objective of social order and individual freedom more efficiently than constitutional democracy. Similarly, there is no other economic system better equipped to generate prosperity for the greatest number while preserving individual freedom than economic democracy. Therefore, the establishment of political and economic democracy is the ninth humanist rule.[2]

Finally, as each individual progresses in life, the attainment of maximum physical and intellectual autonomy is closely associated with the quality and quantity of education available, especially in the formative years. Many of the social and economic problems prevailing in the world today can be traced back to insufficient or inappropriate educational training for the individual. The right to education is a fundamental humanist right, and no child, wherever he or she lives, should be deprived of access to education and training, for financial or other reasons. General access to education and learning is the tenth humanist rule both for the individual and for society, any society.

On a global ethical level, it is our contention that the world must free itself from the yolk of ancient religions if we want to avoid being destroyed by them. Indeed, parallel to the humanist message of this book, there is also the view that if people want to be genuinely moral, on a personal and global basis, they must rid themselves of the old, narrow religious morality.

It is a dismal historical fact that organized religions, especially the more politicized and proselytizing ones, have, for centuries and even millennia, supplied the intellectual and ideological support for innumerable crimes against humanity, while aligning themselves time and again with totalitarian and oppressive political regimes. That is why they must accept a shared responsibility for the human disasters and exactions that have beset humanity over the ages, in the form of wars of aggression, religion-inspired massacres, executions and persecutions, genocides, pillages, rapes and murders, as well as slavery and exploitations of all kinds. Religious morality has been, at best, a mixed blessing for humanity.

What does this mean for the future? Presently, with the spread of nuclear armaments, the world is on a path toward self-destruction. It is time to stop, think, and change course, before it is too late. Morally, it all boils down to whether we have enough courage and foresight to adopt a better moral code, and whether we have enough confidence in the human intellect and human conscience to build a better future, a more moral future for all, and a more ethical humanist civilization, in harmony with nature. Obviously, humanists, and all those who adopt the humanist worldview and who share the vision of the common brotherhood of all humankind, believe so. For all of us, therefore, in the future, as in the past, the greatest human challenge will be to see to it that the power of reason and science triumphs over the ravages of superstition and fanaticism.

ANNEX:
COMPARATIVE MORAL COMMANDMENTS

MOSES' TEN COMMANDMENTS

Exodus 20: 1–17 (ca. 1200 BC)

1. You shall have no other gods before me.
2. You shall not make for yourself an idol.
3. You shall not make wrongful use of the name of the Lord your God.
4. Remember the Sabbath, and keep it holy.
5. Honor your father and your mother.
6. You shall not kill.
7. You shall not commit adultery.
8. You shall not steal.
9. You shall not bear false witness against your neighbor.
10. You shall not covet your neighbor's wife [neighbor's house, etc.]

JESUS CHRIST'S COMMANDMENTS

Matthew 19: 16–22

1. Do not kill.
2. Do not commit adultery.
3. Do not steal.
4. Do not give false testimony.
5. Honor your father and mother.
6. Love your neighbor as yourself.

THE TEN PRINCIPLES FOR A GLOBAL RATIONAL HUMANISM

The Code for Global Ethics

1. DIGNITY: Proclaim the natural dignity and inherent worth of all human beings.
2. RESPECT: Respect the life and property of others.
3. TOLERANCE: Be tolerant of others' beliefs and lifestyles.
4. SHARING: Share with those who are less fortunate and assist those who are in need of help.
5. NO DOMINATION: Do not dominate through lies or otherwise.
6. NO SUPERSTITION: Rely on reason, logic, and science to understand the Universe and to solve life's problems.
7. CONSERVATION: Conserve and improve the Earth's natural environment.
8. NO WAR: Resolve differences and conflicts without resorting to war or violence.
9. DEMOCRACY: Rely on political and economic democracy to organize human affairs.
10. EDUCATION: Develop one's intelligence and talents through education and effort.

NOTES

PREFACE: TOWARD A NEW PLANETARY HUMANISM

1. See *Humanist Manifesto 2000* (Prometheus Books, Amherst, NY: 2000), chapter 4.

2. *Humanist Manifesto I and II* (Prometheus Books, Amherst, NY: 1973).

INTRODUCTION: THE ETHICAL INFRASTRUCTURE OF EVERY SOCIETY

1. For a comprehensive history of the development of the term "humanism" and its influences over the ages, see Tony Davies, *Humanism.* In the United States, one may want to consult the works of the great free-thinker Robert G. Ingersoll (1833–1899): *The Works of Robert Ingersoll,* vols. 1–12.

2. For a succinct view of humanism as a philosophy of life, see Corliss Lamont, *The Philosophy of Humanism.*

3. There are two recent examples of such moral ambiguity. The first is personified by Osama bin Laden, the self-proclaimed religious leader of the al-Qaeda terrorist movement, who harbors two moralities simultaneously: one drawn from the Qur'an enjoining him "not to kill," and another one—also inspired by the Qur'an—that says that it is good to kill certain innocent people "for the cause of God (Allah)." The second example is the self-styled deeply religious former American president, George W. Bush, who presum-

ably considered himself religiously moral after ordering an illegal and unprovoked war of aggression against Iraq in 2003, an onslaught that resulted in the killing of many hundreds of thousands of people—men, women, and children.

4. For theories of animal ethics, see S. Armstrong, ed., *The Animal Ethics Reader* and Mark Rowlands, *Animals Like Us*. For a book that changed our way of looking at animals, see Peter Singer, *Animal Liberation*.

5. For studies about how humans have an intuitive sense of right and wrong in their brains, see D. J. Linden, *The Accidental Mind: How Brain Evolution Has Given Us Love, Memory, Dreams, and God*. Also M. R. Trimble, *The Soul in the Brain: The Cerebral Basis of Language, Art, and Belief*.

6. The idea that man has naturally become more moral over time is derived from evolutionary ethics. *Evolutionary ethics* is the study of ethics from a biological point of view, rather than from a purely philosophical point of view. The biological explanation of morality states that the moral sense or conscience of humans stems from progressive natural evolution and natural selection, as more intellectual and more moral species displaced less intellectual and less moral species over time. Thus, moral values are essentially human values. See Charles Darwin, *The Descent of Man, and Selection in Relation to Sex* (1871). Also Edward O. Wilson, *Consilience: The Unity of Knowledge*.

7. For a study of natural empathy and morality, see Michael Slote, *The Ethics of Care and Empathy*.

8. For a book about the science of morality and moral judgments, see Marc D. Hauser, *Moral Minds: How Nature Designed Our Universal Sense of Right and Wrong*.

9. For practical advice on how to find happiness and meaning in life, see Jonathan Haidt, *The Happiness Hypothesis: Finding Modern Truth in Ancient Wisdom*.

10. For a religious approach to global ethics, see Hans Küng, *A Global Ethic for Global Politics and Economics*.

11. In the last third of the eighteenth century, the rational humanist ideas of Seneca the Younger (ca. 4 BCE–65 CE), of Marcus Aurelius (121–180), of Erasmus (1467–1536) and of Baruch Spinoza (1632–1677) were reinterpreted and developed by the German philosopher Immanuel Kant (1724–1804). Kant did not use the word "humanism," but his moral doctrine is closely associated with rational humanism. In fact, the first one to use the word humanism, a word derived from the fifth-century Italian term *uminista*, which was used to designate a teacher or student of classic literature, was the German philosopher F. J. Niethammer. According to the

Kantian principle of rational humanism, there exists a fundamental relationship between rationality and human morality.

12. For a related Asian and international basis for universal ethics, see Eiji Uehiro, *Practical Ethics for Our Time* and Carl B. Becker, *Asian and Jungian Views of Ethics.*

13. Biologist James D. Watson, one of the main researchers behind the discovery of the structure of DNA, defines humanism as "a system of thoughts and actions in which man's interests, values, and dignity are paramount." We subscribe to Watson's view that in the present, as for millennia to come, the dominant human figure will be Darwin, not Christ or Muhammed, because, "Darwin has identified what we are and has shown that human beings are a product of evolution and are not a predetermined product of a supernatural entity." See James Watson, "Biotechnology and Humanism," conference on intellectual property and living matter, Paris.

14. To understand why the belief in gods remains strong, see A. Newberg, E. D'Aquili, and V. Rause, *Why God Won't Go Away: Brain Science and the Biology of Belief.*

15. See his essay, *The Humanism of Existentialism.*

16. For an attack of traditional views of morality and for the proposition that there is no universal moral code, see Friedrich Nietzsche, *Beyond Good and Evil*, a book first published in 1886.

17. If we were to compare two US presidents, who would seriously say that enlightened secularist Thomas Jefferson (1743–1826) was less moral than deeply religious George W. Bush?

18. For various studies and ideas on the relationship between human morality and organized religions, see: William K. Frankena, "Is Morality Logically Dependent on Religion?" *Religion and Morality: A Collection of Essays*, edited by Gene Outka and J. P. Reeder Jr.; E. D. Klemke, "On the Alleged Inseparability of Religion and Morality," *Religious Studies*; Kai Nielsen, *Ethics without God*; Alasdair MacIntyre and Paul Ricoeur, *The Religious Significance of Atheism*; George Mavrodes, "Religion and the Queerness of Morality," *Rationality, Religious Belief and Moral Commitment: New Essays in the Philosophy of Religion*, edited by Robert Audi and W. Wainwright; Patrick Nowell-Smith, "Religion and Morality," *Encyclopedia of Philosophy*, edited by Paul Edwards, pp. 150–58; Robert Young, "Theism and Morality," *Canadian Journal of Philosophy* 7, no. 2:341–51; James Rachels, "God and Human Attitudes," *Religious Studies* 7:325–37; and Philip Quinn, "Religious Obedience and Moral Autonomy," *Religious Studies* 11:265–81.

Here is a partial list of philosophers throughout history who have developed a moral idealism and an ethic without religion: Confucius (551–479 BCE): "Do not do to others what you do not want done to yourself"; Protagoras (485–410 BCE): "Man is the measure of everything"; Democrites (460–370 BCE): "Divinities are produced by the human reason"; Epicurius (341–270 BCE); Lucretius (98–55 BCE); Baruch Spinoza (1632–1677); Jean Meslier (1664–1729); David Hume (1711–1776); Immanuel Kant (1724–1804); Arthur Schopenhauer (1788–1860); Auguste Comte (1798–1857); Ludwig Feuerbach (1804–1872); John Stuart Mill (1806–1873); Friedrich Nietzsche (1844–1900); Sigmund Freud (1856–1939); Emile Durkheim (1858–1917); Bertrand Russell (1872–1970); Jean Rostand (1894–1977); Jean-Paul Sartre (1905–1980); Albert Camus (1913–1960); Hans Küng (1928–present); André Comte-Sponville (1952–present); Michel Onfray (1959–present).

For a repudiation of the false and self-serving beliefs that without a god or organized religions human life is meaningless and that there is no natural human morality, see Erik J. Wielenberg, *Value and Virtue in a Godless Universe.* See also, Erik J. Wielenberg, *God and the Reach of Reason.*

19. For arguments on why, in an age of weapons of mass destruction, religious beliefs are a hazard of great proportions, see Sam Harris, *The End of Faith: Religion, Terror, and the Future of Reason.*

20. The nuclear bombing of the civilian populations of Hiroshima and Nagasaki, during the summer of 1945, established a terrible precedent. At that time, a moral choice was made by the Truman administration, which put the United States in danger of one day being the target of a similar attack. No government before, and no government since, has taken on the heavy responsibility of massacring enemy noncombatants with nuclear weapons of mass destruction. On August 6, 1945, the first nuclear bomb was dropped over the Japanese city of Hiroshima and claimed 70,000 lives. Within two weeks, about 90,000 were dead and the final count has been put as high as 200,000 people. On August 9, 1945, a second American-made nuclear bomb was dropped on Nagasaki, killing 74,800 more. See Sherwood Ross, "From Guernica to Hiroshima: How America Reversed Its Policy on Bombing Civilians," *Humanist* (July/August 2005).

ONE. DIGNITY AND EQUALITY

1. In Kant's formulation of his *categorical imperative*, it is stated that we should never act in such a way that we treat human beings as means or

instruments, only and always as ends in themselves. See Immanuel Kant *Groundwork for the Metaphysics of Morals.*

2. The universal altruistic "golden rule" or *reciprocity principle* of morality dates at least as far back as Confucius (ca. 551–479 BCE), and possibly much further, in different philosophies as distinct as Zoroastrianism, Buddhism, and Judaism. Because Confucius's teachings emphasize human excellence with the purpose of searching for the greater good and of building the ideal society, without resorting to deities or abstract principles, it can be said that Confucianism is a form of Chinese humanism. Just as with rational humanism, Confucius's moral system was based upon empathy and understanding others, rather than divinely ordained rules.

3. Here is an example of amorality on the part of a fanatically religious person:

> In 2006, an extremist Israeli rabbi, Yousef Falay, who lives at the Yitzhar settlement on illegally seized Palestinian land in the northern part of the West Bank, wrote an article in a Zionist magazine under the title "Ways of War," in which he called for the killing of all Palestinian males refusing to flee their country, describing his idea as the practical way to ensure the nonexistence of the Palestinian race. That was his practical way to solve the Palestinian problem.
> [See "Jewish Rabbi Calls for Extermination of all Palestinian Males," *International Middle East Media Center* (IMEMC), September 16, 2006.]

4. Exodus 22: 18: "Thou shalt not suffer a witch to live." For an apologetic presentation of the values that one can find in the Bible, see Thomas Cahill, *The Gifts of the Jews, How a Tribe of Desert Nomads Changed the Way Everyone Thinks and Feels.*

5. The Second Lateran Council, in 1139, decreed that all marriages of priests were null and void and that existing marriages had to be severed before a man could be ordained to the priesthood. See A. W. R. Sipe, *A Secret World: Sexuality and the Search for Celibacy,* Brunner/Masel, 1990.

6. Other religions have promoted celibacy. Some Buddhist groups, for example, such as the Jains, believe that celibacy is absolutely necessary to achieve nirvana or moksha. Conversely, Judaism and Islam do not have celibate traditions. Similarly, Christian traditions following the Protestant Reformation almost universally allow clerical marriage.

7. Under such laws, in the case of rape or adultery for example, the woman had no recourse, but the father or husband could receive compensation. Other ancient societies were more socially advanced. For instance, in ancient Egyptian society, women and men were considered equal under the law.

8. There are other practices that the Bible accepts as normal, such as genocide, torturing prisoners, raping female prisoners of war, executing religious minorities, burning prostitutes alive, and so on.

9. Jefferson Davis, "Inaugural Address as Provisional President of the Confederacy," Montgomery, AL, February 18, 1861, *Confederate States of America*, Congressional Journal, 1:64–66.

10. John T. Noonan Jr., *A Church that Can and Cannot Change: The Development of Catholic Moral Teaching*, 2005. In 1993, in his encyclical *Veritatis Splendor*, Pope John Paul II extended Vatican II's views on social evils: "homicide, genocide, abortion, euthanasia and voluntary suicide…mutilation, physical and mental torture and attempts to coerce the spirit; whatever is offensive to human dignity, such as subhuman living conditions, arbitrary imprisonment, deportation, slavery, prostitution and trafficking in women and children; degrading conditions of work which treat laborers as mere instruments of profit, and not as free responsible persons." Where Vatican II had called such practices shameful (*probra*), Pope John Paul II called them "intrinsically evil."

11. V. A. Gunasekara, *Essays on Islamic Theory and Practice Considered from a Humanist Perspective.*

12. A research report written by sociologists of religion at Baylor University concluded that people's views of God reveal their personal values and politics. For instance, the more conservative Americans believe in an authoritarian god (31.4 percent) or in a benevolent god (23 percent) who intervenes in human affairs. The more liberal among Americans rather believe either in a critical god (16 percent) or in a distant god (24.4 percent) who does not intervene directly in human affairs. See: "American Piety in the Twenty-First Century: New Insights to the Depths and Complexity of Religion in the US," *Selected findings*, Baylor Institute for Studies of Religion, Baylor University, September 11, 2006.

13. See Rochel Yaffe, *Rambam: The Story of Rabbi Moshe Ben Maimon.*

14. The expansionist editor John L. O'Sullivan coined the famous expression in 1845, when he wrote of "our manifest destiny to overspread the continent allotted by Providence for the free development of our yearly multiplying millions." See John Mack Faragher, *Manifest Destiny and Mission in American History.*

15. See R. Tremblay, *The New American Empire*; Robert Jewett and John Shelton Lawrence, *Captain America and the Crusade against Evil: The Dilemma of Zealous Nationalism*; Anthony D. Smith, *Chosen Peoples: Sacred Sources of National Identity*; Conrad Cherry, ed., *God's New Israel: Religious Interpretations of American Destiny*; Ernest Lee Tuveson, *Redeemer Nation: The Idea of America's Millennial Role*; Russel B. Nye, *This Almost Chosen People*; A. K. Weinberg, *Manifest Destiny: A Study of Nationalist Expansionism in American History*. It is possible that since September 11, 2001, a new type of "holy war" has begun. This time, the new crusade with strong religious overtones would seem to pit fundamentalist Christian America and its allies against political Islam and the Islamist al-Qaeda terrorist organization. On September 16, 2001, then President George W. Bush set the tone when he said, *"This crusade, this war on terrorism, is gonna take awhile."*

16. See Jean Bricmont, *Humanitarian Imperialism: Using Human Rights to Sell War.*

Two. Respect Life and Property

1. To understand how an economy need not be centrally planned but is molded from the bottom up by an invisible hand, see Adam Smith, *The Wealth of Nations*.

2. There are limitations in the Bible (Old Testament) to prevent ongoing economic exploitation, excessive wealth inequality, and too much concentration in property ownership. Every fifty years, according to the Jubilee principle, it is recommended that there be a cancellation of old debts in order for the poor to regain some property and for the slaves to be free. Leviticus 25, 810: "Ye shall hallow the fiftieth year, and proclaim liberty throughout the land unto all its inhabitants; and ye shall return every man unto his possession, and ye shall return every man unto his family." From a purely economic point of view, such a situation of income and wealth inequalities can be Pareto efficient, in the sense that no one person could be made better off without making some other person worse off through government intervention. However, if such inequalities threaten to undermine democracy through the excessive concentration of economic and political power, social and political considerations would overrule the narrow definition of common good. Political democracy and large income and wealth inequalities are contradictory.

3. On these issues, see Robert Cook-Deegan, *The Gene Wars: Science, Pol-*

itics, and the Human Genome; James D. Watson, *The Double Helix: A Personal Account of the Discovery of the Structure of DNA*; Kevin Davies, *Cracking the Genome*; J. Craig Venter, *A Life Decoded: My Genome, My Life.*

4. See T. Lister, *Chemistry and the Human Genome.*

5. Harvard University president and economist Larry Summers in Thomas Friedman, *Longitudes and Attitudes: The World in the Age of Terrorism*, p. 273.

6. For books on euthanasia and the right to die with dignity, see Derek Humphry, *Final Exit: The Practicalities of Self-Deliverance and Assisted Suicide for the Dying*; Gerald Dworkin, R. G. Frey, and Sissela Bok, *Euthanasia and Physician-Assisted Suicide (For and Against)*; Barry Rosenfeld, *Assisted Suicide and the Right to Die: The Interface of Social Science, Public Policy, and Medical Ethic*; Ian Dowbiggin, *A Merciful End: The Euthanasia Movement in Modern America*; Timothy E. Quill, *Physician-Assisted Dying: The Case for Palliative Care and Patient Choice.*

7. See Stanley K. Henshaw et al., *The Incidence of Abortion Worldwide.*

8. Most people have rejected the religious fight against the use of contraception. For instance, a vast majority of Catholics around the world ignore the church's teaching on contraception matters, as presented in Pope Paul VI's 1968 encyclical *Humanae Vitae*. This encyclical forbade the use of contraceptive methods, even among married couples. See Damon Linker, *The Theocons: Secular America under Siege*, pp. 200–201.

9. There are three main approaches to morality: virtue or integrity ethics, which focuses on the moral character of an individual (see Aristotle); consequential or empirical ethics, which focuses on the consequences or results of one's acts (see David Hume); and principled ethics or ethics based on rationality, which focuses on universal principles that apply to all people, everywhere, and all the times (see Immanuel Kant).

THREE. TOLERANCE: THE EMPATHY PRINCIPLE

1. For an analysis of the central role that empathy plays in the moral development of children, see Martin L. Hoffman, *Empathy and Moral Development: Implications for Caring and Justice.*

2. For a book about a secular system of "provisional ethics" that allows for tolerance and diversity, see Michael Shermer, *The Science of Good and Evil: Why People Cheat, Gossip, Care, Share, and Follow the Golden Rule.* Also, for a book about developments in the field of evolutionary psychology and the question of utilitarian morality, see Robert Wright, *The Moral Animal.*

3. According to Immanuel Kant, a good moral rule should satisfy the

condition of universalisability, that is to say that it could consistently be willed as a law that everyone ought to obey. The humanist Super Golden Rule meets this criterion.

4. For a challenge to the myth that *multiculturalism* is always good for immigrants or to their welcoming societies, see Ruud Koopmans, Paul Statham, Marco Giugni, and Florence Passy, *Contested Citizenship: Immigration and Cultural Diversity.* In Canada, see Neil Bissoondath, *Innocence of Age.*

5 Salman Rushdie, in a speech at the New York Society for Ethical Culture, October 11, 2006.

6. Abdulla al-Tarekee, "A Muslim's Relations with Non-Muslims— Enmity or Friendship," Institute for Islamic and Arabic Sciences in America, p. 28. See also Karl Ericson, "Creation of Delusions," *International Bulletin of Political Psychology* 15, no. 2 (September 5, 2003). On spiritual delusions, see Charles MacKay, *Extraordinary Popular Delusions: The Madness of Crowds.*

7. The issue of ostensible religious behavior in public has been solved in the following manner in the Mexican Constitution (Article 24) "Every [person] is free to pursue the religious belief that best suits him, and to practice its ceremonies, devotions or cults, as long as they do not constitute a crime. Congress cannot dictate laws that establish or abolish any given religion. Ordinarily, all religious acts will be practiced in temples, and those that extraordinarily are practiced outside temples must adhere to law."

Every society must find what is acceptable and what is not acceptable in public religious manifestations and in the public display of religious symbols.

FOUR. SHARING

1. John Rawls, *A Theory of Justice.* According to the *maximin* principle of redistributive justice, a just society is one that adopts an economic and social system that is economically efficient and that maximizes the welfare of the least advantaged person. Economic and social inequalities, to be tolerated, must be beneficial to all and generate the best possible outcome for the poorest members of society. As a corollary, economic optimality requires that the state promote equal opportunity for all because economic and social inequalities, which tend to become cumulative over time, hinder social mobility, prevent new talents from blossoming, and are detrimental to innovation.

2. In economic theory, the term *moral hazard* refers to the possibility that the redistribution of income or of risk changes people's behavior in a perverse way. Kenneth Arrow introduced the term into economic theory in 1963.

3. Julian Wolpert, *What Charity Can and Cannot Do.*

4. See Derek Croxton and Anuschka Tischer, *The Peace of Westphalia: A Historical Dictionary.*

5. In 2000, in the United States alone, there were 47,000 tax-free foundations. See Randall G. Holcombe, *Writing Off Ideas: Taxation, Foundations, and Philanthropy in America.*

6. For example, if we assume a worldwide level of taxable annual consumption expenditures equal to $30 trillion, a small consumption tax of 0.001 would generate a fiscal revenue equal to $30 billion.

FIVE. NO DOMINATION, NO EXPLOITATION

1. For questions asked throughout history about the nature of sex and love, see Alan Soble, *The Philosophy of Sex and Love: An Introduction.*

2. The Roman Catholic Church instituted the sale of indulgences in the early sixteenth century as a means to raise funds to build cathedrals. People could purchase forgiveness of past sins by handing over money or possessions to the Church or to its institutions. For a modern view of the religion-based so-called capital sins (greed, anger, envy, gluttony, lust, pride, sloth), initially proposed by (Saint) Augustine of Hippo, see Aviad Kleinberg and Susan Emanuel, *Seven Deadly Sins: A Very Partial List.*

3. It is also gaining strength in Brazil, where Pentecostal Christians number twenty-four million.

4. For a report on how the new breed of televangelists corrupts the American political system, see Sarah Posner, *God's Profits: Faith, Fraud, and the Republican Crusade for Values Voters.*

5. Indeed, some people take their Bible seriously. They still worship the Golden Idol (Exodus 32:1–4). Similarly, since many churches contain large amounts of gold, especially in Europe, those who attend these churches can be said to worship the Golden Calf.

6. To understand why some people may be irrational about money matters, see Michael Shermer, *The Mind of the Market: Compassionate Apes, Competitive Humans, and Other Tales from Evolutionary Economics.*

7. Paul Zane Pilzer, *God Wants You to Be Rich.*

8. Peter H. Stone, *Heist: Superlobbyist Jack Abramoff, His Republican Allies, and the Buying of Washington.*

SIX. NO SUPERSTITION

1. Following Emmanuel Kant (in his *Critique of Pure Reason*), British scientist Richard Dawkins has refuted the three main deductive arguments for the alleged existence of an eternal god: the *ontological argument* (God is perfect and it is more perfect to exist than not to exist); the *cosmological argument* (the Universe must have an external cause); and the creationist *design argument* (the Universe is suitable to intelligent life and this requires a purposive cosmic designer). For a humorous refutation of twelve of the most common arguments for the existence of an all-powerful god, see John Allen Paulos, *Irreligion: A Mathematician Explains Why the Arguments for God Just Don't Add Up.* Also, see Richard Dawkins, *The God Delusion.* Similarly, see J. L. Mackie, *The Miracle of Theism: Arguments For and Against the Existence of God.* For an excellent presentation of why there is no evidence for the existence of God, see Victor J. Stenger, *God: The Failed Hypothesis.* Also, for a philosophic attack upon the rationality of religious belief, see David Hume, *Dialogues Concerning Natural Religion.*

2. To be *delusional* is to harbor false certitudes, even after they have been demonstrated to be contrary to reality and proven false. A *belief* is a knowledge or conviction with a doubt. When a belief becomes a certitude, it has the possibility of leading to delusional thinking. For example, if one believes that the Sun revolves around Earth, and this is proven false and contrary to reality, yet one persists in the false belief, then that is delusional, the result of losing contact with reality. A certain number of delusional traditions that some religions have practiced to appease their gods, such as the rite of human sacrifice, have by now—thankfully—been abandoned. For a history of religious and ritual killings, see Nigel Davies, *Human Sacrifice in History and Today.*

3. E. Bleuler, *Textbook in Psychiatry.*

4. B. Spinoza, *The Letters*, trans. S. Shirley, with introductions by S. Barfore, L. Rice, and J. Adler.

5. See Adam Smith, *The Theory of Moral Sentiments.*

6. See Adam Smith, *The Wealth of Nations* (1776):

> The teachers of [religion], in the same manner as other teachers, may either depend altogether for their subsistence upon the voluntary contributions of their hearers; or they may derive it from some other fund to which the law of their country may entitle them... Their exertion, their zeal and industry, are likely to be much greater

in the former situation than the latter. In this respect the teachers of
new religions have always had a considerable advantage in attacking
those ancient and established systems of which the clergy, reposing
themselves upon their benefices, had neglected to keep up the
fervor of the faith and devotion in the great body of the people.

...Such a clergy, [when attacked by a set of popular and bold,
though perhaps stupid and ignorant enthusiasts]...have no other
resource than to call upon the magistrate to persecute, destroy, or
drive out, their adversaries, as disturbers of the public peace.

7. There is possibly no other country in the world where this is done on a
grander scale than in the United States, where legions of evangelical radio stations and television networks mix "faith-based" news, right-wing politics, and
talk shows that exert a tremendous influence on American culture. The end of
the twentieth century and the beginning of the twenty-first probably represent
the golden age of such propagandist activities. As the Internet, an active
medium for distributing and for obtaining information, gradually becomes the
main communication instrument in the decades to come, radio and television
will lose some of their propaganda efficiency. Religious propagandists should
then also lose their current stranglehold on American politics. See Mariah
Blake, "Stations of the Cross," *Columbia Journalism Review*, (May/June 2005).

8. See John Campbell Oman, *Cults, Customs and Superstitions of India:
Being a Revised and Enlarged Edition of "Indian Life, Religious and Social."*

9. Anyone who believes in the religious idea of an afterlife or in any
supernatural or paranormal activity, and can prove and demonstrate their
existence, can claim a prize of $1,000,000 from the James Randi Educational
Foundation (JREF) by going to the following Web site: http://www.randi
.org/. To this day, no one has passed the tests and claimed the prize.

10. Religions that advance the idea that each individual's mind, spirit, or
soul is immortal and survives the body's death have the burden of proof to
establish why something that appears at the birth of a person would not disappear at the death of that person.

11. Joseph Weber with Peter Coy, "Economists Are Getting Religion,"
Business Week, December 6, 2004.

12. About fifty thousand years ago, the human mind experienced a
sudden expansion of cognitive abilities, placing humans in a unique position
in the animal kingdom.

13. Evolutionary psychology can explain why religious belief seems to
be universal among *Homo sapiens*. See Richard Dawkins, *The God Delusion*.

14. For a view of such sociological developments, see Barbara J. King, *Evolving God, A Provocative View on the Origins of Religion.*

15. For a study of the role of mass violence in politics, see E. Staub, *The Roots of Evil: The Origins of Genocide and Other Group Violence.* For a study of how biological and social forces shape many of our ethical beliefs, see Arthur G. Miller, *The Social Psychology of Good and Evil.*

16. Max Weber, *The Protestant Ethic and the Spirit of Capitalism.*

17. For a thesis proposing that in the past anti-Semitism has in fact been a positive force in Jewish life, see Dan Cohn-Sherbok, *The Paradox of Anti-Semitism.*

18. Different religions have different and contradictory explanations of reality. For example, the three main monotheist religions—Christianity, Islam, and Judaism—have contradictory beliefs in regards to the historical figure of Jesus of Nazareth. Christian churches profess that Jesus Christ is God incarnate; Islam considers Jesus an inspired prophet but no match for their prophet, Muhammad; and, for Judaism, Jesus Christ was a sort of impostor because he wrongly claimed to be the Messiah, and his followers falsely ascribed to him the title of Messiah. See Daniel C. Dennett, *Breaking the Spell: Religion as a Natural Phenomenon.*

19. The average life span of humans is around eighty years, while it is about seventy years for the elephant. When they age, elephants suffer diseases similar to humans. They are prone to cardiovascular diseases and age-related arthritis.

20. For a presentation of how myth-making and religious rituals have played a central role in the development of the human species and of how religious traditions have been transmitted from one generation to the next, see Roy A. Rappaport, *Ritual and Religion in the Making of Humanity.*

21. See Mark Twain, *The War Prayer* (published posthumously in 1916).

22. When children believe in Santa Claus or the Tooth Fairy—that is, until they reach ages seven or eight—they are predisposed to magical thinking, believing that wishing can make things come true. Therefore, when they are taught to pray to obtain something, just by magic, such practice is only the continuation of a frame of mind that children had when they believed in magic. In this sense, praying is tantamount to magical thinking.

23. The three small gravestones of Captain Collier's boys can be seen today in the cemetery of Marco Island, Forida. This story was reported in the *Marco Eagle,* January 3, 2007, 11A.

24. See Felix Adler, *Life and Destiny: or Thoughts from the Ethical Lectures of Felix Adler.*

25. People can actually develop a form of personal or cultural dependency upon various religious practices. This is clearly the case, for example, for different rituals or rites of passage (births, weddings, deaths, etc.), where the ceremonial side of events acquires a symbolic value. See Roy A. Rappaport, *Ritual and Religion in the Making of Humanity.*

26. Becker's prognosis for humanity is built upon the premise that we are "stuck with" human nature and that it cannot be changed. This premise is flawed. For an alternative, visit http://www.actualfreedom.com.au. See Ernest Becker, *The Denial of Death.*

27. In the early twenty-first century, it was truly amazing that three individuals with great public responsibility all seemed to have had frequent conversations with God. Osama bin Laden said, "I ask God to help us champion His religion and continue jihad for His sake until we meet Him and He is satisfied with us. And He can do so. Praise be to Almighty God" (November 14, 2002). Mahmoud Ahmadinejad said, "I often connect with Allah and he has assured me that the infidels will never be able to overpower the faithful" (October 20, 2005). And then US president George W. Bush dared to say: "I trust God speaks through me. Without that, I couldn't do my job" (July 9, 2004).

28. See Max Weber, *Economy and Society.*

29. To see why there are sometimes hidden incentives and an unexpected logic behind some people's seemingly irrational behavior, see Tim Harford, *The Logic of Life: The Rational Economics of an Irrational World.* Also, Rodney Stark, Laurence R. Iannaccone, and Roger Finke, "Religion, Science, and Rationality," *American Economic Review Papers and Proceedings*, May 1996, pp. 433–37.

30. The human brain is an organ that contains some one hundred billion neurons or nerve cells, which are capable of electrical and chemical communication with tens of thousands of other nerve cells. It is the center of human consciousness and of mental activity. See Neil A. Campbell and Jane B. Reece, *Biology.* See also John McCrone and John Gribbin, *How the Brain Works.*

31. REM means "rapid eye movement." The REM stage of sleep is one of five stages of sleep in humans. It is marked by rapid eye movement and by extensive physiological changes, such as accelerated respiration, increased brain activity, and muscle relaxation.

32. See Cornelia Dean, "Science of the Soul? 'I Think, Therefore I Am' Is Losing Force," *New York Times*, June 26, 2007.

33. It can be argued that there is only one monotheistic religion in the world: Judaism/Christianity/Islam. Indeed, these closely related religions

worship the same deity and have similar moral codes. All three have adopted the flawed concept of a dichotomy between the human body and the human mind, and all three have built entire moral structures on this shaky ground, while claiming to possess the absolute truth. Asiatic religions (Hinduism, Buddhism, Confucianism, Taoism, as well as several others) are more practical. They are essentially secular, nonorganized forms of spiritual philosophies, systems, or schools of thought and traditions, relying on the principle of self-responsibility and self-improvement, using such techniques as meditation, relaxation, physical self-awareness, harmony, and human development.

34. According to research in neuroscience, moral behaviors originate from three areas in the human brain: the amygdala, the inhibitory networks, and the mirror-neuron system. See Laurence R. Tancredi, *Hardwired Behavior: What Neuroscience Reveals about Morality*. See also Matthew Alper's *The God Part of the Brain*. Alper stresses that humans are genetically hardwired to be spiritual or religious.

35. See Patrick Bracken and Philip Thomas, "Time to Move beyond the Mind-Body Split," editorial, *British Medical Journal* (*BMJ*), December 21, 2002, pp. 1433–34.

36. Marcus J. Borg, *Reading the Bible Again for the First Time: Taking the Bible Seriously but Not Literally*. See also Obery M. Hendricks, *The Politics of Jesus: Rediscovering the True Revolutionary Nature of Jesus' Teachings and How They Have Been Corrupted*.

37. The most famous case of the difficulty scientists encounter in their work when they are at odds with the Roman Catholic Church and its institutions is Galileo's trial and forced recantation. See also Sam Harris, *Letter to a Christian Nation*.

38. For a study of how freedom of scientific inquiry came about and to learn why modern science arose only in the West, despite the fact that medieval Islam and China were more scientifically advanced, see Toby E. Huff, *The Rise of Early Modern Science, Islam, China, and the West*.

39. The Muslim world desperately needs a new Atatürk to bring it into the twenty-first century. Mustafa Kemal Atatürk (1881–1938) founded the modern Turkish secular republic out of the ashes of the Muslim Ottoman Empire. Over the course of a dozen years (1923–35), Atatürk undertook to modernize Turkey and introduce a positive science mentality in all aspects of the social and economic life of his nation. As a consequence, Turkey is today one of the most advanced nations among the predominantly Muslim countries. See Andrew Mango, *Ataturk: The Biography of the Founder of Modern Turkey*.

40. The theologian-novelist Arthur A. Cohen has questioned the theo-

logical appropriateness of the term *Judeo-Christian* and suggested that it is essentially an invention of American politics, of Christian Americans wishing to distinguish themselves from anti-Semite Christian Germans after World War II. See Arthur A. Cohen, *The Myth of the Judeo-Christian Tradition: And Other Dissenting Essays.* For an analysis of hateful passages found in the Christian Bible that have been used to promote violence, see Chris Hedges, *American Fascists: The Christian Right and the War on America.*

41. Doug Saunders, "US Got What It Deserves, Falwell Says," *Globe & Mail*, September 15, 2001, A2.

42. The government of Israel punished Robertson by pulling out of a $50 million deal it had with the American TV evangelist to build a biblical theme park by the Sea of Galilee.

43. The Cathar religion, which flourished in the Southwest of France during the twelfth and thirteenth centuries, subscribed to a common Gnostic idea and believed that an evil god had created our physical world. All things material, including the human body, were considered evil. The Cathars thought that the human body was a prison of flesh from which the soul wished to escape.

44. Gottfried Leibniz, *Theodicy: Essays on the Goodness of God the Freedom of Man and the Origin of Evil.*

45. Bertrand Russell, *Why I Am Not a Christian*, 1957, p. 30. Also Michel Onfray, *Atheist Manifesto: The Case Against Christianity, Judaism, and Islam*; Victor J. Stenger and Christopher Hitchens, *God: The Failed Hypothesis*; Dan Barker, *Losing Faith in Faith: From Preacher to Atheist.*

46. For a rebuttal of Christian fundamentalism, see Robert M. Price, *The Reason-Driven Life: What Am I Here on Earth For?*

47. 1954 Revenue Act, 501 (c) (3).

48. There are numerous humanist associations that organize ritual ceremonies. There exists also a Unitarian Universalist movement, or Unitarian Universalist Church, which is nondogmatically deist, and which promotes humanist principles and also supplies the infrastructure for humanist-based ceremonies.

SEVEN. CONSERVATION

1. Earth is the only planet currently known to harbor life. This is due to the special composition of its atmosphere, which is 79 percent nitrogen and 21 percent oxygen, with traces of carbon dioxide, methane, and argon.

Other planets, such as Venus and Mars, have atmospheric conditions that are hostile to life. Their atmosphere is 95–96 percent carbon dioxide and 3–4 percent nitrogen, with traces of oxygen, argon, and methane. Earth has not always had an environment suitable to life, and it is possible, in a far-away future, that this could again be the case. The idea that planet Earth is a self-regulating system is sometime referred to as the Gaia hypothesis, a name taken from the Greek goddess of the Earth. See James Lovelock, *The Ages of Gaia: A Biography of Our Living Earth.*

2. A social cost or benefit includes both the private cost, or benefit derived from a good, plus any public cost or benefit supported or enjoyed by society as a whole.

3. For a classical presentation of humanist economics, see E. Fritz Schumacker, *Small Is Beautiful, 25th Anniversary Edition: Economics as If People Mattered: 25 Years Later... With Commentaries.*

4. It is estimated that our Sun will have a physical life of about 10 billion years before exploding and turning into a gaseous red giant. It is now about 5 billion years old. Therefore, Earth and the rest of the solar system will undergo a fundamental transformation in about 5 billion years. This is, of course, if the predicted collision of our galaxy, the Milky Way, with the Andromeda galaxy, merging each other's black holes, does not happen before. A gigantic collision of our massive galaxy and its 200 billion stars, with the equally massive Andromeda galaxy and other smaller galaxies in the same gravity pull, such as the Magellanic Clouds, has been predicted, and is scheduled to occur about four billion years from now. Then our solar system will vaporize in the ensuing chaos and be recycled within a new, giant, elliptical galaxy. Presently, the Milky Way and Andromeda are rushing toward each other at the speed of 500,000 kilometers per hour, or 310,000 miles per hour. Paradoxically, other distant galaxies, those not bound to our galaxy by gravity, will move further away, and over a very long time, become invisible from Earth.

5. The cyclical model of the Universe emerged from the idea that each Big Bang was followed by another, and that this could go on for eternity. The whole Universe might have existed forever, and there would have been a series of these Big Bangs, stretching back into the infinite past, and into the infinite future. See Paul J. Steinhardt and Neil Turok, *Endless Universe: Beyond the Big Bang.* See also, Paul J. Steinhardt and Neil Turok, "The Endless Universe: A Brief Introduction to the Cyclic Universe," *Science on line*, April 25, 2002; and *Science Magazine*, May 24, 2002. Similarly, see Fred Hoyle, Geoffrey Burbidge, and Jayant Vishnu Narlikar, *A Different Approach to Cosmology: From a Static Universe through the Big Bang towards Reality.*

The idea that the cosmic Big Bang is a very long repetitive cycle has received a mathematical confirmation by three physicists at the Institute for Gravitational Physics and Geometry at Penn State University. Their calculations indicate that the Universe may have undergone numerous bangs in its past history. See Penn State University and *World Science*, "Another Universe May Have Preceded Ours, Study Finds," May 14, 2006, http://www.world-science.net/othernews/060514_bouncefrm.htm

See also, Bill Bryson, *A Short History of Nearly Everything*.

6. Stanford University professor Andrei Linde's inflationary cosmology model is currently the best model of the early Universe. It postulates an eternally self-replicating "multiverse" during a very long, circular time cycle where there is always a past and always a future. Big Bangs are being followed by Big Crunches with each succeeding universe having its own laws of physics. See A. D. Linde, *Particle Physics and Inflationary Cosmology*.

7. In fact, the Universe is 10,000 times older than man. If one day were equal to its age, man's time on Earth would equal about eight seconds. The solar system—the Sun and its planets—is understood to be 4.5 billion years old. Earth, therefore, is about 4.5 billion years old. The Sun's diameter is about 109 times that of Earth. When we discovered that our own solar system is only a small part of our galaxy, the Milky Way, which has about 200,000,000 stars, and that our galaxy is only one among countless other galaxies, we got a better idea of our relative insignificance in the total scheme of things "on our planet"/"in our time"... or something along these lines?

8. See M. J. Benton, *When Life Nearly Died: The Greatest Mass Extinction of All Time*.

9. On March 16, 2880, an asteroid called Asteroid 1950 DA is scheduled either to hit the Earth or pass very close by. It has been calculated that there is a one-in-300 possibility that Asteroid 1950 DA will slam into Earth. If this were to occur, the end result could be another massive extinction of life. If it were to hit the Earth, the asteroid could create a crater 10 miles (16 km) wide . The energy released by the impact of such a large asteroid, which is about one kilometer in diameter, would be on the order of 100,000 megatons, which is 10,000 times the energy released by a standard atom bomb. The hypothetical collision of Asteroid 1950 DA with our planet would have a devastating impact on human life and human civilization. See Steven N. Ward and Erik Asphaug, "Asteroid Impact Tsunami of 2880 March 16," *Geophysical Journal International* (June 2003).

10. Eugene Linden, *The Winds of Change: Climate, Weather, and the Destruc-

tion of Civilizations. For more historical examples of ecological disasters, see Jared Diamond, *Collapse: How Societies Choose to Fail or Succeed.*

11. See "Greenland Ice Core Analysis Shows Drastic Climate Change Near End of Last Ice Age," *Science News,* June 19, 2008.

12. According to the "Report of the Intergovernmental Panel on Climate Change, 2001" (United Nations IPCC 2001 report), the temperature on Earth's surface increased by about 0.6° Centigrade (approximately 1° degree Fahrenheit), during the twentieth century. Over the millennium that preceded the twentieth century, the mean global temperature curve for the northern hemisphere fluctuated as much as 0.4° Centigrade. Some scientists speculate that the rise of approximately 0.6° Centigrade in temperature during the twentieth century may, to a large extent, have been caused by a long-period internal mode of the climate system, or by small long-term changes in solar radiation.

13. A major concern is the possibility that the current melting of Arctic ice is unstoppable, even with future reductions in greenhouse gas emissions. This could raise sea levels substantially, possibly by as much as twenty feet, with most of the world's cities disappearing into the sea. See the UN Intergovernmental Panel on Climate Change (IPCC), *Climate Change 2007* (February 2007).

14. The albedo effect is the capacity of a surface or a body to reflect sunlight. The albedo ratio is the percentage of reflected sunlight in relation to various surface conditions of Earth. This ratio ranges from up to 90 percent for fresh snow, to about 4 percent for charcoal, one of the darkest substances. The average albedo ratio of Earth is about 30 percent. See also, United Nations Intergovernmental Panel on Climate Change, (fourth report, IPCC, 2007).

15. Indeed, the observed acceleration in global warming is a combination of many factors. But one reason it is progressing faster than as expected from the sole increase in man-made levels of CO^2 may be due to a concomitant increase in solar radiation on Earth. There are reports that the ice caps on planet Mars are also shrinking, which would suggest that an increase in solar radiation is also affecting that planet.

16. See Benjamin Creme, ed., *Maitreya's Teachings: The Laws of Life.*

17. Scientists have mapped a kind of *highway of extinction* and estimated the effects of man-made global warming on humans and on many other species. For every degree Celsius (1.8° Fahrenheit) of temperature rise, between 400 million and 1.7 billion more people could be affected through water shortages and infectious diseases, while some animal species would become extinct.

18. See "Goodbye Sunshine," *Guardian*, December 18, 2003.

19. After the phenomenon of global dimming was discovered, new climate models speculatively suggested that the drought was likely caused by air pollution generated in Europe and North America. The pollution changed the properties of clouds over the Atlantic Ocean, disturbing the monsoons and shifting the tropical rains southward.

20. Indeed, scientists have estimated that over the last few decades, the global warming effects of pollution have been stronger than its cooling effects. Without the cooling effects of pollution, indeed, the Earth's surface temperature would have risen by about 1.8° Centigrade (about 3° Fahrenheit), over the last few decades. However, because of the cooling effect of global dimming, estimated at around 1° Centigrade (less than 1.5° Fahrenheit), the Earth's temperature rose only between 0.6° and 0.8° Centigrade.

21. Orrin H. Pilkey and Linda Pilkey-Jarvis studied the difficulties encountered in modeling Nature and in predicting climate changes and their myriad effects long in advance: *Why Environmental Scientists Can't Predict the Future.*

22. See James Lovelock, *The Revenge of Gaia, Earth's Climate in Crisis and the Fate of Humanity.*

23. Deoxyribonucleic acid (DNA) is a nucleic acid that contains the genetic instructions for the biological development of a cellular form of life. The nucleus of the average human cell is only six micrometers in diameter, yet it contains about 1.8 meters of DNA, distributed among 46 chromosomes, each consisting of a single DNA molecule about 40 millimeters (1.5 inches) long. See "The Nucleus Structural Organization of the Nucleus DNA Packaging," *Encyclopædia Britannica* (2005).

24. "Scientists Decipher the Chimpanzee's DNA," *Sci-Tech Today*, August 31, 2005.

25. *Homo erectus,* the earliest human ancestor, first appeared 1.6 million to 1.9 million years ago. His brain was 50 percent larger and his teeth were markedly smaller than that of his predecessor, *Homo habilis.* Later on, among the earliest humanoid species, came the *Neanderthals* and the *Cro-Magnons.* The current human and Neanderthal lines of descent began to separate about 700,000 years ago and diverged permanently about 330,000 years ago. *Neanderthals* appeared first in Europe and in Western Asia. The Neanderthals were more apelike; their skull shape had larger and thicker brow ridges. They coexisted with the more advanced *Cro-Magnons* for thousands of years before disappearing, about thirty to thirty-five thousand years ago, as more modern humans moved from Africa to Europe. It is a matter of

speculation if there was any contact between the two before the extinction of the former. The Cro-Magnons survived and are the earliest known European examples of modern humans, or *Homo sapiens* (*sapiens* means "wise" or "intelligent"), who have existed since about 200,000 to 250,000 years ago. See Ian Tattersall, *The Last Neanderthal: The Rise, Success, and Mysterious Extinction of Our Closest Human Relatives.*

26. To see why all people alive today can trace some of their genetic heritage through their mothers back to this one woman, see Rebecca L. Cann, Mark Stoneking, and Allan C. Wilson, "Mitochondrial DNA and Human Evolution," *Nature,* January 1, 1987.

27. See Jack Cohen and Ian Stewart, *Figments of Reality: The Evolution of the Curious Mind,* 1999, p. 88.

28. The human version of the gene FOXP2, in its critical segments, differs by only two molecules, out of 715, from the version carried by chimpanzees. See W. Enard et al., "Molecular Evolution of FOXP2, a Gene Involved in Speech and Language," *Nature,* August 14, 2002.

29. For a study of the evolution of humans from the earliest primates through the emergence of fully modern humans in the past 200,000 to 250,000 years, see Richard G. Klein, *The Human Career: Human Biological and Cultural Origins*; and Richard G. Klein, *The Dawn of Human Culture.*

30. See Jared Diamond, *The Third Chimpanzee: The Evolution and Future of the Human Animal.*

31. Until approximately 60,000–70,000 years ago, the total human population was relatively small, perhaps not numbering more than 10,000 breeding people.

32. See Nicholas Wade, "Humans Have Spread Globally, and Evolved Locally," *New York Times,* Evolution: A Special Issue, June 26, 2007. See also Nicholas Wade, *The Faith Instinct: How Religion Evolved and Why It Endures.*

33. See Spencer Wells, *The Journey of Man: A Genetic Odyssey.*

34. See Neil Shubin, *Your Inner Fish: A Journey into the 3.5-Billion-Year History of the Human Body.*

35. For a presentation of *creationism* as essentially an American political-religious phenomenon, nearly absent in the rest of the word, see Michael Ruse, *The Evolution-Creation Struggle.*

36. Genesis 1:25–26 and Genesis 2:18–20.

37. A 2005 poll by the Pew Research Center revealed that 64 percent of Americans favor the teaching of intelligent design or creationism in public schools. Some 42 percent totally reject evolution or believe that present forms of life existed since the beginning of time, while 38 percent would

teach only creationism instead of evolutionary theory. Only 26 percent agree with the predominant scientific view that life evolved by the process of natural selection without the need for divine intervention. The capacity of viruses to survive, mutate, and reproduce by natural selection requires the development of new vaccines to fight disease. This is also the reason why biologists have to invent new antibiotics to fight antibiotic-resistant bacteria that have changed and adapted to survive. A rejection of evolution would also be a rejection of scientific progress in fighting human diseases. Since creationism supposes that a god creates all organisms, this would imply that such a god is also continually creating new diseases!

38. See Kevin Phillips, *American Theocracy: The Peril and Politics of Radical Religion, Oil, and Borrowed Money in the Twenty-First Century.*

39. To understand how the skeletons of the vertebrates that inhabit the Earth today carry within them the imprint of an evolutionary process that has lasted several billion years, see Jean-Baptiste de Panafieu, Patrick Gries, and Linda Asher, *Evolution.*

40. In 1802 French biologist Jean-Baptiste Lamarck (1744–1829) published a book in which he advanced the idea that living species change over time to adapt to their environment. Yet it was Darwin who developed the definitive explanation of the phenomenon with his theory of natural selection. See Jean-Baptiste Lamarck, *Recherches sur l'Organisation des Corps Vivants,* 1802; and Charles Darwin, *Origin of Species,* 1859.

41. See Edward J. Steele et al., *Lamarck's Signature: How Retrogenes Are Changing Darwin's Natural Selection Paradigm.*

42. See Spencer Wells, *The Journey of Man.*

EIGHT. VIOLENCE, WAR, AND PEACE

1. On the Kantian ideal of a perpetual peace, see James Bohman and Matthias Lutz-Bachmann, *Perpetual Peace: Essays on Kant's Cosmopolitan Ideal.*

2. There are four main academic centers that track world conflicts: the Stockholm International Peace Research Institute; the International Peace Research Institute in Oslo, Norway; the Center for International Development and Conflict Management at the University of Maryland in College Park, and the Human Security Centre at the University of British Columbia in Vancouver, Canada.

3. For a presentation of a somewhat utopian interventionist international morality, see John Rawls' eight principles of international relations:

1. People (as organized by their government) are free and independent, and their freedom and independence is to be respected by other peoples.
2. Peoples are equal and parties to their own agreements.
3. Peoples have the right of self-defense but no right to war.
4. Peoples are to observe a duty of nonintervention.
5. Peoples are to observe treaties and undertakings.
6. Peoples are to observe certain specified restrictions on the conduct of war (assumed to be in self-defense).
7. Peoples are to honor human rights.
8. Peoples have a duty to assist other peoples living under unfavorable conditions that prevent their having a just or decent political and social regime.

(Source: John Rawls, *The Law of Peoples.*)

4. See Catherine Wessinger, ed., *Millennialism, Persecution and Violence: Historical Cases (Religion and Politics).*

5. Given power under authority, many persons may be willing to abuse their power and use violence and brutality against other persons. In the early 1960s, Yale University psychologist Stanley Milgram conducted a series of obedience experiments proving that average citizens would readily inflict painful electric shocks on strangers if they were instructed or encouraged to do so by an authority figure. In fact, nearly two-thirds of participants in the experiments were willing to brutalize and inflict pain on another person. See Stanley Milgram and Jerome S. Bruner, *Obedience to Authority.*

6. In the Stanford University experiment, college students were randomly assigned to be either prisoners or guards in a simulated prison. It was found that group members (acting as guards) could not resist the pressure of their assumed positions to use their group power to brutalize and sadistically abuse those who had less power (the prisoners). See C. Haney, W. C. Banks, and P. G. Zimbardo, "Interpersonal Dynamics in a Simulated Prison," *International Journal of Criminology and Penology* (1973): 69–97.

For a similar experiment but with less severe conclusions, see: Stephen. D. Reicher and S. Alexander Haslam, "The Psychology of Tyranny: The BBC Prison Study," *British Journal of Social Psychology* (March 2006): 1–40. See also, S. Alexander Haslam and Stephen D. Reicher, "The Psychology of Tyranny," *Scientific American Mind* (October 2005): 45–51.

7. See Philip G. Zimbardo, *The Lucifer Effect: Understanding How Good People Turn Evil.* See also Marilyn Elias, "Do We All Have a Dark Side? Psychologist Argues We Do in 'The Lucifer Effect,'" *USA Today*, March 14, 2007, 7D.

8. In European countries, the tendency is to be skeptical of religions in general. For example, a poll taken in Great Britain at the end of 2006 by the British newspaper *The Guardian* indicated that more people in Britain think religion causes harm than believe it does good. An overwhelming majority see religion as a cause of division and tension, greatly outnumbering the smaller majority who also believe that it can be a force for good. See "Religion Does More Harm Than Good—Poll," *Guardian,* January 5, 2007.

9. See James N. Gardner, "Broken Spells and Unveiled Secrets," *Skeptic Magazine* 12, no. 4 (2006): 71.

10. See Steven Weinberg, *Dreams of a Final Theory: The Scientist's Search for the Ultimate Laws of Nature.*

11. One factor in the unending Israeli-Palestinian conflict may be this idea of a "chosen" Jewish people. It is drawn from the Torah (first five books of the Bible) in the book of Deuteronomy 7:1–8: "When the Lord your God brings you into the land you are to possess and cast out the many peoples living there, you shall then slaughter them all and utterly destroy them.... You shall make no agreements with them nor show them any mercy.... You shall destroy their altars, break down their images, cut down their groves and burn their graven images with fire. For you are a holy people unto the Lord thy God, and He has chosen you to be a special people above all others upon the face of the Earth."

12. See Robert O. Paxton, *The Anatomy of Fascism.*

13. For how religious thinkers can twist reality to justify practically any war of aggression, see Damon Linker, *The Theocons.*

14. See "Yesha Rabbinical Council: During Time of War, Enemy Has No Innocents," *Yediot Aharonot,* July 30, 2006. "Yesha Rabbis Call for 'Extermination of the Enemy,'" *Jerusalem Post,* July 12, 2006. In March 2008, the Association of rabbis for the People and Land of Israel reconfirmed this position and issued a religious ruling stating that the Torah permits the shelling and bombing of Palestinian civilians.

15. See "A Statement from Qaidat al-Jihad Regarding the Mandates of the Heroes and the Legality of the Operations in New York and Washington," *Middle East Policy Council Journal,* April 24, 2002.

16. As Bertrand Russell observed, "I do not myself feel that any person who is really profoundly humane can believe in everlasting punishment.... [This doctrine of hell] put cruelty into the world and gave the world generations of cruel torture; and the Christ of the Gospels...would certainly have to be considered partly responsible for that." See Russell, *Why I Am Not a Christian,* pp. 17–18.

17. It is to be noted that the doctrine of hell was explicitly and categorically abandoned by the Church of England in 1995, but not, however, by the Roman Catholic Church.

18. See Mark Twain, *The War Prayer*.

19. For example, in the United States, religious people appear to be more warmongering than secular people. At the beginning of the war against Iraq, in March 2003, a Gallup poll indicated that 63 percent of practicing individuals of all religious denominations supported the war, while the same percentage was 59 percent for the overall population. See Richard N. Ostling, "US Churches' Clergy-Laity Split on War," *AP*, March 18, 2003. See also, Cheryl K. Chumley, "War Seen as in Line with Christian View," *Washington Times*, April 15, 2003.

20. Indeed, German biblical scholar Raymund Schwager has found in the Old Testament six hundred passages of explicit violence, one thousand descriptive verses of God's own violent actions of punishment, and one hundred passages where God expressly commands others to kill people. See Raymund Schwager, *Must There Be Scapegoats? Violence and Redemption in the Bible*, (German: *Brauchen wir einen Sündenbock?*), translated by M. L. Assad, Crossroad, 2000.

21. There is even advice in the Bible on how to wage war against others. Proverbs 24:6, for example, encourages deception: "By way of deception thou shalt make war." Therefore, lying and killing could be acceptable, provided it is to wage war! It all depends on how a sentence is translated from the Hebrew. Indeed, the sentence "be-tachbūlōt ta`aseh lekha milchāmāh" is sometimes translated as meaning "By way of deception thou shalt make war" and sometimes by the less explicit form "for by wise counsel thou shalt wage thy war." This is a recurring problem with different translations of the Bible. Some translations attempt to soften the original meaning of the text to make it more acceptable to modern eyes. "By way of deception thou shalt make war" is also the motto adopted by Israel's Intelligence Agency, the Mossad or, in Hebrew, Ha-Mossad Lé-Modiin. See Victor Ostrovsky, *By Way of Deception: The Making and Unmaking of a Mossad Officer*.

22. For a long list of contradictions in the Bible, see Paul N. Tobin, *Rejection of Pascal's Wager*.

23. See Andrew M. Lobaczewski, *Political Ponerology: A Science on the Nature of Evil Adjusted for Political Purposes*.

24. In contemporary America, the character profiles of some politicians offer a clue behind some life-and-death decisions. For an analysis of such psychological traits, see Martha Stout, *The Sociopath Next Door*.

25. See Hannah Arendt and Amos Elon, *Eichmann in Jerusalem: A Report on the Banality of Evil.* See also Christopher R. Browning, *Ordinary Men: Reserve Police Battalion 101 and the Final Solution in Poland.*

26. See an adaptation of this section: Rodrigue Tremblay, "Just War Theory" *Humanist* (May/June 2003): 15–18.

27. Judith Wagner DeCew, "Codes of Warfare," *Encyclopedia of Applied Ethics* 4.

28. For a study of the issue of war, and particularly of the primitive ideology of the ban (*herem*) or of ethnic cleansing (total annihilation of the enemy without regard to sex, age, or military status) in the Hebrew Bible, see Susan Niditch, *War in the Hebrew Bible: A Study in the Ethics of Violence.*

29. The religious warfare ideology of Islam is summarized in the Islamic concept of holy war, or jihad, meaning "to strive" in Arabic. For a differentiation between a military jihad that is waged in self-defense and the expansionist or imperialist military jihad, which is waged against atheists and non-Muslims, see John L. Esposito, *Unholy War: Terror in the Name of Islam.*

30. The unambiguous portrayal of Jews as being responsible for the state execution of Jesus of Nazareth (ben Yeshua) really began when Paul of Tarsus brought the Jewish Christian faith to Rome, the center of the Roman Empire, and turned it into a Roman Christian faith. For this transformation to take place, however, the responsibility for Jesus' crucifixion had to be shifted somewhat from the occupying Roman political and military authorities, especially from the Roman governor Pontius Pilate, to the local Jewish religious authorities. This has had tragic historical consequences because such a shift of responsibility has served over the centuries as a religious basis for recurrent bouts of anti-Semitism and of persecutions of the Jews in Christian and even in Muslim countries. In a sense, Jews became the scapegoats for Jesus' execution at the hands of the Romans.—At the Council of Vatican II in the 1960s, the Roman Catholic Church solemnly affirmed that Jews were not responsible for the death of Jesus. This came, however, after many centuries of ambivalence about the question.

31. The US military has thousands of nuclear bombs, the largest being the nine-megaton B-53 nuclear bombs. A neutron bomb is a thermonuclear weapon that produces minimal blast and heat but releases large amounts of lethal radiation that can penetrate armor and is especially destructive to human tissue.

32. American strategists have calculated the proportion of civilians killed in the twentieth century's major wars. In World War I, 5 percent of those killed were civilians, in the World War II, 48 percent, while in a hypo-

thetical World War III, 90–95 percent would be civilians. See Colin Ward, *Anarchy in Action.*

33. Cluster bombs are composed of 202 bomblets that can be dispersed at superhigh speed over an area as large as 22 football fields. These bomblets are packed with razor-sharp shrapnel that can penetrate human bodies.

34. The Geneva Protocol Relating to the Protection of Victims of International Armed Conflicts, article 51, bans these weapons. The attitude toward war varies greatly between Americans and Europeans. A poll conducted in June 2003 by the US-based German Marshall Fund asked the following question: "Under certain conditions, is war necessary to obtain justice?" The answer was yes for 55 percent of Americans, 35 percent of British citizens, 22 percent of the Dutch, and for only 12 percent of the French and of the Germans. See Laurent Zecchini, "La Question de l'Usage de la Force et le Rôle Dominant des États-Unis Divisent Américains et Européens," *Le Monde*, September 5, 2003.

35. To understand how the war mentality infiltrated the American Republican Party and led to the Iraq War, see Anne Norton, *Leo Strauss and the Politics of American Empire* and Rodrigue Tremblay, *The New American Empire.*

36. Reuters, "Pope Urges World to Avoid 'Dramatic Conflict,'" *New York Times*, March 5, 2003.

37. See Mister Thorne, "Atheists in Foxholes, Christians in Uniform," *Humanist* (May/June 2003): 19–23.

38. Neoconservative Christians and US televangelists are among the few who believe that offensive wars, such as the United States–led 2003 war against Iraq, are moral. One month before the war, televangelist Charles Stanley decreed, "*God approves of war...and hates peaceniks.*" Mister Thorne, "Atheists in Foxholes, Christians in Uniform."

39. See Peter Godwin, "The Future of War," *Men's Journal* (April 2008): 96–100, 140.

40. See Bruce Hoffman, *Inside Terrorism.*

41. Muhammad himself justified his imperialistic wars of aggression in these terms: "I was commanded to fight people until they say there is no God but the only God, and Muhammad is the apostle of God, and they perform all the Islamic ordinances and rituals" (Sahih of al-Bukhari vol. 1, p. 13). This is a conversion in response to the threat of death and it is a negation of freedom of conscience and of fundamental human rights.

42. The Qur'an itself does not mention the act of apostasy. However, Islamic Law and the hadiths (anecdotes of the sayings and doings of Muhammad) do. Since Islam is a very politicized religion and has a tendency

to merge state and religion, apostasy came to be considered an act of treason
to the rulers or to the Islamic political empire of the day, as much as a dis-
approval of the official religion. According to Muslim Law (Shari'a), a male
apostate, or *murtadd*, is liable to be put to death. The exception is when a
person becomes a Muslim upon compulsion and afterward apostatizes; he is
not to be put to death. Moreover, a male Muslim apostate is disabled from
selling or otherwise disposing of his property. A female apostate is not subject to capital punishment, but she may be kept in confinement until she
recants. If either the husband or the wife apostatizes from the faith of Islam,
a divorce takes place *ipso facto*; the wife is entitled to her whole dower, but no
sentence of divorce is necessary. If the husband and wife both apostatize
together, their marriage is generally allowed to continue. If an under-age
boy apostatizes, he is not to be put to death but to be imprisoned until he
comes to full age, when, if he continues in the state of unbelief, he must be
put to death (Hidayah, vol. 3, 467).

See Robert Spencer, *The Myth of Islamic Tolerance: How Islamic Law Treats
Non-Muslims* and Robert Spencer, *The Truth about Muhammad, Founder of the
World's Most Intolerant Religion*. See also Irshad Manji, *The Trouble with Islam
Today: A Muslim's Call for Reform in Her Faith*.

43. Many in the most fundamentalist Islamic countries recoil at the
thought of assigning to religion the main domestic reason why their countries lag behind Europe, North America, and Asia in economics, technology
and science. They prefer to blame external factors, such as economic globalization, colonization, and the triumph of materialist values.

44. Even though the culture of takfir-inspired violence against people
accused of being heretic goes back to 632, the year of Muhammad's death,
and the emergence of a radical group known as Khawarij whose members
argued that committing a single sin constituted heresy, it is considered that the
father of modern takfir ideology is Taqi al-Din Ibn Taymiyyah, a thirteenth-
century theologian.

45. An example of how religious scriptures can be interpreted differently is the Islamic concept of *jihad*. There are two meanings of *jihad*, a
peaceful one and a violent one. Muhammad defined the greater jihad as the
struggle to elevate oneself spiritually and morally. There is also the lesser
jihad, which refers to the need to defend one's family and community. This
usually means self-defense. However, some may define self-defense so
broadly that it can justify aggression and attacks against others. See Akbar
Ahmed, *Journey Into Islam: The Crisis of Globalization*. On the various meanings of "jihad," see also Ayesha Jalal, *Partisans of Allah: Jihad in South Asia*.

46. The word *Qur'an* means "recitation" or "reading." According to Muhammad, the angel Gabriel revealed the word of God to him. Muslims believe that the original text of the book is in heaven and that Gabriel dictated the sacred words from it. The revelations began in 610 CE, and were completed in 632 CE, when Muhammad died.

47. The myth of Islamic tolerance is belied by the massacre and extermination of the Zoroastrians in Iran; a million Armenians in Turkey, in 1915; the Buddhists and Hindus in India (in 1399, Taimur killed 100,000 Hindus in a single day); the more than six thousand Jews in Fez, Morocco, in 1033; the hundreds of Jews killed in Cordoba between 1010 and 1013; the entire Jewish community of Granada in 1066; the Jews in Marrakesh in 1232; the Jews of Tetuan, Morocco in 1790; and the Jews of Baghdad in 1828. See Robert Spencer, *The Myth of Islamic Tolerance: How Islamic Law Treats Non-Muslims.* Also see I. Manji, *The Trouble with Islam Today.* The idea of forced conversion under threat of death is also present in the so-called verse of the sword: *"Fight and kill the disbelievers wherever you find them, take them captive, lie in wait and ambush them using every stratagem of war, but if they repent, establish regular prayers, and practice regular charity, then open the way for them, for God is oft-forgiving, Most Merciful"* (9:5).

48. For a study of why Europe was behind the Muslim world for many centuries, see David Levering Lewis, *God's Crucible: A Lesson for the 21st Century.*

49. It should be recalled that in 1204, European Christian Crusaders sacked and destroyed Constantinople's great libraries. One also has to remember that in the early years of the Reformation (1517–1648), European Protestant mobs went on a rampage and destroyed scores of ecclesiastical art because they deemed images of the divine to be idolatrous. This was stopped only after Martin Luther (1483–1546) himself objected. Therefore, Muslims have no monopoly in destroying art for religious reasons.

50. Ironically, in Islamic history, the time before the coming of the Prophet Muhammad is called the *jahiliyya*, the Age of Ignorance.

51. For an account on how total warfare has impacted civilization for the worse, see David A. Bell, *The First Total War: Napoleon's Europe and the Birth of Warfare as We Know It.*

52. For an example of how intellectual freedom is considered to be dangerous and a threat to religious orthodoxy in a nonscientific climate, see Karen Armstrong, *Through the Narrow Gate: A Memoir of Spiritual Discovery,* p. 197.

53. Humans have free will even though human actions are the effects of prior causes or circumstances. This is known as *compatibilism*. The enemy of

human freedom is not causation but constraints to its application. See D. C. Dennett, *Breaking the Spell: Religion as a Natural Phenomenon.*

54. Another utterance by a religious leader gives food for thought: *"Bless the guns if, in the gaps they open, the Gospel can flourish."*—Mgr. V. Camara, Bishop of Cartagena in Spain, during the Spanish civil war (1936–1939).

NINE. DEMOCRACY

1. For new thinking about democracy today, see Jürgen Habermas, *Democracy and the Public Sphere.*

2. For an in-depth analysis of constitutional democracy, see Walter F. Murphy, *Constitutional Democracy: Creating and Maintaining a Just Political Order.*

3. US Supreme Court Justice Robert Jackson aptly put it when he wrote in 1943, "The very purpose of a Bill of Rights was to withdraw certain subjects from the vicissitudes of political controversy . . . and to establish them as legal principles to be applied by the Courts. . . . Fundamental rights may not be submitted to vote; they depend on the outcome of no election."

4. On the need for decentralization and separation of powers in a democracy, see Montesquieu, *The Spirit of the Laws,* (initially published anonymously in two volumes in 1748).

5. For a philosophical defense of democracy against arbitrary power, see Baruch (Benedict de) Spinoza et al., *A Theologico-Political Treatise.*

6. It has been observed that countries that have their collectivist identity in their official name have a good chance of being countries from which people are not allowed to escape. A contemporary example would perhaps be the Democratic People's Republic of North Korea (DPRK). Countries that include their official religion in their name are also likely to be countries where political freedom is kept to a minimum. A contemporary example would perhaps be the Islamic Republic of Iran.

7. The principles advanced by the American Revolution are *Life, Liberty, and the Pursuit of Happiness;* those of the French Revolution are *Liberty, Equality, and Fraternity.* This contrasts, for instance, with the principles preached by the Roman Catholic Church: *Faith, Hope, and Charity.*

8. For instance, the powers of democratic decision making should never be bypassed through totalitarian maneuvers, such as the Royal Prerogative in the United Kingdom or the Executive Privilege in the United States, which can be used arbitrarily to overrule democratic demands and can serve as stratagems to declare wars of aggression or initiate other unpopular measures.

9. It is Proudhon, however, who was among the first to propose the establishment of credit unions, an idea which has proved to be very socially efficient in many countries.

10. See Pierre-Joseph Proudhon, *The Philosophy of Misery.*

11. See Danny Danziger and John Gillingham, *1215, The Year of Magna Carta*, p. 253.

12. Not all Muslims live in totalitarian societies. For instance, out of 1.25 billion Muslims world wide, roughly half live in democratic nations, in countries such as Indonesia (220 million), Malaysia (25 million), Bangladesh (150 million), India (Muslim minority of 150 million), and Turkey (80 million). Can it therefore be inferred from this fact that the antidemocracy Islamic bias is stronger in Arab countries than elsewhere?

13. According to Israel's Central Bureau of Statistics, at the end of 2004, of Israel's 6.9 million people, 76.2 percent were Jews, 19.5 percent were Arabs, and 4.3 percent had other religious afflictions.

14. See Jimmy Carter, *Palestine: Peace Not Apartheid.*

15. For the importance of religion and of secret societies in American politics, see Jeff Sharlet, *The Family: The Secret Fundamentalism at the Heart of American Power.*

16. It is thought that all four canonical Christian Gospels were originally written in Greek, the *lingua franca* of the Roman Oriental Empire, not in Hebrew and not in Aramaic, the language spoken by Jesus. Consider the myth of the Virgin Mary. Matthew and Luke, two of the four evangelists, (the other two being Mark and John), in their efforts to make the life of Jesus Christ conform to a prophecy in the Old Testament (Isaiah 7:14), spread the myth that Mary conceived as a virgin. To do so, they relied on the Greek translation of Isaiah where the Hebrew word *alma* for "young woman" is erroneously translated by the Greek word *parthenos,* meaning "virgin." A simple mistranslation is thus the basis of a myth that has been espoused for centuries. This error could explain the sexual neurosis that transpires in many of the Catholic Church's teachings. More damaging to the legend, however, is the knowledge that thousands of years before the advent of Christianity, there also existed a legend that the Hindu god Krishna was conceived by a virgin and his birth was attended by angels, wise men, and shepherds. See Michael Baigent, *The Jesus Papers: Exposing the Greatest Cover-Up in History.*

17. For all these reasons, one must be careful when reading old religious books. Many of the religious stories they contain are no more than a haphazard compilation of a few traditions, a jumble of ethnic-centered historical accounts, and fairy tales for grownups. Fairy tales abound in the Bible.

One can read the fictitious story of Adam and Eve or about magic talking donkeys, bushes on fire that are not consumed, giant slayers, worldwide floods, man-eating fish, a miracle lunch for thousands, and so on.

18. See John Hagee, *From Daniel to Doomsday: The Countdown Has Begun.*

19. See Michael O. Hill, *Dreaming the End of the World: Apocalypse as a Rite of Passage.*

20. The last book of the Bible, Revelation, was not even considered part of the Scriptures before the fourth century.

21. See the nonsensical fiction of Hal Lindsey, *The Late Great Planet Earth.*

22. In the delusional Armageddon fantasy, democracy is abolished and the world is supposed to be ruled for one thousand years by Jesus and his army of all-knowing saints in an earthbound theocracy, in which teachers will use the Bible as their only textbook. See Edward Humes, *Monkey Girl, Evolution, Education, Religion, and the Battle for America's Soul*, p. 21.

23. For an analysis of pop prophets, see "Religion: The Pop Prophets," *Newsweek*, May 24, 2004. For a study of the prophecy merchants and their predictions of Armageddon, see Richard Abanes, *End-Time Visions: The Road to Armageddon.*

24. American fundamentalist groups spread the idea that the reunification of Europe is an indication of the return of the Roman Empire and the emergence of the Antichrist.

25. For Jews, these books of religious fiction and political propaganda are a double-edged sword. The story says that after the last battle with the Antichrist in Jerusalem, two thirds of the Jews will accept Jesus as the true Messiah, but the others will be killed or will be forever damned. It would be the end of Judaism.

26. Islamic Muslims and Evangelical Protestants have one thing in common: they interpret the contents of the Qur'an and of the Bible textually, considering everything they find there to be true. Catholics and mainstream Protestants, however, tend to interpret the Bible in a metaphoric fashion, its fables, legends, and myths not to be taken literally.

27. Former US President George W. Bush once uttered this unbelievable, immoral sentence: "We will export death and violence to the four corners of the Earth in defense of this great country and rid the world of evil." See Bob Woodward's book *Bush at War*. In *The New American Empire*, I wrote: "The world should take notice when someone...with a fanatic mind and with powerful means, receives his marching orders from Heaven" (p. 18).

Knowing Bush's hang-ups on religion and his penchant for thinking that he was somehow on a "mission from God," the Pentagon went so far as to use biblical quotes in secret wartime memos to cast the 2003 American invasion of Iraq as a holy Christian crusade. The quotes included some of the most warlike verses of the Bible: "Commit to the Lord, whatever you do, and your plans will succeed" (Proverbs 16:3); or, "Open the gates that the righteous nation may enter, the nation that keeps the faith" (Isaiah 26:2); or again, "Therefore put on the full armor of God, so that when the day of evil comes, you may be able to stand your ground, and after you have done everything, to stand" (Ephesians 6:13). See Robert Draper, "And He Shall Be Judged," *GQ magazine*, May 17, 2009.

28. Speech on September 12, 1960. For a study of the American tradition of religious freedom, See Martha Nussbaum, *Liberty of Conscience: In Defense of America's Tradition of Religious Equality.*

29. For a study of the crisis of democracy, see Jeffrey Stout, *Democracy and Tradition.*

30. For instance, let us compare two societies which both have five members.

In society X, income distribution is as follows: individual A has an income equal to 4; individual B receives 5; individual C receives 6; individual D has 15; and individual E has an income equal to 20. The median income is 6 and the average income is $50/5 = 10$. Therefore, the median income is lower than the average income. This means a majority of the population receives below-average incomes.

In society Y, however, income distribution takes this form: individual A has an income equal to 5; individual B receives 6; individual C receives 11; individual D has 13; and individual E has an income equal to 15. The median income in this second society is 11, and the average income is $50/5 = 10$. Here, the median income is above the average income, and a majority of the population receives incomes above the average.

31. See Edward D. Mansfield and Jack Snyder, *Electing to Fight: Why Emerging Democracies Go to War.*

32. For an analysis of the phenomenon of *pathocracy* in government, see Andrew M. Lobaczewski, *Political Ponerology.*

33. Richard A. Viguerie et al., *America's Right Turn: How Conservatives Used New and Alternative Media to Take Power.*

34. Serge Chakotin, *The Rape of the Masses: The Psychology of Totalitarian Political Propaganda.*

35. To understand how some political leaders use propaganda to rally support for themselves and their causes by invoking external threats and

resorting to belligerent, nationalist rhetoric and slogans, see Edward D. Mansfield and Jack Snyder, *Electing to Fight.*

36. James Bovard, *Attention Deficit Democracy.*

37. James Bamford documented extensively the propaganda techniques that the Bush-Cheney administration used to sell its war against Iraq to the American public, how it presented false information, employed fake journalists, and manipulated the media. See Bamford, A *Pretext for War: 9/11, Iraq, and the Abuse of America's Intelligence Agencies.*

38. In a speech on May 15, 1951, the American general Douglas MacArthur eloquently denounced such a propaganda of fear: "It is part of the general pattern of misguided policy that our country is now geared to an arms economy which was bred in an artificially induced psychosis of war hysteria and nurtured upon an incessant propaganda of fear."

39. On this score, it is worth noting that an open society and an open government do not function in secret but always in the sunshine. Secret societies and organizations are hostile to true democracy. As President John F. Kennedy said on April 27, 1961, in an address to newspaper publishers, "The very word 'secrecy' is repugnant in a free and open society; and we are as a people inherently and historically opposed to secret societies, to secret oaths and to secret proceedings. We decided long ago that the dangers of excessive and unwarranted concealment of pertinent facts far outweighed the dangers, which are cited to justify it."

40. As an example, and to understand the extent to which money corrupts the American democracy, see Robert G. Kaiser, *So Damn Much Money: The Triumph of Lobbying and the Corrosion of American Government.*

41. See John Locke, *The Second Treatise on Civil Government.*

42. See Alan Wolfe, "The Coming Religious Peace; And the Winner Is...," *Atlantic* (March 2008): 55–63.

43. For analyses of this economic, social, and demographic phenomenon, see Pippa Norris and Ronald Inglehart, *Sacred and Secular: Religion and Politics Worldwide.*

44. The institution of microfinancing to make personal loans to low-income entrepreneurs in the developing world is a good example of how working capital can be raised in small amounts to help people empower themselves to earn their way out of poverty. See about the Kiva organization at: http://www.kiva.org/.

45. For an analysis of why culture and religion are important in explaining economic development, see David Landes, *The Wealth and Poverty of Nations: Why Some Are So Rich and Some So Poor.*

46. See Timur Kuran, *Islam and Mammon: The Economic Predicaments of Islamism.*

47. However, the election of a Democratic majority in November 2008, and the election of President Barack Obama, has reversed the antiscientific approach to these issues.

48. See Rodney Stark, *The Victory of Reason: How Christianity Led to Freedom, Capitalism, and Western Success.*

49. See Max Weber, *The Protestant Ethic and the Spirit of Capitalism (Die protestantische Ethik und der 'Geist' des Kapitalismus).*

50. Martin Luther (1483–1546) published his *95 Theses* in 1517.

TEN. EDUCATION

1. In French, there are two distinct words, one for formal education and another for the wider concept of general formation: *instruction* signifies learning in school and *education* refers to the formation of a child in all aspects of life.

2. See Carl Zimmer, *Soul Made Flesh: The Discovery of the Brain—and How it Changed the World.* In the fourth century BCE, Greek physicians, such as Herophilus and Erasistratus, in Alexandria, overcame ancient taboos and dissected hundreds of cadavers and, in the process, discovered the nervous system.

3. See Norman Doidge, *The Brain that Changes Itself: Stories of Personal Triumph from the Frontiers of Brain Science.*

ELEVEN. MORALITY IN EVERYDAY LIFE

1. To read about the question of selfishness and objectivist ethics, see Ayn Rand, *The Virtue of Selfishness.*

2. For teaching humanist morality to children aged nine to twelve years, see Helen Bennett, *Humanism, What's That? A Book for Curious Kids*; see also Dale McGowan, *Raising Freethinkers: A Practical Guide for Parenting beyond Belief.*

Conclusion. For a Better and More Moral Future

1. For a view of education and an ethic of caring, see Nel Noddings, *Caring: A Feminine Approach to Ethics and Moral Education.*

2. Observations seem to indicate that *economic* freedom is even more important than *political* freedom in fostering conditions for economic development. See Aparna Mathur and Kartikeya Singh, "Foreign Direct Investment, Corruption, and Democracy," *AEI Working paper*, May 15, 2007.

APPENDIX

MAIN HUMANIST AND ETHICAL ORGANIZATIONS

INTERNATIONAL

• Center for Inquiry Transnational
3965 Rensch Rd
Amherst, NY 14228
(716) 636-4869
info@centerforinquiry.net
www.centerforinquiry.net

• International Humanist and Ethical Union (IHEU)
1, Gower Street,
London WC1E 6HD,
United Kingdom
UK: 0870 288 7631
International: + 44 870 288 7631
iheu-office@iheu.org
www.iheu.org

UNITED STATES

• American Humanist Association (AHA)
1777 T St, NW,
Washington, DC 20009-7125
(202) 238-9088
Toll-Free: (800) 837-3792
info@thehumanist.org
www.americanhumanist.org

• The Humanist Society
1777 T Street, NW
Washington, DC 20009-7125
 (202) 238-9088
Toll-Free: (800) 837-3792
info@humanist-society.org
www.humanist-society.org

• Americans United for Separation of Church and State
518 C Street NE,
Washington, DC 20002
(202) 466-3234
americansunited@au.org
http://www.au.org/

• Council for Secular Humanism
PO Box 664
Amherst, New York 14226-0664
Toll-Free: (800) 818-7071
info@secularhumanism.org
www.secularhumanism.org/

• Center for Inquiry/Head Office
3965 Rensch Rd.
Amherst, NY 14228
(716) 636-4869

info@centerforinquiry.net
www.centerforinquiry.net

CANADA

• Humanist Association of Canada
PO Box 8752, Station T
Ottawa, Ontario, K1G 3J1
Toll-Free: (877) 486-2671
hac@humanists.ca
http://humanists.ca

• Mouvement Laïque Québécois
CP 32132, Succ. St-André
Montréal (Québec)
H2L 4Y5
514-985-5840
braun.claude@uqam.ca
http://www.weltethos.org

• Center for Inquiry/Toronto
216 Beverley Street
Toronto, Ontario M5T 1Z3
www.centerforinquiry.net/toronto

BRITAIN

• British Humanist Association
1, Gower Street,
London WC1E 6HD,
United Kingdom
020 7079 3580
info@humanism.org.uk
www.humanism.org.uk

BOOKS CITED OR RECOMMENDED

Abanes, Richard. *End-Time Visions: The Road to Armageddon.* Four Walls Eight Windows, 1998.

Abbott, Elizabeth. *A History of Celibacy: From Athena to Elizabeth I, Leonardo da Vinci, Florence Nightingale, Ghandi, and Cher.* Scribner, 2000.

Abootalebi, Ali Reza. *Islam and Democracy: State-Society Relations in Developing Countries, 1980–1994.* New York: Routledge, 2000.

Acemoglu, Daron, and James A. Robinson. *Economic Origins of Dictatorship and Democracy: Economic and Political Origins.* Cambridge University Press, 2005.

Aczel, Amir D. *God's Equation, Einstein, Relativity, and the Expanding Universe.* MJF Books, 1999.

Adams, Marilyn McCord. "The Problem of Hell: A Problem of Evil for Christians." In *God and the Problem of Evil,* edited by William Rowe. Blackwell, 2001.

Adams, Robert Merrihew. *A Theory of Virtue: Excellence in Being for the Good.* Oxford University Press, 2006.

Adler, Felix. *Creed and Deed: A Series of Discourses.* Arno Press, 1972.

———. *Life And Destiny; or Thoughts From The Ethical Lectures Of Felix Adler.* Kessinger, 2007.

Ahmed, Akbar. *Islam under Siege: Living Dangerously in a Post-Honour World.* Polity Press, 2003.

———. *Journey Into Islam: The Crisis of Globalization.* Brookings Institution Press, 2007.

Alexander, Michael. *The Kondratiev Cycle: A Generational Interpretation.* Writers Club Press, 2002.

Alexander, Richard. *The Biology of Moral Systems.* Aldine Transaction, 1987.

Ali, Tariq. *The Clash of Fundamentalisms: Crusades, Jihads, and Modernity.* Verso, 2006.

Allen, Brooke. *Moral Minority: Our Skeptical Founding Fathers.* Ivan R. Dee, 2006.

Allen, Douglas. *Religion and Political Conflict in South Asia: India, Pakistan, and Sri Lanka.* Greenwood Press, 1992.

Allen, Steve. *Steve Allen On the Bible, Religion, and Morality.* Prometheus Books, 1990.

Alper, Matthew. *The God Part of the Brain.* Rogue Press, 2001.

Alperovitz, Gar. *The Decision to Use the Atomic Bomb.* Vintage, 1996.

Anderson, Abraham. *Treatise of the Three Impostors and the Problem of Enlightenment.* Rowman & Littlefield, 1997.

Anderson, J. Kirby. *Moral Dilemmas.* Word, 1998.

Anderson, G. W. *A Critical Introduction to the Old Testament.* Duckworth, 1964.

Anscombe, G. E. M. *Ethics, Religion and Politics.* Blackwell, 2002.

Anthony, Dick, and Thomas Robbins. "Religious Totalism, Violence and Exemplary Dualism: Beyond the Extrinsic Model." In *Millennialism and Violence,* edited by Michael Barkun. Frank Cass, 1996.

Arendt, Hannah, and Amos Elon. *Eichmann in Jerusalem: A Report on the Banality of Evil.* 1964. Penguin Classics, 1994.

Arendt, Hannah, and Margaret Canovan. *The Human Condition* 2nd ed. University of Chicago Press, 1998.

Aristotle. *The Basic Works of Aristotle.* Edited by Richard McKeon. Modern Library, 2001.

Armstrong, Karen. *A History of God: The 4,000-Year Quest of Judaism, Christianity, and Islam.* Ballantine Books, 1994.

———. *The Great Transformation: The Beginning of Our Religious Traditions.* Knopf, 2006.

———. *Through the Narrow Gate, A Memoir of Spiritual Discovery.* 1981. St Martin's Griffin, 2005.

———. *The Spiral Staircase: My Climb Out of Darkness.* Reprint, Anchor, 2005.

Armstrong, S., ed. *The Animal Ethics Reader.* Routledge, 2003.

Arnhart, Larry. *Darwinian Natural Right: The Biological Ethics of Human Nature.* State University of New York Press, 1998.

Aron, Raymond. *The Opium of the Intellectuals.* With a foreword by Daniel J. Mahoney. Transaction, 2001.

Aronson, Ronald. *Living without God: New Directions for Atheists, Agnostics, Secularists, and the Undecided.* Counterpoint Press, 2008.

Asad, Talal. *Formations of the Secular: Christianity, Islam, Modernity.* Stanford University Press, 2003.

Asimov, Isaac. *The Relativity of Wrong.* Doubleday, 1988.

Atran, Scot. *In Gods We Trust: The Evolutionary Landscape of Religion.* Oxford University Press, 2004.

Audi, Robert, and W. Wainwright. *Rationality, Religious Belief, and Moral Commitment: New Essays in the Philosophy of Religion.* Cornell University Press, 1986.

Babbitt, Irving. *Democracy and Leadership.* Liberty Fund, 1979.

Baier, Kurt. *Problems of Life and Death: A Humanist Perspective.* Prometheus Books, 1997.

———. *The Rational and the Moral Order: The Social Roots of Reason and Morality.* Open Court, 1995.

Baigent, Michael. *The Jesus Papers: Exposing the Greatest Cover-Up in History.* HarperOne, 2007.

Bakan, Joel. *The Corporation: The Pathological Pursuit of Profit and Power.* Free Press, 2005.

Ball, George W., and Douglas B. Ball. *The Passionate Attachment: America's Involvement with Israel, 1947 to the Present.* W. W. Norton, 1992.

Bamford, James. *A Pretext for War: 9/11, Iraq, and the Abuse of America's Intelligence Agencies.* Doubleday, 2004.

Barber, Benjamin R. *Consumed: How Markets Corrupt Children, Infantilize Adults, and Swallow Citizens Whole.* W. W. Norton, 2007.

Barker, Dan. *Godless: How an Evangelical Preacher Became One of America's Leading Atheists.* Ulysses Press, 2008.

———. *Losing Faith in Faith: From Preacher to Atheist.* Freedom from Religion Foundation, 1992.

Baskin, Wade, ed. *Jean-Paul Sartre, Essays in Existentialism.* Citadel Press, 1993.

Becker, Carl B. *Asian and Jungian Views of Ethics.* Greenwood Press, 1999.

———. *Breaking the Circle: Death and the Afterlife in Buddhism.* Southern Illinois University Press, 1993.

Beinhocker, Eric D. *The Origin of Wealth: Evolution, Complexity, and the Radical Remaking of Economics.* Harvard Business School Press, 2007.

Bell, Daniel, ed. *The New American Right.* Criterion Books, 1955.

———. *The Radical Right.* Anchor Books, 1963.

Bell, David A. *The First Total War: Napoleon's Europe and the Birth of Warfare as We Know It.* Houghton Mifflin, 2007.

Bennett, Helen. *Humanism, What's That?: A Book for Curious Kids.* Prometheus Books, 2005.

Benton, M. J. *When Life Nearly Died: The Greatest Mass Extinction of All Time.* Thames & Hudson, 2003.

Berger, Peter L. *The Other Side of God: A Polarity in World Religions.* Anchor Press/Doubleday, 1981.

Berlet, Chip, and Matthew N. Lyons. *Right-Wing Populism in America: Too Close for Comfort.* Guilford Press, 2007.

Berlinski, David. *Newton's Gift: How Sir Isaac Newton Unlocked the System of Our World.* Simon & Schuster, 2000.

Bernays, Edward. *Propaganda.* 1928. Ig, 2004.

Berry, Brian J. L. *Long-Wave Rhythms in Economic Development and Political Behavior.* Johns Hopkins University Press, 1991.

Bissoondath, Neil. *Innocence of Age.* Penguin Books Canada, 1993.

Blass, Thomas. *The Man Who Shocked the World: The Life and Legacy of Stanley Milgram.* Basic Books, 2004.

Bleuler, Eugene. *Textbook of Psychiatry.* Arno Press, 1976.

Blum, William. *The Rogue State.* Zed Books, 2006.

Bohman, James, and Matthias Lutz-Bachmann. *Perpetual Peace: Essays on Kant's Cosmopolitan Ideal.* MIT Press, 1997.

Booth, Ken, Michael Cox, and Timothy Dunne. *How Might We Live? Global Ethics in the New Century.* Cambridge University Press, 2001.

Borg, Marcus J. *Jesus: Uncovering the Life, Teachings, and Relevance of a Religious Revolutionary.* HarperSanFrancisco, 2006.

———. *Reading the Bible Again for the First Time: Taking the Bible Seriously But Not Literally.* HarperSanFrancisco, 2002.

Bovard, James. *Attention Deficit Democracy,* Palgrave Macmillan, 2006.

Boyd, Gregory A. *God at War: The Bible & Spiritual Conflict.* Inter Varsity Press, 1997.

Boyer, Pascal. *Religion Explained: The Evolutionary Origins of Religious Thought.* Basic Books, 2002.

Boyer, Paul. *When Time Shall Be No More.* Harvard University Press, 1992.

———. "When US Foreign Policy Meets Biblical Prophecy." *AlterNet,* February 20, 2003, available online at: http://www.alternet.org/story/15221.

Bracken, Patrick, and Philip Thomas. "Time to Move beyond the Mind-Body Split." *British Medical Journal (BMJ),* December 21, 2002, editorial, no. 325, pp. 1433–34.

Bradbury, Ray. *Fahrenheit 451.* Ballantine Books, 1987.

Brenner, Lenni, ed. *Jefferson and Madison on the Separation of Church and State.* Barricade Books, 2004.

Bricmont, Jean. "Humanitarian Imperialism: Using Human Rights to Sell War." Monthly Review Press, 2006.

Brockman, John. *The New Humanists: Science at the Edge.* Barnes & Noble, 2003.

Bronner, Stephen Eric. *Reclaiming the Enlightenment: Towards a Politics of Radical Engagement.* Columbia University Press, 2004.

Broom, Donald M. *The Evolution of Morality and Religion.* Cambridge University Press, 2004.

Brown, Laurence B. *The First & Final Commandment: A Search for Truth in Revelation within the Abrahamic Religion.* Amana, 2004.

Browning, Christopher R. *Ordinary Men: Reserve Police Battalion 101 and the Final Solution in Poland.* Harper Perennial, 1993.

Bronowski, Jacob. *Science and Human Values.* Harper Perennial, 1990.

Butler, Samuel, and Lewis Mumford. *Erewhon and Erewhon Revisited.* Kessinger, 2005.

Bryson, Bill. *A Short History of Nearly Everything.* Broadway Books, 2003.

Brzezinski, Zbigniew, and Kenneth Velasquez. *The Grand Chessboard— American Primacy and Its Geostrategic Imperatives.* Easton Press, 1997.

Brubaker, Elizabeth. *Property Rights in the Defense of Nature.* Earthscan, 1995.

Buckman, Robert. *Can We Be Good without God? Biology, Behavior, and the Need to Believe.* Prometheus Books, 2002.

Bunge, Mario. *Chasing Reality: Strife over Realism.* University of Toronto Press, 2006.

———. *Philosophy in Crisis: The Need for Reconstruction.* Prometheus Books, 2001.

———. *Scientific Realism: Selected Essays.* Prometheus Books, 2001.

Burger, A. J. *The Ethics of Belief.* Dry Bones Press, 2001.

Burke, Edmund. *A Philosophical Enquiry into the Origin of Our Ideas of the Sublime and Beautiful.* Oxford University Press, 1998, written in 1757.

Burleigh, Michael. *Earthly Powers: The Clash of Religion and Politics in Europe from the French Revolution to the Great War.* HarperCollins, 2005.

Burstein, Dan, ed. *Secrets of the Code: The Unauthorized Guide to the Mysteries Behind the Da Vinci Code.* CDS Books, 2004.

Bush, George W., and Karen Hughes. *A Charge to Keep,* William Morrow, 1999.

Buss, Doris, and Didi Herman. *Globalizing Family Values: The Christian Right in International Politics.* University of Minnesota Press, 2002.

Cahill, Thomas. *The Gifts Of the Jews, How a Tribe of Desert Nomads Changed the Way Everyone Thinks and Feels.* 1998. Lion Hudson Plc, 2006.

Campbell, Neil A., and Jane B. Reece. *Biology.* Benjamin Cummings, 2005.

Camus, Albert. *The Myth of Sisyphus: And Other Essays.* Reprint, Vintage, 1991.

Canguilhem, Georges. *A Vital Rationalist: Selected writings from Georges Canguilhem.* Edited by F. Delaporte. Zone Books, 1993.

Carlson, Richard. *Don't Sweat the Small Stuff About Money.* Hyperion, 2001.

Carrier, Richard. *Sense And Goodness without God: A Defense of Metaphysical Naturalism.* Authorhouse, 2005.

Carroll, Robert Todd. *The Skeptic's Dictionary: A Collection of Strange Beliefs, Amusing Deceptions, and Dangerous Delusions.* Wiley, 2003.

Carter, Jimmy. *Palestine: Peace Not Apartheid.* Simon & Schuster, 2007.

Cassidy, John. *How Markets Fail: The Logic of Economic Calamities.* Farrar, Straus & Giroux, 2009.

Cederquist, Druzelle. *The Story of Baha'u'llah, Promised One of All Religions.* Baha'i, 2005.

Chakotin, Serge. *The Rape of the Masses: The Psychology of Totalitarian Political Propaganda.* Labour Book Service, 1940.

Chancellor, Edward. *Devil Take the Hindmost: A History of Financial Speculation.* Reprint, Plume, 2000.

Chebel, Malek. *L'Islam et la Raison: Le Combat des Idées.* Librairie Académique Perrin (Tempus), 2006.

Cherry, Conrad, ed. *God's New Israel: Religious Interpretations of American Destiny.* 1st ed. 1971. Reprint, University of North Carolina Press, 1998.

Chopra, Deepak. *Life After Death: The Burden of Proof.* Harmony, 2006.

Clark, Rodney. *One True God: Historical Consequences of Monotheism.* Princeton University Press, 2003.

———. *The Victory of Reason: How Christianity Led to Freedom, Capitalism, and Western Success.* Random House, 2005.

Clifford, William K., and Timothy J. Madigan. *The Ethics of Belief and Other Essays.* 1877. Reprint, Prometheus Books, 1999.

Coates, Anthony Josef. *The Ethics of War.* Manchester University Press, 1997.

Cohen, Arthur A. *The Myth of the Judeo-Christian Tradition: And Other Dissenting Essays.* Harper & Row, 1970. (Also Schocken Books, 1971).

Cohen, Jack, and Ian Stewart. *Figments of Reality: The Evolution of the Curious Mind.* Cambridge University Press, 1999.

Cohn-Sherbok, Dan. *The Paradox of Anti-Semitism.* Continuum International, 2006.

Collins, Francis. *The Language of God: A Scientist Presents Evidence for Belief.* Free Press, 2007.

Cook, Jonathan. *Blood and Religion: The Unmasking of the Jewish and Democratic State.* Pluto Press, 2005.

Cook, William. *Psalms for the 21st Century.* Mellen Poetry Press, 2003.

Cook-Deegan, Robert. *The Gene Wars: Science, Politics and the Human Genome.* W. W. Norton, 1995.

Coon, Carl. *One Planet, One People: Beyond "Us versus Them."* Prometheus Books, 2004.

Corrigan, John, Eric Crump, and John Kloos. *Emotion and Religion: A Critical Assessment and Annotated Bibliography.* Greenwood Press, 2000.

Coward, Harold G. *Population, Consumption, and the Environment: Religious and Secular Responses.* State University of New York Press, 1995.

Coyne, Jerry A. *Why Evolution is True.* Viking Adult, 2009.

Crawford, Alan. *Thunder on the Right.* Pantheon, 1981.

Creme, Benjamin, ed. *Maitreya's Teachings: The Laws of Life.* Share International Fdn, 2005.

Croxton, Derek, and Anuschka Tischer. *The Peace of Westphalia: A Historical Dictionary.* Greenwood Press, 2001.

Crozier, W. Ray, and Paul Greenhalgh. "Beyond Relativism and Formalism: The Empathy Principle." *Leonardo* 25, no. 1 (1992): 83–87.

Crowley, Roger. *1453: The Holy War for Constantinople and the Clash of Islam and the West.* Hyperion, 2005.

Dacey, Austin. *The Secular Conscience: Why Belief Belongs in Public Life.* Prometheus Books, 2008.

Daly, Lew, and James Carroll. *God and the Welfare State.* MIT Press, 2006.

Danziger, Danny, and John Gillingham. *1215, The Year of Magna Carta.* Touchstone, 2003.

Dark, K. R. *Religion and International Relations.* Palgrave MacMillan, 2000.

Darwin, Charles. *On the Origin of Species.* 1859. Gramercy, 1995.

———. *The Descent of Man, and Selection in Relation to Sex.* John Murray, 1871.

———. *On the Origin of Species.* With an introduction by Julian Huxley. 1859. Signet Classics, 2003.

Davich, Victor N. *8-Minute Meditation: Quiet Your Mind. Change Your Life.* Perigee Books, 2004.

———. *The Best Guide to Meditation.* With a foreword by Jack Canfield. Renaissance Books, 1998.

Davies, Kevin. *Cracking the Genome.* Johns Hopkins University Press, 2002.

Davies, Nigel. *Human Sacrifice: In History and Today.* Dorset, 1988.

Davies, Tony. *Humanism.* Routledge, 2008.

Dawkins, Richard. *The Blind Watchmaker: Why the Evidence of Evolution Reveals a Universe without Design.* W. W. Norton, 1996.

———. *The God Delusion.* Houghton Mifflin, 2006.

———. *The Selfish Gene.* Oxford University Press, 1976.

De Panafieu, Jean-Baptiste, Patrick Gries, and Linda Asher. *Evolution.* Seven Stories Press, 2007.

De Wall, Frans. *Primates and Philosophers: How Morality Evolved.* Princeton University Press, 2006.

Delos, Andrew C. *Myths We Live By: From the Times of Jesus and Paul.* Book-Surge, 2006.

Dennett, Daniel C. *Breaking the Spell: Religion as a Natural Phenomenon.* Viking, 2006.

———. *Darwin's Dangerous Idea, Evolution and the Meanings of Life.* Simon and Schuster, 1995.

Dershowitz, Alan. *Blasphemy: How the Religious Right is Hijacking our Declaration of Independence.* John Wiley & Sons, 2007.

Detmer, David. *Challenging Postmodernism: Philosophy and the Politics of Truth.* Humanity Books, 2003.

Dewey, John. *A Common Faith.* Yale University Press, 1960.

D'Holbach, Baron, *Good Sense without God; or Freethoughts Opposed to Supernatural Ideas, A Translation Of Baron D'Holbach's "le Bon Sens."* Kessinger, 2004.

Diamond, Jared. *Collapse: How Societies Choose to Fail or Succeed.* Viking Adult, 2004.

———. *The Third Chimpanzee: The Evolution and Future of the Human Animal.* Harper Perennial, 1992.

Diamond, Larry, Marc F. Plattner, and Philip J. Costopoulos. *World Religions and Democracy.* Johns Hopkins University Press, 2005.

Diamond, Sara. *Roads to Dominion.* Guilford Press, 1995.

———. *Spiritual Warfare: The Politics of the Christian Right.* South End Press, 1989.

Dobrin, Arthur. *Ethics for Everyone: How to Increase Your Moral Intelligence.* John Wiley & Sons, 2002.

Doidge, Norman. *The Brain That Changes Itself: Stories of Personal Triumph from the Frontiers of Brain Science.* Viking, 2007.

Dostoevsky, Fyodor, with Marie Jaanus and Constance Garnett. *The Brothers Karamazov.* Barnes & Noble, 2004.

Dowbiggin, Ian. *A Merciful End: The Euthanasia Movement in Modern America.* Oxford University Press, 2003.

Ducomte, Jean-Michel. *La Loi de 1905 : Quand l'Etat Se Séparait des Eglises.* Milan, 2005.

Durant, Will, and Ariel Durant. *The Story of Civilization, Part X, Rousseau and Revolution.* Simon and Schuster, 1967.

Durkheim, Emile, and Anthony Giddens. *Emile Durkheim: Selected Writings.* Cambridge University Press, 1972.

Durkheim, Emile, Anthony Giddens, Mark S. Cladis, and Carol Cosman. *The Elementary Forms of Religious Life.* Oxford University Press, 2001.

Dworkin, Gerald, R. G. Frey, and Sissela Bok. *Euthanasia and Physician-Assisted Suicide (For and Against).* Cambridge University Press, 1998.

Edis, Taner. *An Illusion of Harmony: Science and Religion in Islam.* Prometheus Books, 2007.

Ehrman, Bart D. *Misquoting Jesus: The Story behind Who Changed the Bible and Why.* HarperSanFrancisco, 2005.

Ellens, Harold. *The Destructive Power of Religion: Violence in Judaism, Christianity, and Islam.* 4 vols. Praeger, 2003.

Eller, David. *Natural Atheism.* American Atheist Press, 2004.

Elliott Abrams, ed. *The Influence of Faith: Religious Groups & US Foreign Policy.* Rowman & Littlefield, 2001.

Ellis, Albert. *Case Against Religion: A Psychotherapists View and the Case Against Religiosity.* American Atheist Press, 1980.

Epstein, Greg. *Good without God: What a Billion Religious People Do Believe.* William Morrow, 2009.

Ericson, Karl. "Creation of Delusions." *International Bulletin of Political Psychology* 15, no. 2 (September 2003).

Esposito, John L. *Unholy War: Terror in the Name of Islam.* Oxford University Press, 2003.

Faber, M. D. *The Psychological Roots of Religious Belief: Searching for Angels and the Parent-God.* Prometheus Books, 2004.

Faragher, John Mack. *Manifest Destiny and Mission in American History.* Harvard University Press, 1995.

Fearn, Nicholas. *The Latest Answers to the Oldest Questions: A Philosophical Adventure with the World's Greatest Thinkers.* Grove Press, 2007.

Fellows, Otis E., and Norman L. Torrey, eds. *The Age of Enlightenment.* F. S. Crofts, 1942.

Fenves, Peter. *Raising the Tone of Philosophy: Late Essays by Immanuel Kant.* Johns Hopkins University Press, 1998.

Feuerbach, Ludwig. *The Essence of Christianity.* 1841. Prometheus Books, 2008.
———. *The Essence of Religion.* 1845. Prometheus Books, 2004.

Fieser, James. *Metaethics, Normative Ethics, and Applied Ethics: Contemporary and Historical Readings.* Wadsworth, 1999.

Finke, Roger, and Rodney Stark. *The Churching of America, 1776–2005: Winners and Losers in Our Religious Economy.* Rutgers University Press, 2005.

Firestone, Reuven. *Jihad: The Origin of Holy War in Islam.* Oxford University Press, 2002.

Fisk, Robert. *The Great War for Civilization: The Conquest of the Middle East.* Alfred A. Knopf, 2005.

France, John. *Western Warfare in the Age of the Crusades, 1000–1300.* Cornell University Press, 1999.

Frank, Leonard Roy. *Freedom: Quotes and Passages from the World's Greatest Freethinkers.* Random House Reference, 2003.

Frank, Robert G. *Harvey and the Oxford Physiologists: Scientific Ideas and Social Interaction.* University of California Press, 1980.

Frankena, William K. "Is Morality Logically Dependent on Religion?" In *Religion and Morality: A Collection of Essays,* edited by Gene Outka and J. P. Reeder Jr. Doubleday, 1973.

Freud, Sigmund, James Strachey, and Peter Gay. *The Future of an Illusion.* Reprint, W. W. Norton, 1987.

Friedman, Benjamin M. *The Moral Consequences of Economic Growth.* Knopf, 2005.

Friedman, Richard E. *Who Wrote the Bible?* HarperSanFrancisco, 1997.

Fromkin, David. *Europe's Last Summer: Who Started the Great War in 1914?* Reprint, Vintage, 2005.

Fry, Iris. *The Emergence of Life on Earth: A Historical and Scientific Overview.* Rutgers University Press, 2000.

Fuller, Steve. *Science v. Religion? Intelligent Design and the Problem of Evolution.* Polity Press, 2007.

Gabriel, Mark A. *Islam and the Jews.* Charisma House, 2003.

Garety, Philippa A., and Daniel Freeman. "Cognitive Approaches to Delusions: A Critical Review of Theories and Evidence." In *British Journal of Clinical Psychology* 38 (1999): 113–54.

Gaustad, Edwin Scott, Philip L. Barlow, and Richard W. Dishno. *New Historical Atlas of Religion in America.* Oxford University Press, 2001.

Gaylor, Annie L. *Woe to the Women: The Bible Tells Me So.* Freedom From Religion Foundation, 1981.

———, ed. *Women without Superstition: No Gods—No Masters.* Freedom From Religion Foundation, 1997.

Gaylor, Annie L., and Alma Cuebas. *Woe to the Women: The Bible, Female Sexuality and the Law: The Bible Tells Me So.* Freedom From Religion Foundation, 2004.

Gensler, Harry. *Ethics: Contemporary Readings.* Routledge, 2003.

———. *Formal Ethics.* Routledge, 1996.

Gibbs, John C. *Moral Development & Reality: Beyond the Theories of Kohlberg and Hoffman.* Allyn & Pacon, 2009.

Gittler, J. B. *Ideas of Concord and Discord in Selected World Religions.* JAI Press, 2000.

Gleditsch, Kristian. "A Revised List of Wars between and within Independent States, 1816–2002." *International Interactions* 30, no. 3 (July–September 2004): 231–62.

Gottlieb, Anthony. *The Dream of Reason: A History of Philosophy from the Greeks to the Renaissance.* W. W. Norton, 2001.

Goring, Rosemary. *Dictionary of Beliefs and Religion.* Larousse, 1994.

Gottesman, Ronald, and Richard M. Brown. *Violence in America: An Encyclopedia.* Charles Scribner's Sons, 1999.

Gould, Stephen Jay. *The Structure of Evolutionary Theory.* Belknap Press, 2002.

Gould, Stephen Jay, Oliver Sacks, and Stephen Rose. *The Richness of Life: The Essential Stephen Jay Gould.* W. W. Norton, 2007.

Goyette, John, Mark S. Latkovic, and Richard S. Myers. *St. Thomas Aquinas and the Natural Law Tradition: Contemporary Perspectives,* Catholic University of America Press, 2004.

Grassian, Victor. *Moral Reasoning: Ethical Theory and Some Contemporary Moral Problems.* 1981. Prentice Hall, 1992.

Grayling, A. C. *Among the Dead Cities: The History and Moral Legacy of the WWII Bombing of Civilians in Germany and in Japan.* Walker, 2006.

———. *Life, Sex and Ideas: The Good Life without God.* Oxford University Press, 2004.

Grayling, A. C. *Meditations for the Humanist: Ethics for a Secular Age.* Oxford University Press, 2003.

———. *Philosophy 1: A Guide through the Subject.* Oxford University Press, 1999.

———. *Philosophy 2: Further through the Subject.* Oxford University Press, 1999.

Green, Joshua, "God's Foreign Policy." *Washington Monthly,* November 2001, 26–30.

Greene, Joshua D., and Jonathan Haidt, "How (and Where) Does Moral Judgment Work?" *Trends in Cognitive Sciences* 6:517–23.

Greenwald, Glenn. *A Tragic Legacy: How a Good vs. Evil Mentality Destroyed the Bush Presidency.* Crown, 2007.

Griggs, Edward Howard. *The Ethics of Personal Life: A Handbook of Six Lectures.* Kessinger, 2006.

———. *The New Humanism: Studies in Personal and Social Development (1913).* Kessinger, 2008.

Gross, Ronald. *Socrates' Way: Seven Keys to Using Your Mind to the Utmost.* Tarcher, 2002.

Gunasekara, Victor A. *The Philosophical Basis of Humanist Ethics.* Paper presented to the Regional Congress of the IHEU and CAHS, Sydney, Australia, November 2000.

Habermas, Jürgen. *Democracy and the Public Sphere.* Pluto Press, 2005.

———. *Jurgen Habermas on Society and Ethics: A Reader.* Beacon Press, 1989.

Habermas, Jürgen, and Joseph Ratzinger (now Pope Benedict XVI). *The Dialectics of Secularization: On Reason and Religion.* Ignatius Press, 2007.

Hagee, John. *From Daniel to Doomsday: The Countdown Has Begun.* Nelson Books, 2000. (Also revised ed., Frontline, 2007).

Haidt, Jonathan. *The Happiness Hypothesis.* Basic Books, 2006.

———. *The Happiness Hypothesis: Finding Modern Truth in Ancient Wisdom.* Basic Books, 2005.

Haleem, M. A. S. Abdel. *The Quran.* Oxford University Press, 2004.

Halsell, Grace. *Prophecy and Politics: Militant Evangelists on the Road to Nuclear War.* Lawrence Hill Books, 1986.

———. *Prophecy and Politics: The Secret Alliance between Israel and the US Christian Right.* Revised ed., Lawrence Hill Books, 1989.

Hamer, Dean H. *The God Gene: How Faith Is Hardwired into Our Genes.* Doubleday, 2004.

Hamilton, Marci A., and Edward R. Becker. *God vs. the Gavel: Religion and the Rule of Law.* Cambridge University Press, 2005.

Haney, C., W. C. Banks, and P. G. Zimbardo. "Interpersonal Dynamics in a Simulated Prison." *International Journal of Criminology and Penology* (1973): 69–97.

Hare, Robert D. *Without Conscience: The Disturbing World of the Psychopaths among Us,* Guilford Press, 1999.

Harford, Tim. *The Logic of Life: The Rational Economics of an Irrational World.* Random House, 2008.

Harris, Lee. *The Suicide of Reason: Radical Islam's Threat to the West.* Basic Books, 2007.

Harris, Sam. *Letter to a Christian Nation.* Knopf, 2006.

———. *The End of Faith: Religion, Terror, and the Future of Reason,* W. W. Norton, 2006.

Hart, Darryl. *A Secular Faith: Why Christianity Favors the Separation of Church and State.* Ivan R. Dee, 2006.

Hauser, Marc D. *Moral Minds: How Nature Designed Our Universal Sense of Right and Wrong.* Ecco, 2005.

Hawking, Stephen. *A Brief History of Time.* Bantam, 1998.

———. *The Universe in a Nutshell.* Bantam, 2001.

Hawking, Stephen, and Leonard Mlodinow. *A Briefer History of Time.* Bantam, 2005.

Hayek, Friedrich A. *New Studies in Philosophy, Politics, Economics and the History of Ideas.* Routledge and K. Paul, 1978.

————. *The Road to Serfdom.* 1944. Revised ed., Routledge, 1991.

Hayward, Patricia, and Johnathon Noble. *Macquarie HSC Studies of Religion.* 2nd ed. Macmillan Education Australia, 2007.

Hedges, Chris. *American Fascism: The Christian Right and the War on America.* Free Press, 2007.

Heidegger, Martin. *Being and Time.* 1927. Blackwell, 1978.

Heidegger, Martin, and Joan Stambaugh. *On Being and Time.* University of Chicago Press, 2002.

Hendricks, Obery M. *The Politics of Jesus: Rediscovering the True Revolutionary Nature of Jesus' Teachings and How They Have Been Corrupted.* Doubleday, 2006.

Henshaw, Stanley K., Susheela Singh, and Taylor Haas. *The Incidence of Abortion Worldwide: International Family Planning Perspectives* 25 (1999): S30–S8.

Herrick, Jim. *Humanism: An Introduction.* Prometheus Books, 2005.

Hershberg, James G. *James B. Conant: Harvard to Hiroshima and the Making of the Nuclear Age.* Stanford University Press, 1993.

Higginbotham, Joyce. *Pagan Spirituality: A Guide to Personal Transformation.* Llewellyn, 2006.

Hill, Jonathan. *Faith in the Age of Reason: The Enlightenment from Galileo to Kant.* Inter Varsity Press, 2004.

Hill, Michael O. *Dreaming the End of the World.* Spring, 2004.

Hinman, Lawrence M. *Ethics: A Pluralistic Approach to Moral Theory.* 3rd ed. Wadsworth, 2002.

Hitchens, Christopher. *God Is Not Great: How Religion Poisons Everything.* Twelve, 2007.

Hitt, William D. *Ethics and Leadership: Putting Theory into Practice.* Battelle Press, 1990.

Hoffman, Bruce. *Inside Terrorism.* Columbia University Press, 2006.

Hoffman, Martin L. *Empathy and Moral Development: Implications for Caring and Justice.* Cambridge University Press, 2001.

Hoffman, Michael A. *Judaism's Strange Gods.* Independent History & Research, 2000.

Holcombe, Randall G. *Writing Off Ideas: Taxation, Foundations, and Philanthropy in America.* Independent Institute, 2000.

Hood, Ralph W. Jr., Peter C. Hill and W. Paul Williamson. *The Psychology of Religious Fundamentalism.* Guilford Press, 2005.

Hoyle, Fred, Geoffrey Burbidge, and Jayant Vishnu Narlikar. *A Different*

Approach to Cosmology: From a Static Universe through the Big Bang towards Reality. Cambridge University Press, 2000.

Houtart, F., and G. Lemercinier. *The Great Asiatic Religions.* Université Catholique, Louvain, 1980.

Howe, Marvine. *Turkey Today—A Nation Divided over Islam's Revival.* Westview Press, 2000.

Howell-Smith, Arthur Denner. *In Search of the Real Bible.* 2nd ed. Watts, 1947.

Huff, Toby E. *The Rise of Early Modern Science, Islam, China, and the West.* Cambridge University Press, 1993.

Hume, David. *An Enquiry Concerning the Principles of Morals.* 1750. New ed. Oxford University Press, 1998.

———. *Dialogues and Natural History of Religion.* 1779. Reedited, Penguin Classics, 1990.

Humes, Edward. *Monkey Girl, Evolution, Education, Religion, and the Battle for America's Soul.* Ecco, 2007.

Humphry, Derek. *Final Exit: The Practicalities of Self-Deliverance and Assisted Suicide for the Dying.* 3rd ed. Delta, 2002.

Huntington, Samuel P. *The Clash of Civilizations and the Remaking of World Order.* Simon & Schuster, 1998.

Hutcheon, Pat Duffy. *Building Character & Culture.* Praeger, 1999.

Huxley, Aldous. *Brave New World.* 1932. Reprint, Perennial Classics, 1998.

Huxley, T. H. *Evolution and Ethics and Other Essays.* Appleton, 1896.

Ingersoll, Robert G. *Superstition and Other Essays.* Prometheus Books, 2004.

———. *The Works of Robert Ingersoll.* Vols.1–12. Dresden, 1912.

———. *Immortal Infidel: Robert G. Ingersoll.* edited by Orvin Larson, Freedom From Religion Foundation, 1993.

Jacobs, A. J. *The Year of Living Biblically: One Man's Humble Quest to Follow the Bible as Literally as Possible.* Simon & Schuster, 2007.

Jacoby, Susan. *Freethinkers: A History of American Secularism.* Metropolitan Books, 2004.

———. *The Age of American Unreason.* Pantheon, 2008.

Jalal, Ayesha. *Partisans of Allah: Jihad in South Asia.* Harvard University Press, 2008.

James, William. *The Will to Believe, Human Immortality.* Dover, 1956.

———. *Writings 1902–1910: The Varieties of Religious Experience.* Library of America, 1988.

Jenkins, Philip. *The Next Christendom: The Coming of Global Christianity.* Revised ed. Oxford University Press, 2007.

Jewett, Robert, and John Shelton Lawrence. *Captain America and the Crusade against Evil: The Dilemma of Zealous Nationalism.* William B. Eerdmans, 2004.

Johnson, George. *Fire in the Mind: Science, Faith, and the Search for Order.* Vintage, 1996.

Johnson, Suzan. *Live Like You're Blessed: Simple Steps for Making Balance, Love, Energy, Spirit, Success, Encouragement, and Devotion Part of Your Life.* Doubleday Religion, 2006.

Joseph, Rhawn, Andrew Newberg, Carol Albright Rausch, Michael Persinger, William James, Friedrich Nietzsche. *NeuroTheology: Brain, Science, Spirituality, Religious Experience.* University Press, 2003.

Juergensmeyer, Mark. *Comparative Studies in Religion and Society.* Vol. 13 *Terror in the Mind of God: The Global Rise of Religious Violence.* University of California Press, 2003.

Kaiser, Robert G. *So Damn Much Money: The Triumph of Lobbying and the Corrosion of American Government.* Knopf, 2009.

Kamen, Henry. *The Spanish Inquisition.* Weidenfeld & Nicolson, 1965.

Kant, Immanuel. *Critique of Pure Reason.* 1781. Edited by Paul Guyer and Allen W. Wood. Cambridge University Press, 1999.

———. *Groundwork for the Metaphysics of Morals.* Edited and translated by Mary Gregor. Wilder Publications, 2008.

———. *Observations on the Feeling of the Beautiful and Sublime.* Translated by John T. Goldthwait. University of California Press, 2004.

———. *Religion within the Limits of Reason Alone.* HarperOne, 1960.

Katz, Jack. *Seductions of Crime.* Basic Books, 1988.

Katz, Leonard D. *Evolutionary Origins of Morality: Cross-Disciplinary Perspectives.* Imprint Academic, 2000.

Kaufmann, Walter A. *Critique of Religion and Philosophy.* Princeton University Press, 1979.

Keeley, Lawrence H. *War before Civilization: The Myth of the Peaceful Savage.* Oxford University Press, 1997.

Kennedy, Paul. *The Parliament of Man: The Past, Present and Future of the United Nations.* Random House, 2006.

Kepel, Gilles. *The War for Muslim Minds: Islam and the West.* Belknap Press, 2004.

Khadduri, Majid. *War and Peace in the Law of Islam.* Lawbook Exchange, 1965. Reprint, Johns Hopkins Press, 2007.

Khan, Muhammad M., and Muhammad T. Al-Hilali, trans. *The Noble Quran,* fundamentalist version published in and distributed usually for free by the government of Saudi Arabia. Dar-us-Salam, 1999.

King, Barbara J. *Evolving God: A Provocative View on the Origins of Religion.* Doubleday Religion, 2007.

Kirk-Duggan, Cheryl. *Refiner's Fire: A Religious Engagement with Violence,* Augsburg Fortress, 2000.

Klein, Richard G. *The Dawn of Human Culture.* Wiley, 2002.

———. *The Human Career: Human Biological and Cultural Origins.* University of Chicago Press, 1999.

Kleinberg, Aviad, and Susan Emanuel. *Seven Deadly Sins: A Very Partial List.* Belknap Press, 2008.

Klemke, E. D. *The Meaning of Life.* Oxford University Press, 1999.

Knight, Margaret. *Humanist Anthology: From Confucius to Attenborough.* Prometheus Books, 1995.

———. *Morals without Religion and Other Essays.* Dennis Dobson, 1960.

Kling, Arnold, and Nick Schulz. *From Poverty to Prosperity: Intangible Assets, Hidden Liabilities, and the Lasting Triumph over Scarcity,* Encounter Books, 2009.

Koopmans, Ruud, Paul Statham, Marco Giugni, and Florence Passy. *Contested Citizenship: Immigration and Cultural Diversity,* University Of Minnesota Press, 2005.

Kornbluth, Cyril M. *The Marching Morons.* 3rd ed. 1963. Ballantine Books, 1959.

Kung, Hans. *A Global Ethic for Global Politics and Economics.* Oxford University Press, 1997.

———. *Global Responsibility: In Search of a New World Ethic.* Continuum International, 1991.

———. *My Struggle for Freedom.* Continuum International, 2005.

———. *A Global Ethic: The Declaration of the Parliament of the World's Religions.* Edited by Karl-Josef Kuschel. Continuum International Publishing Group, 1993.

Kung, Hans, Josef Van Ess, Heinrich Von Stietencron, and Heinz Bechert. *Christianity and World Religions: Paths of Dialogue with Islam, Hinduism, and Buddhism.* Orbis Books, 1993.

Kuran, Timur. *Islam and Mammon: The Economic Predicaments of Islamism.* Princeton University Press, 2004.

Kurtz, Paul. *Humanist Manifesto 2000: A Call for New Planetary Humanism.* Prometheus Books, 2000.

———. *Humanist Manifestos I and II.* Prometheus Books, 1973.

———. *Living without Religion: Eupraxophy.* Prometheus Books, 1994.

———. *The Courage to Become: The Virtues of Humanism.* Praeger Paperback, 1997.

―――. *The Transcendental Temptation: A Critique of Religion and the Paranormal.* Prometheus Books, 1991.

―――. *Forbidden Fruit: The Ethics of Humanism.* Prometheus Books, 1988.

―――. *Secular Humanist Declaration.* Prometheus Books, 1980.

―――. *Humanist Manifestos One and Two.* Prometheus Books, 1973.

―――. *Moral Problems in Contemporary Society―Essays in Humanistic Ethics.* 2nd ed. Prometheus Books, 1977.

―――. *What Is Secular Humanism,* Prometheus Books, 2007.

Lamont, Corliss. *The Philosophy of Humanism.* Humanist Press, 1997.

―――. "The Affirmative Ethics of Humanism." *The Humanist* 49, no. 2 (March/April 1980).

Landaw, Jonathan. *Buddhism for Dummies.* For Dummies, 2002.

Landes, David. *The Wealth and Poverty of Nations: Why Some Are So Rich and Some So Poor.* W. W. Norton, 1998.

Lao-Tzu. *Lao Tzu: Tao Te Ching: A Book about the Way and the Power of the Way.* Translated by Ursula K. Le Guin. Shambhala, 1998.

Lardner, James, and David A. Smith, eds. *Inequality Matters: The Growing Economic Divide in America and Its Poisonous Consequences.* New Press, 2006.

Lawrence, T.E. *Seven Pillars of Wisdom: A Triumph.* Reissued ed. Anchor, 1991.

Layard, Richard. *Happiness: Lessons from a New Science.* Reprint, Penguin, 2006.

Leibniz, Gottfried W. *Theodicy: Essays on the Goodness of God the Freedom of Man and the Origin of Evil.* 1710. Open Court, 1985.

Leibniz, Gottfried W., Peter Remnant, and Jonathan Bennett. *New Essays on Human Understanding.* 2nd ed. Cambridge University Press, 2003.

Levine, David. *Teaching Empathy: A Blueprint for Caring, Compassion, and Community.* Solution Tree, 2005.

Lewis, David Levering. *God's Crucible: A Lesson for the 21st Century.* Norton, 2008.

Lienesch, Michael. *Redeeming America: Piety and Politics in the New Christian Right.* University of North Carolina Press, 1993.

Lilienthal, Alfred M. *The Zionist Connection II.* Noontide Pr, 1986.

Lilla, Mark. *The Stillborn God: Religion, Politics, and the Modern West.* Knopf, 2007.

Lindberg, David C. *The Beginnings of Western Science: The European Scientific Tradition in Philosophical, Religious and Institutional Context, 600 BC to AD 1450.* University of Chicago Press, 1992.

Linde, A. D. *Particle Physics and Inflationary Cosmology.* CRC Press, 1990.

Linden, David J. *The Accidental Mind: How Brain Evolution Has Given Us Love, Memory, Dreams, and God.* Belknap Press, 2007.

Linden, Eugene. *The Winds of Change : Climate, Weather, and the Destruction of Civilizations*. Simon & Schuster, 2006.

Linker, Damon. *The Theocons: Secular America under Siege*. Doubleday, 2006.

Lipset, Seymour Martin, and Earl Raab. *The Politics of Unreason*. University of Chicago Press, 1978.

Littlejohn, Stephen W. *Theories of Human Communication*. Wadsworth, 2002.

Lister, T. *Chemistry and the Human Genome*. Royal Society of Chemistry, 2007.

Livingstone, E. A. *The Concise Oxford Dictionary of the Christian Church*. 2nd Revised ed. Oxford University Press, 2006.

Lobaczewski, Andrew M. *Political Ponerology: A Science on the Nature of Evil Adjusted for Political Purposes*. Red Pill Press, 2006.

Locke, John. *An Essay Concerning Human Understanding*. Pomona Press, 2007.

———. *The Second Treatise on Civil Government*.1690. Prometheus Books, 1986.

Lofmark, Carl. *What Is the Bible?* Prometheus Books, 1992.

Lopez, Donald S. Jr. *The Story of Buddhism: A Concise Guide to Its History and Teachings*. Reprint, HarperSanFrancisco, 2002.

Lorenz, Konrad. *Civilized Man's Eight Deadly Sins*. Methuen Young Books, 1974.

Lovelock, James. *The Ages of Gaia: A Biography of Our Living Earth*. W. W. Norton, 1995.

———. *The Revenge of Gaia, Earth's Climate in Crisis and the Fate of Humanity*. Basic Books, 2006.

Ludemann, Gerd. *Paul: The Founder of Christianity*. Prometheus Books, 2002.

———. *The Unholy in Holy Scripture: The Dark Side of the Bible*. Westminster John Knox Press, 1997.

Lynn, Barry W., *Piety and Politics: The Right-Wing Assault on Religious Freedom*. Harmony, 2006.

Maccoby, Hyam. *The Mythmaker: Paul and the Invention of Christianity*. Harper & Row, 1986.

———. *Revolution in Judaea: Jesus and the Jewish Resistance, the Jesus of History & the Jesus of Myth*. Specialist Press International, 1986.

MacDonald, Kevin. *A People that Shall Dwell Alone: Judaism as a Group Evolutionary Strategy*. Universe, 2002.

Mackie, J. L. *The Miracle of Theism: Arguments For and Against the Existence of God*. Oxford University Press, 1983.

MacKay, Charles. *Extraordinary Popular Delusions: The Madness of Crowds*. 1841. Three Rivers Press, 1999.

MacLean, Paul D. *The Triune Brain in Evolution: Role in Paleocerebral Functions*. Springer, 2003.

Malinowsk, Bronislaw, and Robert Redfield. *Magic, Science, and Religion and Other Essays, 1948.* Kessinger, 2004.

Manji, Irshad. *The Trouble with Islam Today: A Muslim's Call for Reform in Her Faith.* St. Martin's Griffin, 2005. (In Canada, Vintage Canada, 2005.)

Mango, Andrew. *Ataturk: The Biography of the Founder of Modern Turkey.* Overlook TP, 2002.

Mansfield, Edward D., and Jack Snyder. *Electing to Fight: Why Emerging Democracies Go to War.* MIT Press, 2005.

Maritain, Jacques. *The Rights of Man and Natural Law.* 1942. Gordian Press, 1971.

Marshall, Peter. *Demanding the Impossible: a History of Anarchism.* HarperCollins, 1991.

Martin, Michael. *Atheism, Morality, and Meaning,* Prometheus Books, 2002.

———. *The Cambridge Companion to Atheism.* Cambridge University Press, 2006.

Martin, William. "The Christian Right and American Foreign Policy." *Foreign Policy* 114 (Spring 1999): 66–79.

———. *With God on Our Side: The Rise of the Religious Right in America.* Broadway, 2005.

Masuzawa, Tomoko. *The Invention of World Eeligions, or, How European Universalism Was Preserved in the Language of Pluralism.* Chicago University Press, 2005.

Matafonov, George. *Fire and Water: Market Morality & Civil Society.* BookSurge, 2006.

Mathur, Aparna, and Kartikeya Singh. "Foreign Direct Investment, Corruption, and Democracy." *AEI Working Paper.* May 15, 2007. http://www.aei.org/publications/pubID.26180/pub_detail.asp.

Mayer, Milton. *They Thought They Were Free: The Germans, 1933-45.* University of Chicago Press, 1966.

Mazower, Mark. *Salonica, City of Ghosts: Christians, Muslims and Jews.* HarperCollins, 2004.

McArthur, Bruce. *Your Life: Why It Is the Way It Is and What You Can Do about It—Understanding the Universal Laws.* A. R. E. Press, 1993.

McCrone, John, and John Gribbin. *How the Brain Works.* DK Adult, 2002.

McGowan, Dale. *Raising Freethinkers: A Practical Guide for Parenting beyond Belief.* AMACOM, 2009.

McKibben, Bill. *Deep Economy: The Wealth of Communities and the Durable Future.* Times Books, 2007.

Meadows, Donella H. *Limits to Growth: The 30-Year Update.* Chelsea Green, 2004.

Mearsheimer, John, and Stephen Walt. *The Israel Lobby and US Foreign Policy.* Farrar, Straus and Giroux, 2007.

Mercer, Christia. *Leibniz's Metaphysics: Its Origins and Development.* Cambridge University Press, 2001.

Merton, Robert K. *Sociological Ambivalence and Other Essays.* Free Press, 1976.

Meddeb, Abdelwahab. *La Maladie de l'Islam.* Seuil, 2005.

Melnyk, Andrew. *A Physicalist Manifesto: Thoroughly Modern Materialism.* Cambridge University Press, 2003.

Milgram, Stanley, and Jerome S. Bruner.*Obedience to Authority.* Pinter & Martin, 2005.

Miller, Arthur G. *The Social Psychology of Good and Evil.* Guilford Press, 2005.

Mills, David. *Atheist Universe: The Thinking Person's Answer to Christian Fundamentalism.* Ulysses Press, 2006.

———. *Atheist Universe: Why God Didn't Have a Thing to Do with It.* Xlibris, 2004.

Mintz, Samuel I. *The Hunting of Leviathan: Seventeenth-Century Reactions to the Materialism and Moral Philosophy of Thomas Hobbes.* Cambridge University Press, 1962.

Mises, Ludwig von. *Human Action: A Treatise on Economics.* 1949. Mises Institute, 1966.

———. *Liberalism: The Classical Tradition.* 1927. Liberty Fund, 2005.

Mokyr, Joel. *The Gifts of Athena: Historical Origins of the Knowledge Economy.* Princeton University Press, 2002.

Montesquieu, Charles de Secondat. (On) *The Spirit of the Laws.* Initially published anonymously in two volumes in 1748. Prometheus Books, 2002.

Monbiot, George. *Manifesto for a New World Order.* Reprint, New Press, 2006.

———. *The Age of Consent.* HarperPerennial, 2004.

Mooney, Chris. *The Republican War on Science.* Basics Books, 2005.

Moreland, James Porter, and Dallas Willard. *Love Your God with All Your Mind: The Role of Reason in the Life of the Soul.* Navpress, 1997.

Moreland, James Porter, Dallas Willard, and W. L. Craig. *Philosophical Foundations for a Christian Worldview.* InterVarsity Press, 2003.

Morgan, Christopher W., and Robert A. Peterson, eds. *Hell Under Fire: Modern Scholarship Reinvents Eternal Punishment.* Zondervan, 2004.

Morgan, Peggy, and Clive Lawton. *Ethical Issues in Six Religious Traditions.* Edinburgh University Press, 2006.

Morin, Edgar, and Anne Brigitte Kern. *Homeland Earth: A Manifesto for the New Millennium.* Translated by Sean Kelly and Roger Lapoint. Hampton Press, 1999.

Morris, Thomas V. *God and the Philosophers: The Reconciliation of Faith and Reason.* Oxford University Press, 1996.

Murphy, Walter F. *Constitutional Democracy: Creating and Maintaining a Just Political Order.* Johns Hopkins University Press, 2006.

Narciso, Dianna. *Like Rolling Uphill: realizing the honesty of Atheism.* Llumina Press, 2004.

National Academy of Sciences. *Report on Global Climate Change.* National Academy Press, 2001.

Nelson-Pallmeyer, de Jack. *Is Religion Killing Us? Violence in the Bible and the Qur'an.* Continuum International, 2005.

Newberg, Andrew, Eugene d'Aquili, and Vince Rause. *Why God Won't Go Away: Brain Science and the Biology of Belief.* Ballantine Books, 2002.

Niditch, Susan. *War in the Hebrew Bible: A Study in the Ethics of Violence.* Oxford University Press, 1995.

Nielsen, Kai. *Ethics without God.* Prometheus Books, 1990.

Nietzsche, Friedrich. *Beyond Good and Evil.* 1886. Filiquarian, 2007.

———. *Basic Writings of Nietzsche.* Modern Library, 2000.

Nietzsche, Friedrich, and Walter Kaufmann. *On the Genealogy of Morals and Ecce Homo.* 1887, 1888. Reissue, Vintage, 1989.

Nietzsche, Friedrich, and Douglas Smith. *On the Genealogy of Morals: A Polemic. By Way of Clarification and Supplement to My Last Book* Beyond Good and Evil. Oxford University Press, 1999.

Nietzsche, Friedrich, Keith Ansell-Pearson, and Carol Diethe. *Nietzsche: "On the Genealogy of Morality."* Cambridge University Press, 1994.

Nietzsche, Friedrich, Robert Pippin, and Adrian Del Caro. *Nietzsche: Thus Spoke Zarathustra.* Cambridge University Press, 2006.

Noddings, Nel. *Caring: A Feminine Approach to Ethics and Moral Education.* 2nd ed. with a new preface. University of California Press, 2003.

Noelle-Neumann, E. *The Spiral of Silence: Public Opinion, Our Social Skin.* University of Chicago, 1993.

Noonan Jr., John T. *A Church that Can and Cannot Change: The Development of Catholic Moral Teaching.* University of Notre Dame Press, 2005.

Norris, Pippa, and Ronald Inglehart. *Sacred and Secular: Religion and Politics Worldwide.* Cambridge University Press, 2004.

Numbers, Ronald L., ed. *Galileo Goes to Jail and Other Myths about Science and Religion.* Harvard University Press, 2009.

Nye, Russel B. *This Almost Chosen People.* Michigan State University Press, 1966.

Oderberg, David. *Applied Ethics: A Non-Consequentialist Approach.* Blackwell, 2000.

————. *Moral Theory: A Non-Consequentialist Approach.* Blackwell, 2000.

Oderberg, David, and Timothy Chappell, eds. *Human Values: New Essays on Ethics and Natural Law.* Palgrave Macmillan, 2008.

Oman, John Campbell. *Cults, Customs and Superstitions of India: Being a Revised and Enlarged Edition of "Indian Life, Religious and Social."* 1908. Reprint, Adamant Media, 2005.

Onfray, Michel. *Atheist Manifesto: The Case Against Christianity, Judaism, and Islam.* Arcade, 2008.

Oren, Michael B. *Power, Faith, and Fantasy: America in the Middle East: 1776 to the Present,* W. W. Norton, 2007.

Orwell, George. *1984.* Reissue, Signet Classics, 1990.

————. *Animal Farm.* 50th Anniversary edition, Signet Classics, 1996.

Ostrovsky, Victor. *By Way of Deception: The Making and Unmaking of a Mossad Officer.* Wilshire Press, 2002.

————. *The Other Side of Deception: A Rogue Agent Exposes the Mossad's Secret Agenda.* Harpercollins, 1994.

Outka, Gene, and J. P. Reeder Jr. *Religion and Morality: A Collection of Essays.* Doubleday, 1973.

Paton, H. J. *The Categorical Imperative: A Study in Kant's Moral Philosophy.* University of Pennsylvania Press, 1999.

Pauling, Linus. *Linus Pauling On Peace—A Scientist Speaks Out on Humanism and World Survival.* Edited by Barbara Marinacci and Ramesh S. Krishnamurthy. Rising Star Press, 1998.

Paulos, John Allen. *Irreligion: A Mathematician Explains Why the Arguments for God Just Don't Add Up.* Hill and Wang, 2007.

Paxton, Robert O. *The Anatomy of Fascism.* Alfred A. Knopf, 2004.

Peck, Scott. *People of the Lie.* Touchstone, 1998.

Peikoff, Leonard. *Objectivism: The Philosophy of Ayn Rand.* Reprint, Plume, 1993.

Phillips, Kevin. *American Theocracy: The Peril and Politics of Radical Religion, Oil, and Borrowed Money in the 21st Century.* Viking Adult, 2006.

Pilkey, Orrin H., and Linda Pilkey-Jarvis. *Useless Arithmetic: Why Environmental Scientists Can't Predict the Future.* Columbia University Press, 2007.

Pilzer, Paul Zane. *God Wants You to Be Rich.* Fireside, 1997.

Pinker, Steven. *The Blank Slate: The Modern Denial of Human Nature.* Penguin Books, 2003.

Plato. *Plato's Republic.* Agora, Incorporated, 2001.

————. *The Last Days Of Socrates.* Edited by Harold Tarrant and translated by Hugh Tredennick. Penguin Classics, 2003.

Polastron, Lucien X. *Books on Fire: The Destruction of Libraries throughout History.* Inner Tradition, 2007.

Popper, Karl. *The Logic of Scientific Discovery.* Routledge, 2002.

———. *The Open Society and Its Enemies.* Routledge, 2006.

Posner, Sarah. *God's Profits: Faith, Fraud, and the Republican Crusade for Values Voters.* PoliPointPress, 2008.

Press, Bill. *How the Republicans Stole Religion.* Three Leaves, 2006.

Price, Robert M. *The Reason Driven Life: What Am I Here on Earth For?* Prometheus Books, 2006.

Prior, Michael. *Zionism and the State of Israel: A Moral Inquiry.* Routledge, 1999.

Proudhon, Pierre-Joseph. *The Philosophy of Misery.* 1846. Cosimo Classics, 2007.

———. *What is Property?* 1840. Cambridge University Press, 1994.

Prothero, Stephen. *Religious Literacy: What Every American Needs to Know.* HarperSanFrancisco, 2007.

Provoost, Anne. *In the Shadow of the Ark.* Simon & Schuster, 2005.

Puledda, Salvatore, Mikhail S. Gorbachev, and Andrew Hurley. *On Being Human: Interpretations of Humanism from the Renaissance to the Present.* Latitude Press, 1997.

Pullman, Philip. *His Dark Materials Omnibus (The Golden Compass; The Subtle Knife; The Amber Spyglass).* Initially published separately. Knopf Books for Young Readers, 1996–2007.

Quill, Timothy E. *Physician-Assisted Dying: The Case for Palliative Care and Patient Choice.* Johns Hopkins University Press, 2004.

Rabkin, Yakov M. *A Threat from Within: A Century of Jewish Opposition to Zionism.* Fernwood, 2006.

Rand, Ayn. *Philosophy: Who Needs It.* Reprint, Signet, 1984.

———. *The Ayn Rand Lexicon: Objectivism from A to Z.* Reprint, Plume, 1988.

Rand, Ayn, and Nathaniel Branden. *The Virtue of Selfishness.* Signet, 1964.

Ranke-Heinemann, Uta. *Eunuchs for the Kingdom of Heaven: Women, Sexuality, and the Catholic Church.* Penguin Books, 1991.

Rappaport, Roy A. *Ritual and Religion in the Making of Humanity.* Cambridge University Press, 1999.

Raspail, Jean, with Jeremy Leggatt. *The Camp of the Saints.* Social Contract Press, 1994.

Rawls, John. *A Theory of Justice.* Revised in 1975 and 1999. Belknap Press, 1971.

———. *The Law of Peoples.* Harvard University Press, 2001.

———. *Justice as Fairness: A Restatement.* Edited by Erin Kelly. Belknap Press, 2001.

Reichberg, Gregory M., and Henrik Syse, Endre Begby, eds. *Ethics of War: Classic and Contemporary Readings.* Blackwell, 2006.

Reicher, Stephen D., and S. Alexander Haslam. "The Psychology of Tyranny: The BBC Prison Study." *British Journal of Social Psychology.* March 2006): 1–40.

Reidy, David A. *Rawls's Law of Peoples: A Realistic Utopia?* Blackwell Publishing Professional, 2006.

Reston, James Jr. *Dogs of God, Columbus, the Inquisition, and the Defeat of the Moors.* Doubleday, 2005.

Richardson, H. *Opponents and Implications of a Theory of Justice: The Philosophy of Rawls.* Routledge, 1999.

Richardson, Robert D. *William James: In the Maelstrom of American Modernism.* Houghton Mifflin, 2006.

Ridley, Matt. *The Origins of Virtue: Human Instincts and the Evolution of Cooperation.* Penguin, 1998.

Ridley, Matt, and Francis Crick. *Discoverer of the Genetic Code, Eminent Lives.* HarperCollins, 2006.

Robinson, de Paul F. *Just War in Comparative Perspective.* Ashgate, 2003.

Rogers, G. A. J., ed. *Locke's Philosophy: Content and Context.* Oxford University Press, 1994.

Rogin, Michael Paul. *The Intellectuals and McCarthy: The Radical Specter.* MIT Press, 1969.

Rolston, Holmes. *Genes, Genesis and God: Values and Their Origins in Natural and Human History.* Cambridge University Press, 1999.

Rosenfeld, Barry. *Assisted Suicide and the Right to Die: The Interface of Social Science, Public Policy, and Medical Ethic.* American Psychological Association, 2004.

Roy, Olivier. *Globalised Islam: The Search for a New Ummah.* Hurst, 2004.

Rowe, William, ed. *God and the Problem of Evil.* Blackwell, 2001.

Rowlands, Mark. *Animals Like Us.* Verso, 2002.

Ruether, Rosemary, and Herman Ruether. *The Wrath of Jonah: The Crisis of Religious Nationalism in the Israeli-Palestinian Conflict.* 2nd ed. Augsburg Fortress, 2002.

Ruse, Michael. *The Evolution-Creation Struggle.* Harvard University Press, 2005.

Russell, Bertrand. *A History of Western Philosophy.* 1945. Touchstone, 1967.

———. *Why I am not a Christian: And Other Essays on Religion and Related Subjects,* Touchstone, 1945. (See also the 1957 edition of *Why I am Not a Christian.* Simon & Schuster.)

Sagan, Carl. *The Varieties of Scientific Experiences: A Personal View of the Search of God.* Edited by Ann Druyan. Penguin, 2006.

Sagan, Carl, and Ann Druyan. *The Demon Haunted World: Science as a Candle in the Dark.* Reprint, Ballantine Books, 1997.

Sandhu, Ranjit, and Matthew J. Cravatta. *Media-graphy: A Bibliography of the Works of Paul Kurtz, Fifty-One Years, 1952–2003.* Center for Inquiry Transnational, 2004.

Saranam, Sankara. *God without Religion: Questioning Centuries of Accepted Truths.* Pranayama Institute, 2005.

Sarat, Austin, and Christian Boulanger. *The Cultural Lives Of Capital Punishment: Comparative Perspectives.* Stanford University Press, 2005.

Sartre, Jean-Paul. *Existentialism and Humanism.* Eyre Methuen, 1977.

Saul, John Ralston, and John Saul. *On Equilibrium: Six Qualities of the New Humanism.* Da Capo Press, 2004.

Schopf, J. William. *Life's Origin: The Beginnings of Biological Evolution.* University of California Press, 2002.

Schumacker, E. Fritz. *Small Is Beautiful, 25th Anniversary Edition: Economics as If People Mattered: 25 Years Later…With Commentaries.* 1973. Hartley and Marks, 2000.

Schumpeter, Joseph. *Capitalism, Socialism, and Democracy.* 3rd ed. 1942. Harper Perennial, 1962.

Schwager, Raymund. *Must There Be Scapegoats? Violence and Redemption in the Bible.* (German: Brauchen wir einen Sündenbock?) Translated by M. L. Assad. Crossroad, 2000.

Schweiker, William, Michael A. Johnson, and Kevin Jung. *Humanity Before God: Contemporary Faces of Jewish, Christian, And Islamic Ethics.* Fortress Press, 2006.

Schweitzer, Jeff, and Giuseppe Notarbartolo-Di-Sciara. *Beyond Cosmic Dice: Moral Life in a Random World.* Ingram, 2009.

Scientific American. *Understanding the Genome.* Grand Central, 2002.

Seidman, Barry F., Neil J. Murphy, et al. *Toward a New Political Humanism.* Prometheus Books, 2004.

Segal, Alan. *Life After Death.* Doubleday, 2004.

Shahak, Israel. *Jewish History, Jewish Religion—The Weight of Three Thousand Years.* Pluto Press, 1994.

Shapin, Steven. *The Scientific Revolution.* University of Chicago Press, 1996.

Sharlet, Jeff. *The Family: The Secret Fundamentalism at the Heart of American Power.* Harper, 2008.

Shea, William R. "Galileo and the Church." In *God and Nature: Historical Essays on the Encounter between Christianity and Science,* edited by D. C. Linberg and R. L. Numbers. University of California Press, 1986.

Shermer, Michael. *The Mind of the Market: Compassionate Apes, Competitive Humans, and Other Tales from Evolutionary Economics.* Times Books, 2007.

———. *The Science of Good and Evil : Why People Cheat, Gossip, Care, Share, and Follow the Golden Rule.* Holt Paperbacks, 2004.

———. *Why Darwin Matters: The Case Against Intelligent Design.* Times Books, 2006.

Shreeve, James. *The Neanderthal Enigma: Solving the Mystery of Modern Human Origin.* Avon Books, 1995.

Shubin, Neil. *Your Inner Fish: A Journey into the 3.5-Billion-Year History of the Human Body.* Pantheon, 2008.

Simonnot, Philippe. *Les Papes, l'Église et l'Argent: Histoire Économique du Christianisme des Origines à Nos Jours.* Bayard Centurion, 2005.

Simon, George K. *In Sheep's Clothing: Understanding and Dealing with Manipulative People.* A. J. Christopher, 1996.

Singer, Peter. *A Companion to Ethics.* Blackwell, 1993.

———. *Animal Liberation.* Harper Perennial, 2001.

———. *Applied Ethics.* Oxford University Press, 1986.

———. *Practical Ethics.* Cambridge University Press, 1999.

———. *The Expanding Circle: Ethics and Sociobiology.* Oxford University Press, 1983.

———. *The Life You Can Save: Acting Now to End World Poverty.* Random House, 2009.

———. *Writings on an Ethical Life.* Harper Perennial, 2001.

Singh, Simon. *Big Bang: The Most Important Scientific Discovery of All Time and Why You Need to Know about It.* Fourth Estates, 2004.

Sipe, A.W. R. *A Secret World: Sexuality and the Search for Celibacy.* Brunner/Masel, 1990.

Sizer, Stephen, and David Peterson. *Christian Zionism: Road Map to Armageddon.* InterVarsity Press, 2005.

Slote, Michael. *The Ethics of Care and Empathy.* Routledge, 2007.

Smith, Adam. *The Theory of Moral Sentiments; or, an Essay Towards an Analysis of the Principles by Which Men Naturally Judge.* 1759. Two-Volume edition, 1817. Prometheus Books, 2000.

———. *The Wealth of Nations.* 1776. Bantam Classics, 2003.

Smith, Anthony D. *Chosen Peoples: Sacred Sources of National Identity.* Oxford University Press, 2003.

Smith, B. L. *Religion and Social Conflict in South Asia.* Brill, 1976.

Smith, George H. *Atheism: The Case Against God.* Prometheus Books, 1980.

Smith, John Maynard, and Eörs Szathmáry. *The Origins of Life.* Oxford University Press, 1999.

Smith, Nicholas H. *Charles Taylor: Meaning, Morals and Modernity.* Polity Press, 2002.

Soble, Alan. *The Philosophy of Sex and Love: An Introduction.* Paragon House, 1998.

Spence, Chris. *Global Warming: Personal Solutions for a Healthy Planet.* Palgrave Macmillan, 2005.

Spencer, Herbert. *The Principles of Ethics.* Vol. 1. 1879. Reprint, University Press of the Pacific, 2004.

——. *The Principles of Ethics.* Vol. 2. 1893. Reprint, University Press of the Pacific, 2004.

Spencer, Robert. *The Myth of Islamic Tolerance: How Islamic Law Treats Non-Muslims.* Prometheus Books, 2005.

——. *The Truth about Muhammad, Founder of the World's Most Intolerant Religion.* Regnery, 2006.

Spinoza, Baruch (Benedict de), S. Shirley and S. Feldman. *A Theologico-Political Treatise.* 1670. Hackett, 2001.

——. *The Letters.* Translated by S. Shirley, with introductions by S. Barfore, L. Rice, and J. Adler. Hackett, 1995.

——. *Short Treatise on God, Man and His Well-Being.* Russell & Russell, 1963.

Stark, Rodney. *The Victory of Reason: How Christianity Led to Freedom, Capitalism, and Western Success.* Random House, 2006.

Staub, Ervin. *The Roots of Evil: The Origins of Genocide and Other Group Violence.* Cambridge University Press, 1989.

Steele, Edward J., et al. *Lamarck's Signature: How Retrogenes Are Changing Darwin's Natural Selection Paradigm.* Helix Books Series. Perseus Books Group, 1999.

Steiner, Franklin. *The Religious Beliefs of Our Presidents: From Washington to FDR.* Prometheus Books, 1995.

Steinhardt, Paul J., and Neil Turok. *Endless Universe: Beyond the Big Bang.* Doubleday, 2007.

Stenger, Victor J. *God: The Failed Hypothesis, How Science Shows That God Does Not Exist.* Prometheus Books, 2007.

Stenger, Victor J., and Christopher Hitchens. *God: The Failed Hypothesis.* Prometheus Books, 2008.

Stern, Fritz R. *The Politics of Cultural Despair: A Study in the Rise of the Germanic Ideology.* California Library Reprint Series, 1974.

Stewart, Matthew. *The Courtier and the Heretic.* W.W. Norton, 2006.

Stewart, R. B. Jr. *On the Origin of Gods.* Powell, 2007.

Stickler, Alfons Maria Cardinal. *The Case for Clerical Celibacy: Its Historical Development and Theological Foundations.* Ignatius Press, 1995.

Stone, Peter H. *Heist: Superlobbyist Jack Abramoff, His Republican Allies, and the Buying of Washington*. Farrar, Straus and Giroux, 2006.

Stout, Jeffrey. *Democracy and Tradition*. Princeton University Press, 2005.

Stout, Martha. *The Sociopath Next Door*. Broadway, 2005.

Stover, D., and E. Erdmann. *A Mind For Tomorrow: Facts, Values, and the Future*. Praeger, 2000.

Stoye, John. *The Siege of Vienna: The Last Great Trial between Cross and Crescent*. Pegasus Books, 2006.

Sullivan, Roger J. *An Introduction to Kant's Ethics*. Cambridge University Press, 2005.

Sumner, L. W. *The Moral Foundation of Rights*. Oxford University Press, 1987.

Tainter, Joseph. *The Collapse of Complex Societies*. Reprint, Cambridge University Press, 1990.

Tamarin, G. R. "The Influence of Ethnic and Religious Prejudice on Moral Judgment." *New Outlook* 9, no. 1 (1966): 49–58.

———. *The Israeli Dilemma: Essays on a Warfare State*. Rotterdam University Press, 1973.

Tancredi, Lawrence R. *Hardwired Behavior: What Neuroscience Reveals about Morality*. Cambridge University Press, 2005.

Tarpley, Webster. G. *9/11 Synthetic Terror: Made in USA*. 3rd ed. Progressive Press, 2006.

Tattersall, Ian. *Becoming Human: Evolution and Human Uniqueness*. Harvest Books, 1999.

———. *The Last Neanderthal: The Rise, Success, and Mysterious Extinction of Our Closest Human Relatives*. Westview Press, 1999.

Tattersall, Ian, and Jeffrey H. Schwartz. *Extinct Humans*. Westview Press, 2001.

Tawney, R. H. *Religion and the Rise of Capitalism*. New American Library, 1926.

Taylor, Charles. *A Secular Age*. Harvard University Press, 2007.

———. *Sources of the Self: The Making of the Modern Identity*. Reprint, Harvard University Press, 1992.

———. *The Ethics of Authenticity*. Harvard University Press, 2005.

Taylor, Charles, Marcel Gauchet, and Oscar Burge. *The Disenchantment of the World: A Political History of Religion*. Princeton University Press, 1999.

Telushkin, Joseph. *Jewish Literacy: The Most Important Things to Know about the Jewish Religion, Its People and Its History*. William Morrow, 1991.

Temes, Peter S. *The Just War: An American Reflection on the Morality of War in Our Time*. Ivan R. Dee, 2003.

Templeton, John. *Discovering the Laws of Life*. Continuum International, 1994.

————. *Worldwide Laws of Life: 200 Eternal Spiritual Principles.* Templeton Foundation Press, 1997.

Templeton, Joh, and Norman Vincent Peale. *Discovering the Laws of Life.* Templeton Foundation Press, 2004.

Tickle, Phyllis. *The Words of Jesus: A Gospel of the Sayings of Our Lord with Reflections.* Jossey-Bass, 2008.

Tobin, Paul N. *Rejection of Pascal's Wager.* Octovia Press, 2009.

Tomalin, Claire. *Thomas Hardy.* Penguin, 2007.

Toynbee, Arnold J., and D.C. Somervell. *A Study of History: Abridgement of Volumes I–VI.* Oxford University Press, 1987.

Tremblay, Rodrigue. *The New American Empire.* Infinity, 2004.

Trimble, Michael R. *The Soul in the Brain: The Cerebral Basis of Language, Art, and Belief.* Johns Hopkins University Press, 2007.

Truan, Franklin C. *Metavalues: Universal Principles For A Sane World.* Fenestra Books, 2004.

Tuveson, Ernest Lee. *Redeemer Nation: The Idea of America's Millenial Role.* 1st ed. 1968. Chicago University Press, 1980.

Twain, Mark. *The War Prayer.* HarperCollins, 1984.

Uehiro, Eiji. *Practical Ethics for Our Time.* Translated by Carl Becker. Tuttle, 1998.

United Nations. *Intergovernmental Panel on Climate Change.* Rourth Report, IPCC, 2007.

————. *Intergovernmental Panel on Climate Change.* Third Report, IPCC, 2001.

US National Committee for the International Polar Year 2007–2008. *National Research Council Report: A Vision for the International Polar Year 2007–2008.* National Academies Press, 2004.

————. *Climate Change Science: An Analysis of Some Key Questions.* National Academies Press, 2001.

Van Alstyne, Richard Warner. *The Rising American Empire.* 1st ed. Oxford University Press 1960. W. W. Norton, 1998.

Venter, J. Craig. *A Life Decoded: My Genome: My Life.* Viking Adult, 2007.

Vernon, Mark. *Teach Yourself Humanism.* Teach Yourself Books, 2008.

Viguerie, Richard A., et al. *America's Right Turn: How Conservatives Used New and Alternative Media to Take Power.* Bonus Books, 2004.

Voltaire, (Francois-Marie Arouet de). *Candide.* Translated by John Butt. Penguin Books, 1990.

————. *Fanaticism, or Mahomet the Prophet.* 1745.

Waal, F. B. M. de. *Good Natured: The Origins of Right and Wrong in Humans and Other Animals.* Harvard University Press, 1996.

Wade, Nicholas. *The Faith Instinct: How Religion Evolved and Why It Endures.* Penguin Press HC, 2009.

Walter, Nicolas. *Humanism: What's in the Word.* Rationalist Press Association, 1997.

Waltke, Bruce. *Book of Proverbs: Chapters 1–15.* William B. Eerdmans, 2004.

———. *The Book of Proverbs: Chapters 15–31.* William B. Eerdmans, 2005.

Walzer, Michael. *Just and Unjust Wars: A Moral Argument with Historical Illustrations.* Basic Books, 2006.

Ward, Colin. *Anarchy in Action.* Freedom Press, 1982.

Warren, Rick. *The Purpose-Driven Life: What on Earth Am I Here For?* Zondervan, 2002.

Warsh, David. *Knowledge and the Wealth of Nations: A Story of Economic Discovery.* W. W. Norton, 2006. With illustrations, Basic Books, 2000.

Wasserman, James, Eva von Dassow, Ogden Goelet, and Carol Andrews. *The Egyptian Book of the Dead: The Book of Going Forth by Day.* Chronicle Books, 2008.

Watson, James D. *The Double Helix: A Personal Account of the Discovery of the Structure of DNA.* Touchstone, 2001.

Watson, Robert T., ed. *Climate Change 2001: Synthesis Report: Third Assessment Report of the Intergovernmental Panel on Climate Change.* Cambridge University Press, 2002.

Weber, Max. *The Protestant Ethic and the Spirit of Capitalism.* 1904. BN Publishing, 2008.

Weinberg, A. K. *Manifest Destiny: A Study of Nationalist Expansionism in American History.* 1st ed. Johns Hopkins University Press, 1935. Chicago University Press, 1963.

Weinberg, Steven. *Dreams of a Final Theory: The Scientist's Search for the Ultimate Laws of Nature.* Vintage, 1994.

———. *Facing Up: Science and Its Cultural Adversaries.* Harvard University Press, 2003.

Weinstein, Bruce. *Life Principles: Feeling Good by Doing Good.* Emmis Books, 2006.

Wells, Spencer. *The Journey of Man: A Genetic Odyssey.* Random House, 2004.

Wenham, David. *Paul: Follower of Jesus or Founder of Christianity?* William B. Eerdmans, 1995.

Wessinger, Catherine, ed. *Millennialism, Persecution and Violence: Historical Cases.* Syracuse University Press, 2000.

Wielenberg, Erik J. *God and the Reach of Reason: CS Lewis, David Hume, and Bertrand Russell.* Cambridge University Press, 2007.

————.*Value and Virtue in a Godless Universe.* Cambridge University Press, 2005.

Wilson, Edward O. *Consilience, The Unity of Knowledge.* Vintage Books, 1998.

————. *Sociobiology: The New Synthesis, Twenty-Fifth Anniversary Edition.* 1975. Belknap Press, 2000.

————. *The Creation: A Meeting of Science and Religion.* W. W. Norto, 2006.

Wilson, Edwin H., and Teresa Maciocha, ed. *The Genesis of a Humanist Manifesto.* Humanist Press, 1995.

Woit, Peter. *Not Even Wrong: The Failure of String Theory and the Continuing Challenge to Unify the Laws of Physics.* Jonathan Cape, 2006.

Wolfe Wentzel, Regina. *Ethics and the World Religions: Cross-Cultural Case Studies.* Orbis Books, 1999.

Wolpert, Julian. *What Charity Can and Cannot Do.* Twentieth Century Fund Press, 1996.

Wolpert, Lewis. *Six Impossible Things before Breakfast: The Evolutionary Origins of Belief.* W. W. Norton, 2007.

Woods, Thomas E. *How the Catholic Church Built Western Civilization.* Regnery, 2005.

Woodword, Bob. *Bush at War.* Simon & Schuster, 2003.

Wright, Peter et al. *Primates and Philosophers: How Morality Evolved.* Princeton University Press, 2006.

Wright, Robert. *Nonzero: The Logic of Human Destiny.* Vintage, 2001.

————. *The Evolution of God.* Little, Brown, 2006.

————. *The Moral Animal.* Abacus, 2004.

————. *The Moral Animal: Why We Are, the Way We Are: The New Science of Evolutionary Psychology.* Vintage, 1995.

Xenophon, et al. *Conversations of Socrates.* Penguin Classics, 1990.

Yaffe, Rochel. *Rambam: The Story of Rabbi Moshe Ben Maimon.* Hacha, 1992.

Zimbardo, Zimbardo. *The Lucifer Effect: Understanding How Good People Turn Evil.* Random House, 2007.

Zimmer, Carl. *Soul Made Flesh: The Discovery of the Brain—and How It Changed the World.* Free Press, 2005.

Zimring, Franklin E. *The Contradictions of American Capital Punishment.* Oxford University Press, 2003.

INDEX

ABOUT THE AUTHOR

Rodrigue Tremblay is a Canadian-born economist, humanist, and political figure. Specializing in macroeconomics, international trade and finance, and public finance, he teaches economics at the Université de Montréal. He is a prolific author of books on economics and politics.

Born in Matane, Québec, Professor Tremblay has a BA from the Université Laval (1961) and a BS in economics from the Université de Montréal (1963). He did his graduate work at Stanford University, where he obtained an MA in economics (1965) and a PhD in economics (1968). He has been a professor of economics at the Université de Montréal since 1967 and has been professor emeritus since 2002.

Dr. Tremblay was president of the Association Canadienne de Science Économique (1974–75) and of the North American Economics and Finance Association (1986–87). He was chairman of the Department of Economics of the Université de Montréal (1973–76), member of the Committee of Dispute Settlements of the North American Free Trade Agreement (NAFTA) (1989–93), and vice president of the Association Internationale des Économistes de Langue Française (AIELF) (1999–2005).

Rodrigue Tremblay was elected member of parliament on

November 15, 1976, and served as minister of industry and trade in the government of Québec from 1976 to 1979. He is a public intellectual who is known for his contributions to the understanding of international, Canadian, and Québec politics.

His blog on world geopolitics (www.TheNewAmericanEmpire .com/blog) is read in more than fifty countries and is reproduced in eight languages. His previous book, *The New American Empire*, was published in English, in French under the title *Le nouvel Empire américain*, and in Turkish under the title *Yeni Amerikan Imparatorlugu.*